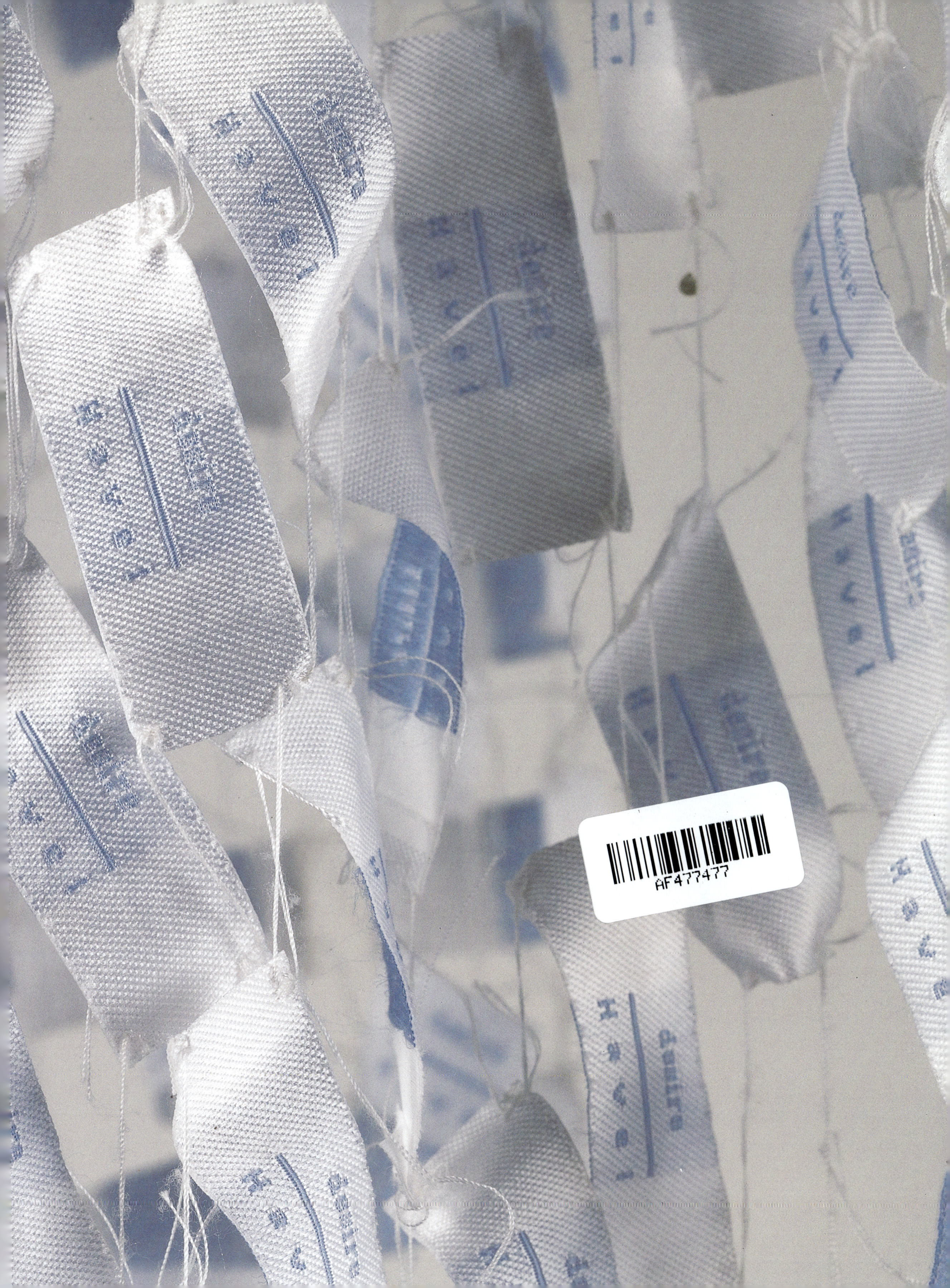

JOSEPH HAVEL:
A DECADE OF SCULPTURE 1996–2006

JOSEPH HAVEL:
A DECADE OF SCULPTURE 1996–2006

With contributions by
Peter Doroshenko, Alison de Lima Greene,
Amelia Jones, and Howard Singerman

SCALA

THE MUSEUM OF FINE ARTS, HOUSTON, IN ASSOCIATION WITH SCALA PUBLISHERS

First published in 2006 by
Scala Publishers Ltd
Northburgh House
10 Northburgh Street
London EC1V OAT

In association with The Museum of Fine Arts, Houston
P.O. Box 6826
Houston, Texas 77265-6826
www.mfah.org

Joseph Havel: A Decade of Sculpture 1996–2006 was published in conjunction with the opening exhibition organized by the Museum of Fine Arts, Houston, and presented there March 26–June 18, 2006.

Major corporate sponsorship is provided by Chubb Group of Insurance Companies.

Additional generous funding was provided by Nona and Richard Barrett, Nancy and Tim Hanley, Eliza Lovett Randall, Stanford and Joan Alexander Foundation, Claire and Doug Ankenman, Carol and Les Ballard, Toni and Jeff Beauchamp, Blake Byrne, Sara Dodd-Spickelmier and Keith Spickelmier, Kay and Al Ebert, Sam Gorman, Diana and Russell Hawkins, Janet and Paul Hobby, Karen and Eric Pulaski, Alice C. Simkins, Emily and Alton Steiner, Herbert C. Wells, Isabel B. and Wallace S. Wilson, Jill and Dunham Jewett, Karol Howard and George Morton, Jan Diesel, and Randee and Howard Berman.

ISBN 0-89090-139-2 (softcover)
ISBN 1-85759-424-X (hardcover)

Library of Congress Cataloguing-in-Publication Data available upon request

Edited by Diane Lovejoy
Designed by Phenon Finley-Smiley
Produced by Scala Publishers Ltd.
Printed and bound in Singapore

Photographs of Joseph Havel's sculpture by Tom Jenkins, unless otherwise noted on pages 171–72.

Cover/Jacket:
Joseph Havel, *Toy, Dream, Rest* (detail), 2003, fabric, shirt labels, and thread, dimensions variable, courtesy of the artist. © Joseph Havel

CONTENTS

LENDERS TO THE EXHIBITION

The Barrett Collection, Dallas, Texas

Collection of Blake Byrne, Los Angeles

Collection of Claire and Doug Ankenman

Collection of Jeffrey and Toni Beauchamp

Collection of Diane and Charles Cheatham

Collection of Mr. and Mrs. Robert H. Dedman, Jr.

Collection of Dr. Carolyn Farb

Collection of Tim and Nancy Hanley

Collection of Mr. and Mrs. Russell Hawkins

Collection of Jeanne and Michael Klein

Collection of Beverly Kopp

Collection of Cornelia and Meredith Long

Collection of Suzanne M. Manns

Collection of Frances and Peter C. Marzio

Collection, Modern Art Museum of Fort Worth

Collection of Nancy M. O'Boyle

Collection of Dr. and Mrs. Bryan Perry, Dallas

Collection of Stedelijk Museum voor Actuele Kunst (S.M.A.K.), Ghent, Belgium

Collection of Nina and Michael Zilkha

Courtesy of the artist

Courtesy of Devin Borden Hiram Butler Gallery

Courtesy of Dunn and Brown Contemporary

Courtesy of Galerie Gabrielle Maubrie

The Museum of Fine Arts, Houston

FOREWORD

Joseph Havel likes the physical facts of sculpture. Dispensing with the glut of imagery from various media in the world, Havel chooses images and shapes from his own life as a way to organize the formal elements of his sculptural works. The exhibition *Joseph Havel: A Decade of Sculpture 1996–2006* is the first major museum exhibition to focus on Havel's investigation of sculptural form and meaning during the last ten years of his critically acclaimed career.

In Havel's sculptures, objects such as buttons, shirt labels, shirts, and bedsheets appear as a means to make his works accessible to a broader audience. Havel uses sculpture as the most recognizable sign of art while introducing installation elements that reflect a new artistic thought. The artworks move between the territories of ephemeral and classical three-dimensional objects.

Havel is interested in how people define sculpture, and in how three-dimensional information is constructed and manifested publicly. Superficially minimalist in style, Havel's works have nothing to do with action or theatrics. In the frozen time frames of the works, viewers can ponder the stillness of the situations they confront.

This exhibition includes thirty-one large-scale sculptures made between 1996 and 2006. During this period, Havel has focused on transforming domestic fabric items into sculptures, starting with men's white shirts, and later expanding to include clothing labels, drapes, bedsheets, and tablecloths. Frequently Havel transforms the objects from fabric into bronze through the process of direct casting. In other instances, metamorphosis occurs through accumulation and assembly.

One of the signature works from this decade is *Curtain*, commissioned by the Museum of Fine Arts, Houston, for the entrance to its Audrey Jones Beck Building (Rafael Moneo, architect). For this exhibition, Havel has planned several new works, including a site-specific installation that will literally break into the gallery design concept of the museum's Caroline Wiess Law Building, designed by legendary architect Ludwig Mies van der Rohe.

I have had the privilege of working with Joseph Havel in his position as director of the Glassell School of Art, the teaching wing of the Museum of Fine Arts, Houston. Special thanks go to all of the funders of this exhibition, which will place Havel's work in the broader context it richly deserves.

Peter C. Marzio
Director
The Museum of Fine Arts, Houston

ACKNOWLEDGMENTS

The concept of the exhibition *Joseph Havel: A Decade of Sculpture* 1996–2006 was born in a discussion between the artist and Peter C. Marzio, director of the Museum of Fine Arts, Houston, in the spring of 2000. Joseph had recently completed *Curtain*, a work commissioned by the museum for the entrance of its then new Audrey Jones Beck Building, and he and I were concurrently discussing a retrospective exhibition.

I was interested in examining the works that Joseph had produced since the initial exhibition of his white shirt and label sculptures, a show I had curated for the Huntington Beach Art Center in California, in 1996. It became clear that the time was right for an in-depth and scholarly examination of the artist's sculptures and that the Museum of Fine Arts, Houston, was the most appropriate venue for this treatment. I am thankful to Dr. Marzio for inviting me to curate this exhibition, enabling me to bring appropriate attention to Joseph's most recent body of work.

A number of individuals have passionately supported this project. I would like to thank the lenders to the exhibition for allowing us to gather the works we needed to best express the artist's accomplishments over the past decade. I would also like to thank the numerous friends who generously supported this exhibition. All of them are recognized on pages 4 and 6 of this catalogue.

I would like to thank Alison de Lima Greene, Amelia Jones, and Howard Singerman for the insightful essays that they contributed to the catalogue. I would also like to thank Alison for her help in coordinating this exhibition for the museum. Her able assistance made the invitation of being a guest curator a true pleasure to accept.

At the Museum of Fine Arts, Houston, many colleagues have helped to make this project a success. I want to thank Diane Lovejoy, publications director, and Phenon Finley-Smiley, graphics manager, for their work on the catalogue. I also wish to thank Scala Publishers for their strong commitment to publishing the book and to distributing it worldwide.

Thanks are also due to Gwendolyn H. Goffe, associate director, finance and administration; Margaret C. Skidmore, former associate director, development; Paul Johnson, associate director, development and membership; and Kathleen Jameson, assistant director of development, program support; Karen Vetter, chief administrator, exhibitions and curatorial; Beth B. Schneider, the W. T. and Louise J. Moran Education Director; Margaret Mims, public programs manager; and Sarah Williams-House, public programs coordinator; Julie Bakke, registrar; Kathleen Crain, exhibitions registrar; and John Obsta, assistant registrar for exhibition; Frances Carter Stephens, public relations director; Lynn Feuerbach, assistant public relations director; Jack Eby, exhibition design director; and Bill Cochrane, exhibition designer; Michael Kennaugh, preparations manager; Marty Stein, photographic services manager; and Thomas R. DuBrock, photographer; Margaret Culbertson, library director; and Jon Evans, associate librarian. Additionally, colleagues at the museum's Glassell School of Art gave vital assistance to this project, including Mary Leclère, assistant director, Core Program; Cheryl Fritsche, executive assistant; and Heather Colvin, former program assistant to the director.

In the museum's curatorial offices, Michelle White, curatorial assistant, is deserving of special thanks for her diligent efforts in preparing this publication's bibliography and securing comparative illustrations, not to mention other myriad aspects of this project. Clifford Edwards, Anna Jordan, and Cristina Lafuente, administrative assistants, were also instrumental to the project's success.

Additional credit is due to my colleagues in Houston, Dallas, and Paris, including most notably Hiram Butler, Devin Borden, and Chad Sager at Devin Borden Hiram Butler Gallery, Houston; Talley Dunn, Lisa Hirschler Brown, Sarah Stork, and Amy Harris at Dunn and Brown Contemporary, Dallas; and Gabrielle Maubrie at Galerie Gabrielle Maubrie, Paris. New photography for this catalogue was undertaken by Tom Jenkins. Aspects of shipping and coordination were expertly handled by Christopher Tribble and Kyle Young at TyArt, Houston, and Tim Nentrup, Casey Rember, and Toby Ferril at Displays Unlimited, Arlington, Texas. Lora Reynolds at Lora Reynolds Gallery, Austin; Barry Whistler at Barry Whistler Gallery, Dallas; and Eva Wittocx at the Stedelijk Museum voor Actuele Kunst expedited several key loans.

Finally, I would like to thank Joseph Havel. It has been my pleasure to work with Joseph on a number of exhibitions for over fourteen years. During that time, I have come to appreciate the depth of his thinking and the generosity with which he shares his ideas. I salute his accomplishments, as reflected by this exhibition, and I treasure his friendship.

Peter Doroshenko
Guest Curator

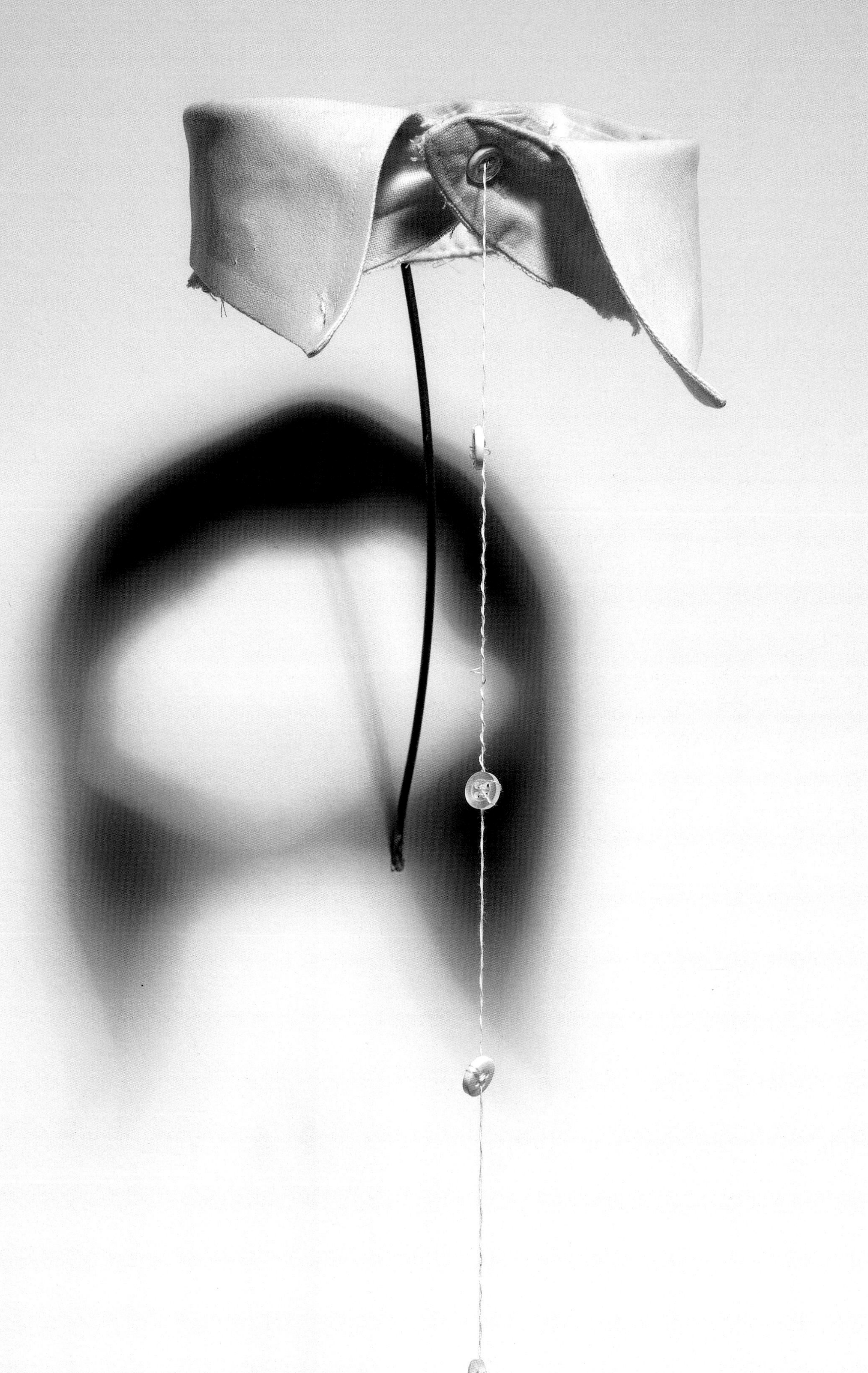

JOSEPH HAVEL'S WHITE COLLAR PRACTICE

Howard Singerman

Writing in 1967 about the work of Carl Andre, Dan Flavin, and Sol LeWitt, the artist Mel Bochner chose a line from eighteenth-century Scottish philosopher David Hume as one of his epigraphs: "No object implies the existence of any other." The argument Bochner enlists Hume for—along with Husserl's "Go to the things themselves" and a longish quote from British analytic philosopher A. J. Ayer—is for a radically autonomous and nonreferential, indeed "solipsistic," art.[1] Bochner's call for works of art as "'things-in-the-world' separate from both maker and observer"[2] is posed implicitly against the metaphorical overreaching of abstract expressionist painting and its critics, but it echoes curiously that earlier generation's embrace of the autonomous, uncommunicative artist: "For them," wrote Alfred Barr of the artists of the New York School, "John Donne to the contrary, each man is an island."[3] The work of what has been broadly termed postminimalism, the idiom in which Joseph Havel came of age in the 1970s, and with which—often quite consciously, referentially—he continues to work, took certain of the basic material and organizational tropes of minimal art to record and then to thematize its contingency: contingent means to need or lean on something, to have been conditioned by something, to have been molded by circumstance.

And against Hume, perhaps, to imply physically, even ontologically, something else. Postminimalism continued minimal art's regularized, gridded forms, its use of repetition and simple, given ordering, as well as its openness to nontraditional materials in what criticism at the time called the "real" or "literal" space of the gallery or studio (as opposed to the idealist space of painting, or of medium). But artists like Eva Hesse, Lynda Benglis, and Keith Sonnier took their new industrial materials from a different part of the hardware store, so to speak, than from where Donald Judd or Dan Flavin took theirs: rather than the rigid construction materials Judd chose, they drew from an equally new stock of caulks, glues, resins, plastics, insulation materials, and so forth, materials marked not by their rigidity but their fluidity, their floppiness or, again, contingency. They are, for the most part, materials that go in between things, that fill in spaces rather than carve them out. They are materials that are in some sense cast, and cast sculpture cannot help but imply the existence of another object. Bruce Nauman's fiberglass *Platform Made Up of the Space between Two Rectilinear Boxes on the Floor* (1966), say, or Lynda Benglis's polyurethane *Phantom* (1971; fig. 1), each, as their titles

PLATE 1

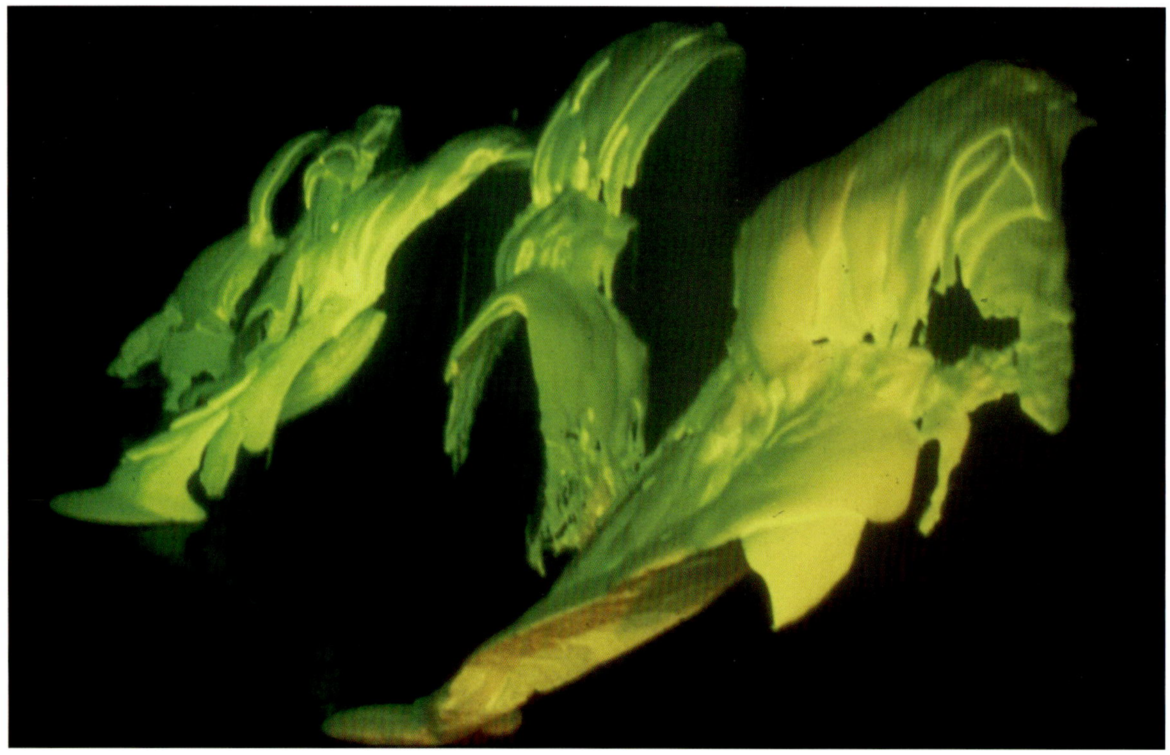

FIGURE 1

suggest, has an other, a ghost that haunts it: the mold that it is a negative or a stamp of. That memory clings ontologically to the cast, which is why it becomes an important method for postminimalism, even as it continues minimal's repetitions and its forms. The cast and the various other processes that leave their contingent traces and marks in malleable materials, allow minimalism's physical presence to figure neediness, absence, a missing part, to reopen to a referent, however close and tangible it may be.

While the work of postminimalism continued minimalism's literalism, its "anti-illusionism," as the title of a 1969 exhibition at the Whitney Museum of American Art had it, postminimalism tended to produce a kind of narrative, even if only the story of its own making, and to take on the body—the body of its maker recorded in its surfaces and folds, as well as the body minimalist presence implied—as a theme. It absorbed the hidden anthropomorphism of minimalism, and insisted not only on the embodiedness but also on the absence of a work like Tony Smith's *Die*. Postminimalism's rejection of the formal rigidity and insistently silent autonomy of minimalism in favor of material working could carry with it a politics as well, at least early on. "The new style's relationship to the women's movement cannot be overly stressed," wrote Robert Pincus-Witten in 1977; "many of its formal attitudes and properties, not to mention its exemplars, derive from methods and substances that hitherto had been sexistically tagged as female or feminine, whether or not the work had been made by women."[4] The recasting of the grid and the repeated unit as a sort of weaving or quilting, as well as the use of screens, industrial felt, and fiberglass cloth, and then various more traditional fabrics themselves, tied the formal and technical tropes of postminimalism to at least one manifestation of the women's movement in the art world. Havel's work in the past decade and a half has addressed, and indeed relied on, the gendered tagging of certain methods, substances, and subjects, and it echoes work by artists such as Lynda Benglis, Rosemarie Castoro, Rosemary Mayer, and Beverly Semmes, all of whom have used expanses of fabric, folds, and casts to figure a body we tend to read as specifically female. Havel's sculpture echoes them differently, one could say, and, to use an analogy drawn from the contemporary university, it suggests the passage so many departments have made in the 1990s from women's studies to gender studies.

Joseph Havel's cast bronze linens and curtains are painstakingly crafted and difficult to make, but their logic is fairly simple: He has taken something limp—unable to support itself or to hold a shape—and hardened it, frozen it in both time and space. Cotton sheets are usually given whatever passing form they may have by being draped horizontally over a bed or a recumbent body; curtains and the men's shirts that Havel has used as an image and a source since the mid-1990s might suggest a kind of verticality, but they too are far from self-supporting; they depend on a support—hangers, curtain rods, clotheslines, torsos—and are given form by pleating and placketing, perhaps, but mostly, again, by gravity. Against the flimsiness and transience of their sources—the shirts and sheets picked up from Target or Kmart or the local thrift store, and that are destroyed in the casting process—the bronzes take on form, permanence, embodiment. One can think of this passage as a kind of transcendence: from pliable, unthinking matter to intended form, as traditional aesthetics has it, from the quotidian and fleeting to the permanent and monumental. It is a transformation, and a series of implications, that Havel works both with and against.

There are other ways to make sheets and shirts stand upright, but unlike the urethane resin that Havel has used to stiffen *Bed Sheet* (2001; plate 33) and the shirts of *Indian Fire* (2003; plate 52), bronze is used not only as a technical material but as an emblem of a time-honored tradition. It is bronze as a medium that suggests the terms of permanence and monumentality, and that signifies, as kind of shorthand, "high art." Cast in bronze, Havel's white-sale specials become drapery, a most traditional, indeed academic, subject for sculptors and painters since the Renaissance. Despite the quotidian ruggedness of their titles, and, we might assume, the incidental nature of their folds and falls, works like *Torn Flannel Duvet Cover* (2003; plate 51) and *Torn and Twisted Curtain* (2004–5; plates 63 and 64) cite the conventions and orders—even the academic lessons—of a history of art since Renaissance times. One could think of them in terms of French academician Roger de Piles's eighteenth-century advice that in "*crafting a drapery*...the disposition of the folds ought rather to seem the effect of mere chance, than of labor and study,"[5] or describe them in terms borrowed from *The Seven Laws of Folds*, a manual published in 1942 by longtime Art Students League instructor George Bridgman, noting *Torn and Twisted*'s "diaper" and "drop," *Torn Flannel*'s "half lock," or the "pipe" and "spiral" of *Black Drape* [6] (2002; plate 50).

"The means to turn cloth into drapery through art…," writes critic and art historian Gen Doy, "were comparable with those used to turn an ordinary naked body into an artistic nude." [7] Indeed, for many commentators, drapery was integral to the classical idea of the nude and (one wants to say literally) dependent on it as a second, unblemished skin. Instructs de Piles: "As the eye must never be in doubt of its object, the chief effect of draperies is, to make us understand what they cover; especially the naked parts of figures; in such manner, that the outward characters of persons, and the exactness of proportions, may appear through them, at least in the main, and as far as probability and art will permit." [8] Cast over the body, falling elegantly from it, drapery at once signifies it as nude and clothes it, but precisely not in the everyday. The drape insists on the body's purity: the draped body is at once "natural" and yet not sexualized, as though all of that white yardage were testament to the body's cleanliness, or a figure for its spiritualization. Thus Hegel can argue that while Greek sculptors rendered youths and athletes completely nude, "we get drapery where a higher intellectual significance, an inner seriousness of the spirit, is prominent and, in short, where nature is not to be made the predominant thing." [9] Nature here is, of course, a kind of "mere" nature; spirit is its sublimation, and the drape is the emblem for that sublimation.

For the sculptors of the baroque, for Gian Lorenzo Bernini in particular, drapery threatened to displace the body, and to become an expressive body of its own; for his numerous critics, Bernini's drapery seemed to engulf and erase the body in its extension and multiplication. Think of *St. Theresa in Ecstasy* (Santa Maria della Vittoria, Rome), say, or his *Tomb of Alexander VII* in St. Peter's (fig. 2). "The *drapery* is altogether a truly deplorable side of this style. How Bernini, in Rome, in the presence daily of the most beautiful draped statues of antiquity, went so astray remains a riddle," complained nineteenth-century cultural historian Jakob Burckhardt, [10] seconding British academician Sir Joshua Reynolds's critique of

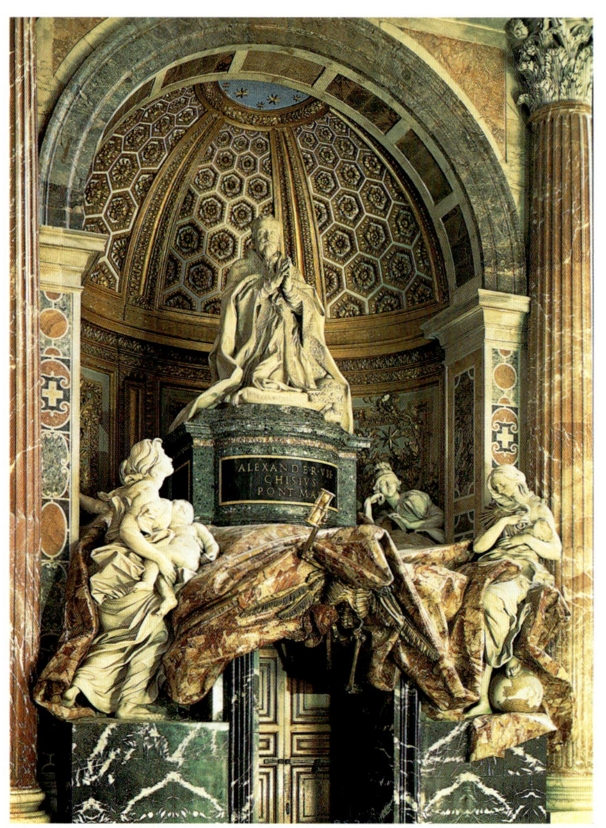

FIGURE 2

Bernini's attempt "to make this species of drapery appear natural": "the ill effect and confusion occasioned by its being detached from the figure to which it belongs, ought to have been sufficient reason to have deterred him from that practice."[11] Against the representational and gravitational decorum of classical drapery, Bernini's flew confusingly and weightlessly free; it had, for Burckhardt, "the appearance of having been…carved with a spoon in almond jelly."[12] Havel's draperies, too, are detached from the body, emotional stand-ins for the figure, but rather than suggesting the celestial, they insist on the literal. His is a low-tech, domestic baroque; his artifice is clear, but his theatricality is given away. His immediate models lie not so much in Bernini, or even in the thinned Giacometti figures that *Three* (1996; plate 10) was at least in part intended to evince, as in children's Halloween party ghosts: empty sheets hanging by a thread. Havel's sculptural forms record simply their having been hung, their propping up and hanging down, their contingency and, maybe, their want to represent, to be other than sheets.

Sheets, after all, are the other of draperies. Unredeemed, untransformed, no longer, or maybe never, the idealized second skin of heroes and saints, sheets—and indeed all of Havel's laundry—are too specific, too much tied to the vicissitudes of market, time, and bodies. One of the jobs of drapery from the Renaissance to the nineteenth century, and one of the ways it suggested the ideal, was to avoid the merely temporal, and precisely the contemporary. "We know, and our first best glance at modern statues or pictures can prove to us," wrote Hegel, "that our modern clothing is wholly inartistic:…even if the most general character of the bodily forms remains, still the beautiful organic undulations are lost and what we see close at hand is something produced for an external purpose, something cut, sewn together here, folded over there, elsewhere fixed, and, in short, purely unfree forms, with folds and surfaces positioned here and there by seams, buttons, and button-holes. In other words, such clothing …precisely conceals what is visibly beautiful, namely their living swelling and curving, and substitutes for them the visible appearance of a material mechanically fashioned."[13] Havel's first fabric works—his first draperies—were made from just the constricting, mechanically constructed clothing Hegel would have him avoid, maybe the very image of that camouflaging armor: the factory-tailored white shirt. Even cast in bronze, the *Laundered Pair* (1996; plate 8) and *Un-Laundered Pair* (1996; plate 9) violate the terms of classical drapery: they are modern dress, and they take their meanings and their specific address from their modernity.

To classicize or idealize means, in part, to leave things out, to refuse the specific, the temporal, the bodily. Bronze is one of the forms of that transformation, and one of its signifiers. But, like drapery, or rather like its "fold"—a term that for Gilles Deleuze and others has come to represent the baroque as the other, the fold-over or intensification, of the classical—bronze too has another, insistently material side. A double sidedness: one that owes to the tradition of high art and to its visual craft, but that owes as well to the material, to the indexicality of casting and the physicality of its transformation. The world necessarily clings to bronze rather differently than it does to marble, a point Robert Morris stresses in theorizing a prehistory for process art. "Rather than modeling parts of the costume in *Judith and Holofernes* (fig. 3), Donatello dipped cloth in hot wax and draped it over the Judith figure. This meant that in casting, the molten bronze had to burn out the cloth as well as the wax. In the process some of the cloth separated from the wax and the bronze replaced part of the cloth, revealing its texture....[H]ere is an early example of a systematic, structurally different process of making being employed to replace taste and labor, and it shows up in the final work. Draping and life casting replace modeling."[14] Look closely at Havel's *Wash* (2004–5; plates 70 and 71), a bronze cast after a Target queen bed sheet, and you'll see the image, or rather the direct and inadvertent trace, of the stitching along the sheet's edge and the folds ironed in at the factory and reinforced by packaging and shelving, and the cast, blank replica of the label that once held a written description of the sheet and its material. It is this blindness that Morris links to automation, to an image (like the photograph) that is forced to appear and that carries the world with it. The world becomes a stain on the bronze, and stains, from the paint slashed across Robert Rauschenberg's *Bed* (1955; fig. 4) to the slept-in sheets of Tracey Emin's *My Bed* (1999), are the marks of a distinctly material, lived-in world.

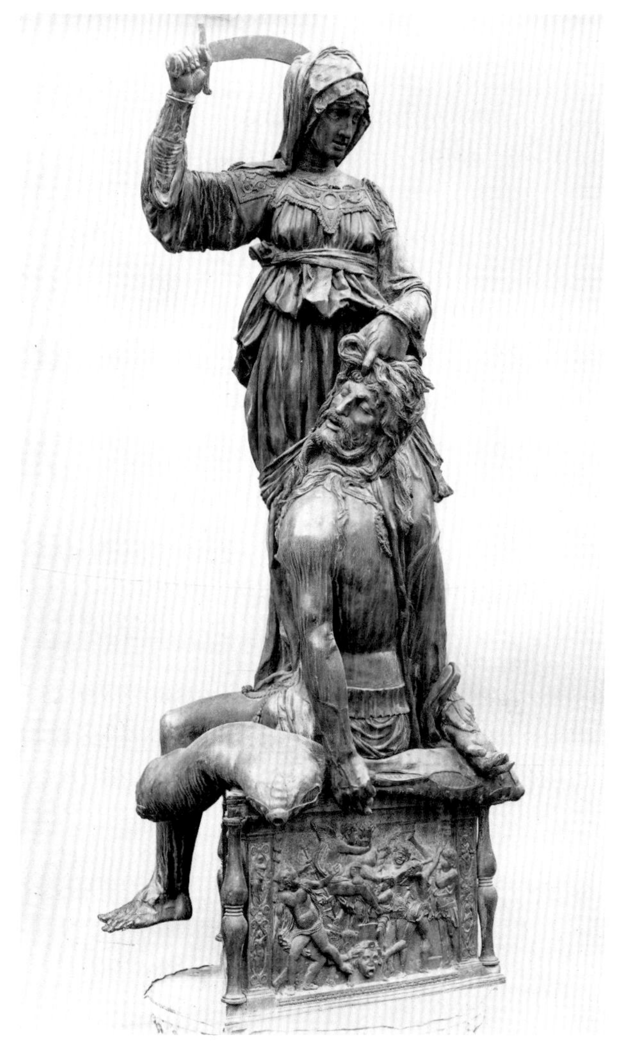

FIGURE 3

Rauschenberg's vertical *Bed* and Emin's piled-up horizontal one both take as their subject something like the specifically lived and, indeed, sexualized nature of Havel's materials, as well as the sense of those materials as surfaces, as bearing traces and evidence, as recording like photo paper—like the blueprint paper Rauschenberg used in a series of direct body prints in the early 1950s—of a human presence now gone. It is disordered, marked by the specifics of class and gender and unfortunate stains of bodies. Emin's rumpled sheets and her bedside are strewn with cigarette packs, pillows, pantyhose, a towel, slippers, and underwear; Rauschenberg's rather straighter ones are covered with a quilt and the drips and thrusts of leftover abstract expressionist painting. According to historian Jonathan Katz, "early reviews of *Bed* claimed that the piece resembled nothing so much as the sight of a rape, or maybe even a murder." [15] Havel's *Wash*, his *Torn Flannel Duvet Cover* are linked to Rauschenberg's and Emin's beds by extension, metonymically, along the over-under spread that Deleuze's fold describes, but his work is far more reticent, far less revelatory than Emin's, even more closeted in its way than Rauschenberg's. And in them the terms of classicizing—of what classicizing he does—might not be those of spiritualization or sublimation, but of repression. Compared to Emin's, Havel's is a kind of buttoned-down, or maybe a buttoned-up world, and that, of course, is an image he has used since the mid-1990s.

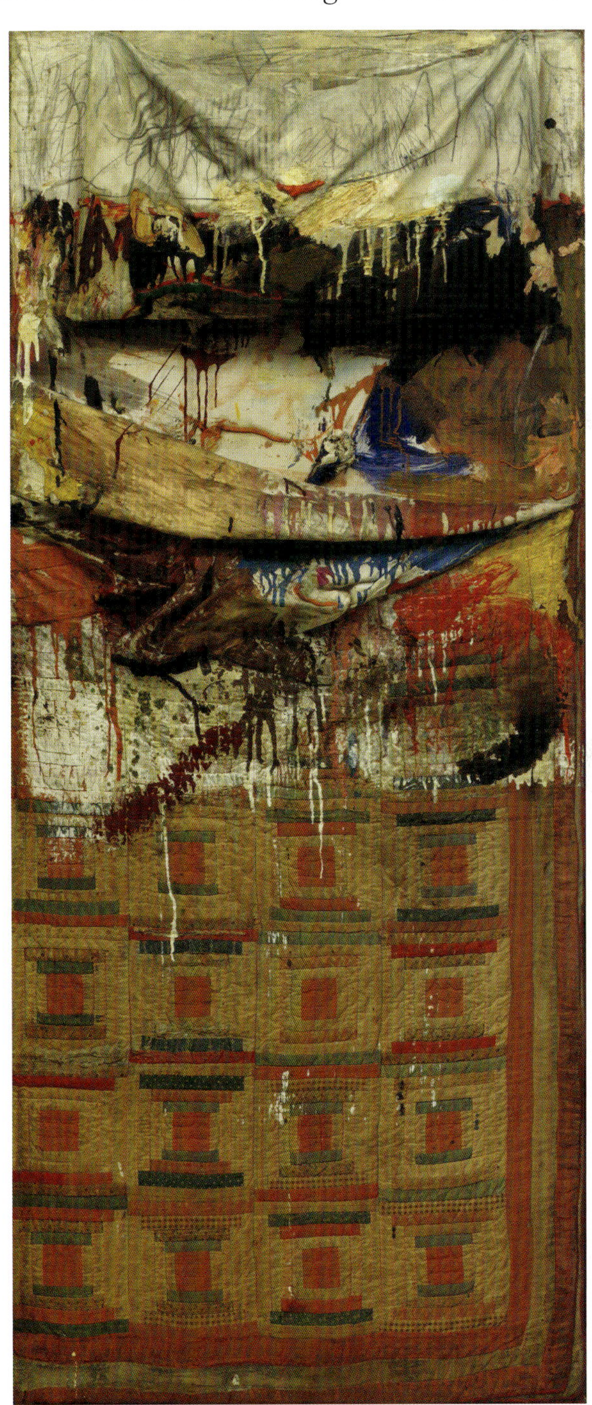
FIGURE 4

My linking of the white collar to repression won't, I hope, seem gratuitous; at least I am not the first to do so. The term "white collar" emerged in America in the 1920s and came to define a large segment of the American workforce across the middle of the century: it labels both a category of jobs—salaried rather than wage labor, technical or clerical rather than manual—and those who filled them: clerks, office workers, sales people, accountants, laboratory technicians, advertising and real estate agents, managers. For the sociologist C. Wright Mills, whose early and still influential study *White Collar: The American Middle Classes* was published in 1953, about the time Havel—and I—were born into white-collar families, that collapse of the employee into the position is fitting; unlike Marx's proletarian, who is taken apart, whose labor is alienated from him, the salaried worker is bought whole, the person, or the display of personality, is part of the bargain. "When white-collar people get jobs, they sell not only their time and energy but their personalities as well. They sell by the week or month their smiles and their kindly gestures, and they must practice prompt repression of resentment and aggression."[16] Here, and indeed across Havel's work, the white collar comes to represent a kind of masquerade, indeed a specifically classed and gendered "male masquerade," and one that opened out even as early as 1951 onto the psychological, at the cost, perhaps, of the political, of a certain kind of consciousness. "The white-collar people slipped quietly into modern society. Whatever history they have is a history without events; whatever common interests they have do not lead to unity; whatever future they have will not be of their own making," wrote Mills. "We need to characterize American society of the mid-twentieth century in more psychological terms, for now the problems that concern us most border on the psychiatric."[17]

Havel's white collar stands for things, for a whole social theory, but also for a sort of person, one characterized increasingly by emptiness precisely in relation to costume—an "empty suit," as they say, an expression that emerges in the 1950s. As Jérôme Sans has written about Havel's work, the white collar "is a sign of discrimination in the world of the worker, the manual laborer. It symbolizes affirmation, effectiveness, assumed responsibility, and consecration. It is an image of power taken and recognized and a universal symbol of decision and money. The color, par excellence, synonymous with the upper class...."[18] But the garment does not merely align its individual wearer on the side of power—prop him up, as it were, it also constricts and dissembles. The white shirt signifies class and gender, but more than that, it signifies a kind of impossible position, a requirement. It is in a sense a disguise, a parade of power, of just adequacy even—an *Aura*, perhaps, to borrow the title of one of the works included here, an empty shirt collar, an invisible shirt, marked only by a lonesome, nearly ephemeral string of buttons—and compensation for its lack. Here we might recall again Hegel's complaint about modern dress, that it is "produced for an external purpose, something cut, sewn together here, folded over there, elsewhere fixed, and, in short, purely unfree forms." Or a little more recently, T. S. Eliot's "The Hollow Men": "We are the hollow men / We are the stuffed men / Leaning together .... Shape without form, shade without colour, / Paralysed force, gesture without motion." Gesture without motion might well describe Havel's starched and abbreviated restaging of Michelangelo's Sistine Chapel creation of Adam in white shirts in *Laundered Pair. Aura* (1995-96; plates 1 and 2) and *Laundered Pair* are characterized most strongly by emptiness and loss, or, to use Lacan's term, by lack, the failure to live up to or to be the image, however one mistrusts or "critiques" it. As my references to Eliot and Mills—and to Lacan for that matter, since his seminal "Signification of the Phallus" was presented as a lecture in 1958—might suggest, these are old but also precisely modern laments. Old enough, one could say, to be his father.

Most of Havel's shirt and collar pieces don't refer as far back as *Laundered Pair*; their formal sources and textual references tend to be mid- to late twentieth century. The twenty-eight bronze patina-white collars of *February* (1996; plate 12), the starched and strung vertical stack of *Spine* (1996; plates 3 and 4) suggest Brancusi's *Endless Column at Tirgu Jiu* (fig. 5) and, after that, say, Donald Judd's mid-1960s wall stacks, ordered, as Judd would say, "one thing after another." Other works too borrow the look and the meanings of minimalism, if only to press against them. Pinned to the wall in shiny, expansive grids or held in the cardboard boxes they are delivered in, open and arranged in rows on the floor, Havel's label pieces take their forms not only from the world of industrial production, assembly-line stitching and the garment shop, but from the work of minimalism. His nods are to Carl Andre and Frank Stella, and in the subtle ranked color of a work like *Lost and Lust* (2004; plates 66 and 67) to Agnes Martin, but, as Hal Foster has noted, those artists' references too were to factory and piece production. "Not until minimalism and pop is serial production made consistently integral to the technical production of works of art."[19] That seriality, the form of industrial production in indefinite series, is the mirror of minimalism's "one thing after another," and it is in part what the art historian Anna Chave characterizes as minimalism's "rhetoric of power."

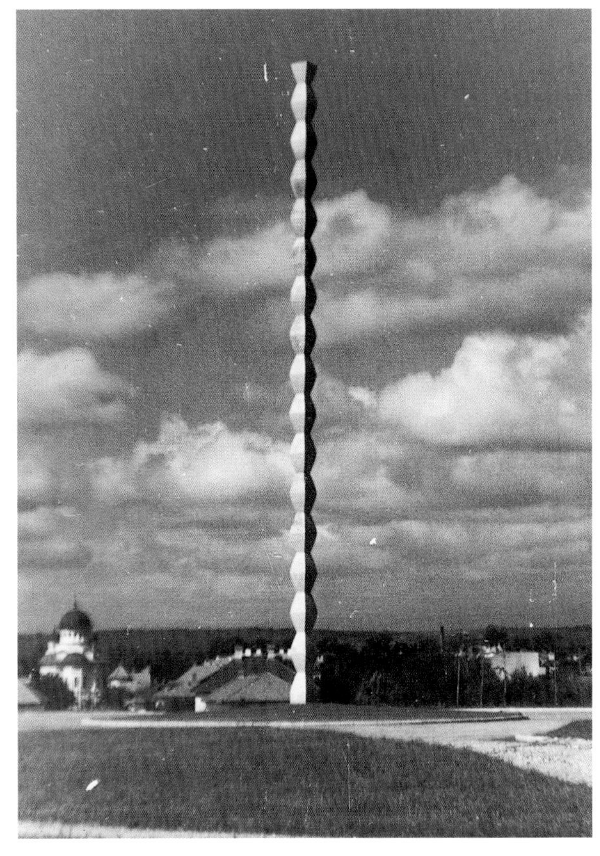

FIGURE 5

"With closer scrutiny," she writes, "the blank face of minimalism may come into focus as the face of capital, the face of authority, the face of the father."[20] Havel's minimalist face is rather crestfallen; its power domesticated. Recasting it not only in the reticent and traditional bronze, but also in the materials of the haberdashery, he has shrunk it, made it intimate, fitted it to the body. Havel's *Wash* is something of a remake of Richard Serra's early 1980s arcs, but its scale is drawn from the domestic sphere; it encloses not as industrial architecture, looming and threatening, or at the very least, insisting, as in Serra's arcs, but as an interior space: the back of *Wash* is like being under the covers. Cowering, perhaps, though that may be too strong of a reading. Still, the language Havel has chosen for the writing in this show, the writing that appears as a sort of caption fastened to the wall on the shirt labels, suggests over and over again—by the hundreds—impotence and powerlessness: *Lost* (2000; plates 31 and 32), *Lost and Lust* (2004; plates 66 and 67), *Bruised* (2004; plates 68 and 69), *Desire* (2003–4; plate 47). *Desire* appears here in two forms, as a decorously soaring, or perhaps gently declining vertical, hung from the ceiling by monofilament, and as *Fading Desire* (plates 43–45), two twelve-foot grids of *Desire* labels washed over and over again to produce that eponymous fade, pinned down one-by-one like specimens or evidence. The words are distanced, damped down both by their photomechanical repetition and by Havel's piecework obsession. They are not even Havel's own words: they are drawn, word by word, from poems by John Berryman and short stories by Samuel Beckett, singled out for what Havel describes as their emotional and contextual fittingness; the labels' typeface—italic or roman, capitalized or lowercase—is borrowed too, taken directly off the page. Berryman's "Dream Song" poems and Beckett's stories share with one another, and with Havel's work, a reticent relation to the present and, even more, to a direct naming of the past; they bury their emotional charge, or deflect it, in strings of words along lines that take the form of sentences but never quite deliver the descriptive or declarative meanings that we expect from sentences.

One could think of this practice as a kind of formalist exercise, the way that formalist modernism makes its meaning; perhaps it is an erasure of the self of the sort that Eliot wrote of in "Tradition and the Individual Talent": "The progress of an artist is a continual self-sacrifice, a continual extinction of the personality....The emotion of art is impersonal." [21] But this reticence, this insistently repeated and yet repeatedly muted complaint, might also suggest a different sort of formalism, one that runs along the lines of class and gender. It might recall once again C. Wright Mill's description of white-collar practice—that practiced "repression of resentment and aggression"—and the damage caused all around by the masculine masquerade.

NOTES

1 Mel Bochner, "Serial Art, Systems, Solipsism," in *Minimal Art: A Critical Anthology*, ed. Gregory Battcock (New York: E. P. Dutton, 1968), 92.

2 Ibid., 101.

3 Alfred Barr, "The New American Painting," in *Abstract Expressionism: A Critical Record*, ed. David Shapiro and Cecile Shapiro (Cambridge, England: Cambridge University Press, 1990), 96.

4 Robert Pincus-Witten, *Postminimalism* (New York: Out of London Press, 1977), 16.

5 Roger de Piles, *The principles of painting, under the heads of anatomy attitude accident ... In which is contained, An account of the Athenian, Roman, Venetian and Flemish schools. To which is added, The balance of painters. ... Written originally in French by Mons. du Piles, ... And now first translated into English. By a painter. London, 1743.* Eighteenth Century Collections Online. Gale Group: http://galenet.galegroup.com/servlet/ECCO. Document Number CW106434694. Facsimile page 110.

6 George B. Bridgman, *The Seven Laws of Folds* (Pelham, N.Y.: Bridgman Publishers, 1942), passim.

7 Gen Doy, *Drapery: Classicism and Barbarism in Visual Culture* (London: I. B. Tauris, 2002), 26.

8 de Piles, 111.

9 G. W. F. Hegel, *Aesthetics: Lectures on Fine Art*, vol. 2, trans. T. M. Knox (Oxford, England: Clarendon Press, 1975), 745. See also Doy, 20–24.

10 Jacob Burckhardt, "The Cicerone: Bernini," in *Bernini in Perspective*, ed. George C. Bauer (Englewood Cliffs, N. J.: Prentice-Hall, 1976), 66.

11 Sir Joshua Reynolds, *Discourses*, ed. Pat Rogers (London: Penguin Books, 1992), 241.

12 Burckhardt, 66.

13 Hegel, 746.

14 Robert Morris, "Some Notes on the Phenomenology of Making," *Artforum* 8 (April 1970): 65.

15 Jonathan Katz, "The Art of Code: Jasper Johns and Robert Rauschenberg," in *Significant Others: Creativity and Intimate Partnership*, ed. Whitney Chadwick and Isabelle de Courtivron (London: Thames and Hudson, 1993), xx.

16 C. Wright Mills, *White Collar: The American Middle Classes* (New York: Oxford University Press, 1953), xvii.

17 Ibid., ix, xx.

18 Jérôme Sans, "White Bodies," in *Joseph Havel: Commun,* exh. cat. (Paris: Galerie Gabrielle Maubrie, 1997), unpaginated.

19 Hal Foster, *The Return of the Real* (Cambridge, MA: MIT Press, 1996), 63.

20 Anna Chave, "Minimalism and the Rhetoric of Power," *Arts Magazine* 64 (January 1990): 51.

21 T. S. Eliot, "Tradition and the Individual Talent," in *Modernism: An Anthology of Sources and Documents*, ed. Vassiliki Kolocotroni, Jane Goldman, and Olga Taxidou (Chicago: University of Chicago Press, 1998), 369, 371.

Plate 1
Aura *(detail)*
1995–96
Shirt collar, needle, thread, and buttons
53 x 7 x 7 inches
Courtesy of Claire and Doug Ankenman

Figure 1
Lynda Benglis
Phantom
1971
Polyurethane foam pigmented with phosphorus
8 x 35 x 8 feet
View of installation at Milwaukee Art Center

Figure 2
Gian Lorenzo Bernini
Tomb of Alexander VII
1672–78
Marble and gilded bronze
Basilica di San Pietro, Vatican State

Figure 3
Donatello
Judith and Holofernes
1455–60
Bronze
Piazza della Signoria, Florence, Italy

Figure 4
Robert Rauschenberg
Bed
1955
Combine painting: oil and pencil on pillow, quilt, and sheet on wooden supports
6 feet 3 1/4 inches x 31 1/2 inches x 8 inches
Collection of the Museum of Modern Art, New York
Gift of Leo Castelli in honor of Alfred H. Barr, Jr. (79.1989)

Figure 5
Constantin Brancusi
Endless Column at Tirgu Jiu
c. 1938
Oak
6 feet 8 inches x 9 7/8 inches x 9 5/8 inches
Musée National d'Art Moderne, Centre Georges Pompidou, Paris, France

Plate 2
Aura
1995–96
Shirt collar, needle, thread, and buttons
53 x 7 x 7 inches
Courtesy of Claire and Doug Ankenman

Plate 3
Spine
1996
Fabric shirt collars and monofilament
156 x 7 1/2 x 7 1/2 inches
Courtesy of Devin Borden Hiram Butler Gallery

Plate 4
Spine *(detail)*
1996
Fabric shirt collars and monofilament
156 x 7 1/2 x 7 1/2 inches
Courtesy of Devin Borden Hiram Butler Gallery

Plate 5
White Virus
1994
White shirts, lampshades, and thread
18 x 25 x 18 inches
Courtesy of the artist

Plate 6
White
1994
White shirts, lampshades, and thread
190 x 49 x 53 inches
Courtesy of the artist

Plate 7
Boogie Woogie
1995
White shirts, pins
48 x 48 x 4 inches
Courtesy of the artist

Plate 8
Laundered Pair
1996
Bronze with patina
82 x 44 x 55 inches
Collection of Nancy M. O'Boyle

Plate 9
Un-Laundered Pair
1996
Bronze with patina
86 x 45 x 45 inches
Collection of Jeanne and Michael Klein

Plate 10
Three
1996
Bronze with patina
114 x 19 1/4 x 14 inches
Collection of Beverly Kopp

Plate 11
Installation of ***Corps Blanc: New Works*** *by Joseph Havel at Barry Whistler Gallery, Dallas*
1995

Plate 12
February
1996
Bronze with patina
94 x 10 x 10 inches
Collection of Dr. Carolyn Farb

Plate 13
Seam
1995–96
Bronze
Dimensions variable
Courtesy of the artist

Plate 14
Seam *(detail)*
1995–96
Bronze
Dimensions variable
Courtesy of the artist

Plate 15
Moon
1998
Fabric shirt collars and monofilament
21 x 21 x 21 inches
Collection of Suzanne M. Manns

Plate 16
Star
1997–98
Bronze with patina
51 1/2 x 51 1/2 x 51 1/2 inches
Collection of Mr. and Mrs. Russell Hawkins

PLATE 2 ***Aura***, *1995–96*

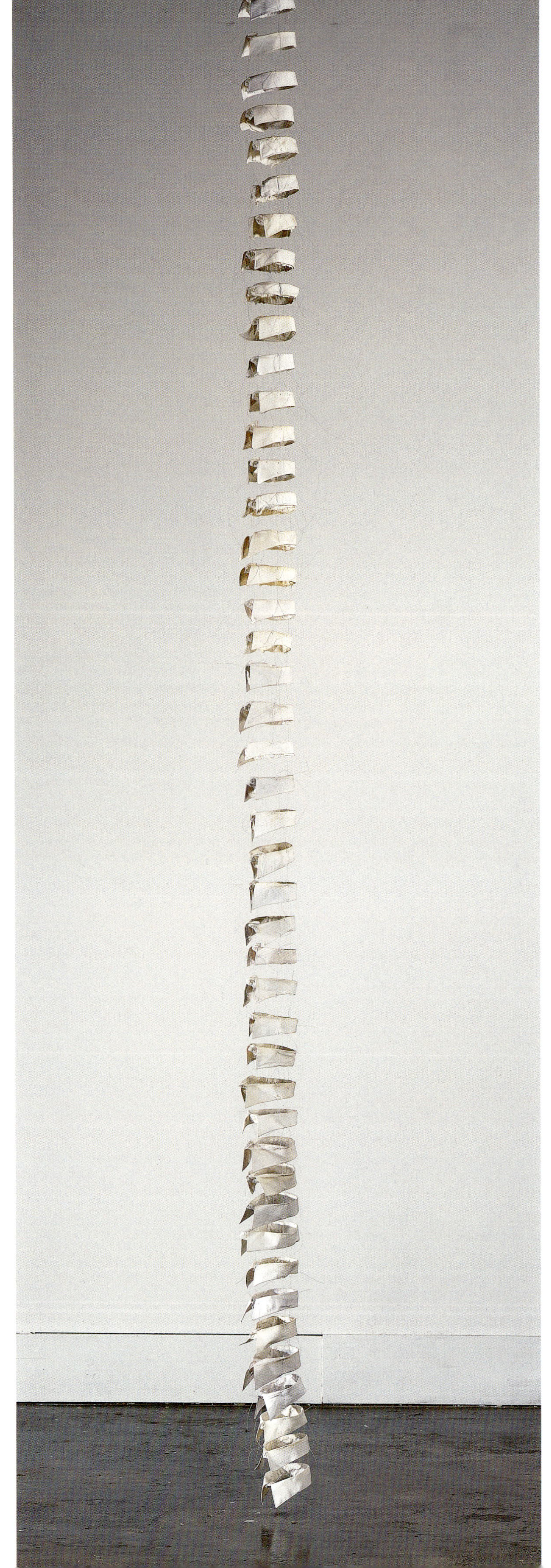

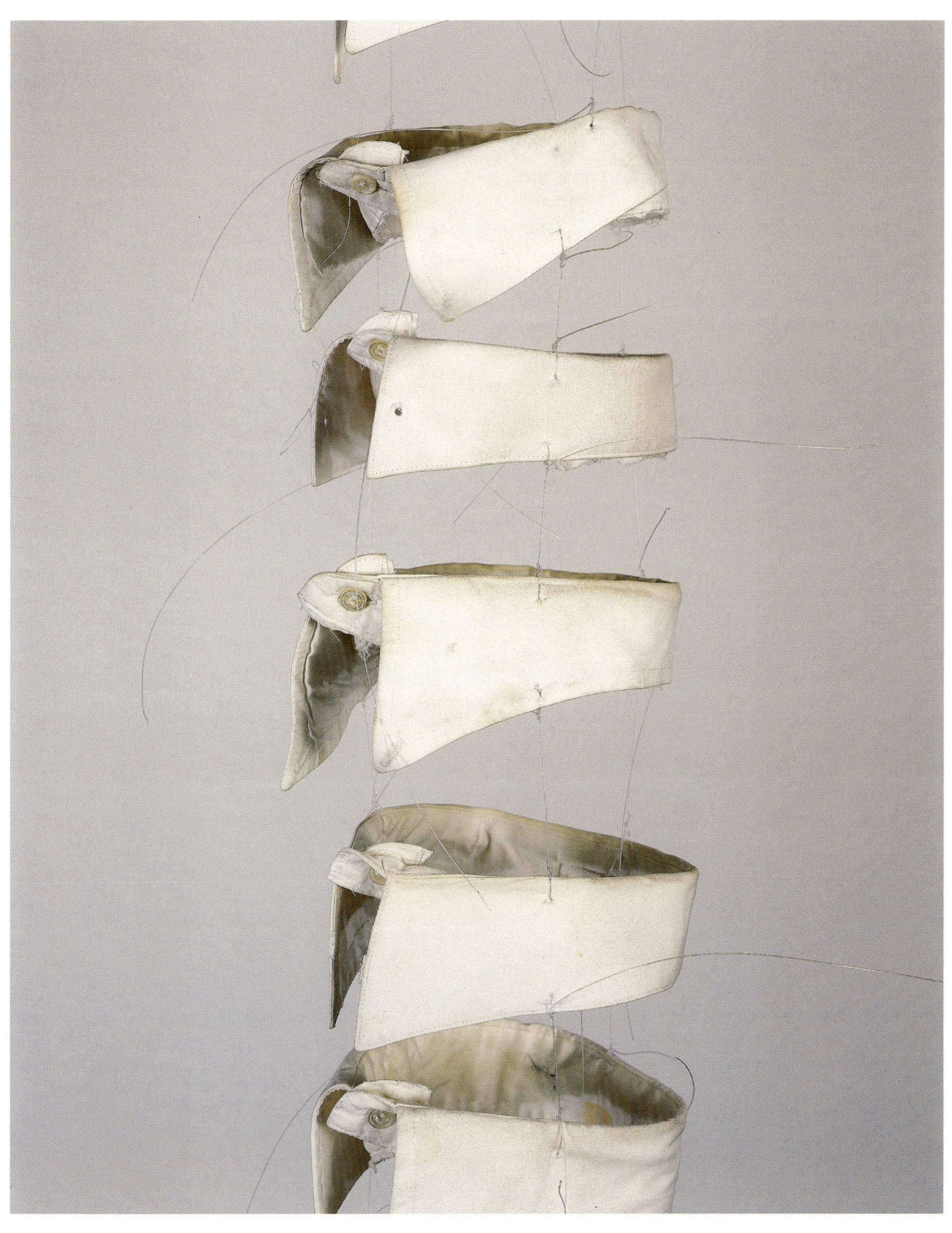

◀ PLATE 3 ***Spine***, *1996*

PLATE 4 ***Spine*** *(detail), 1996* ▶

PLATE 5 ***White Virus**, 1994*

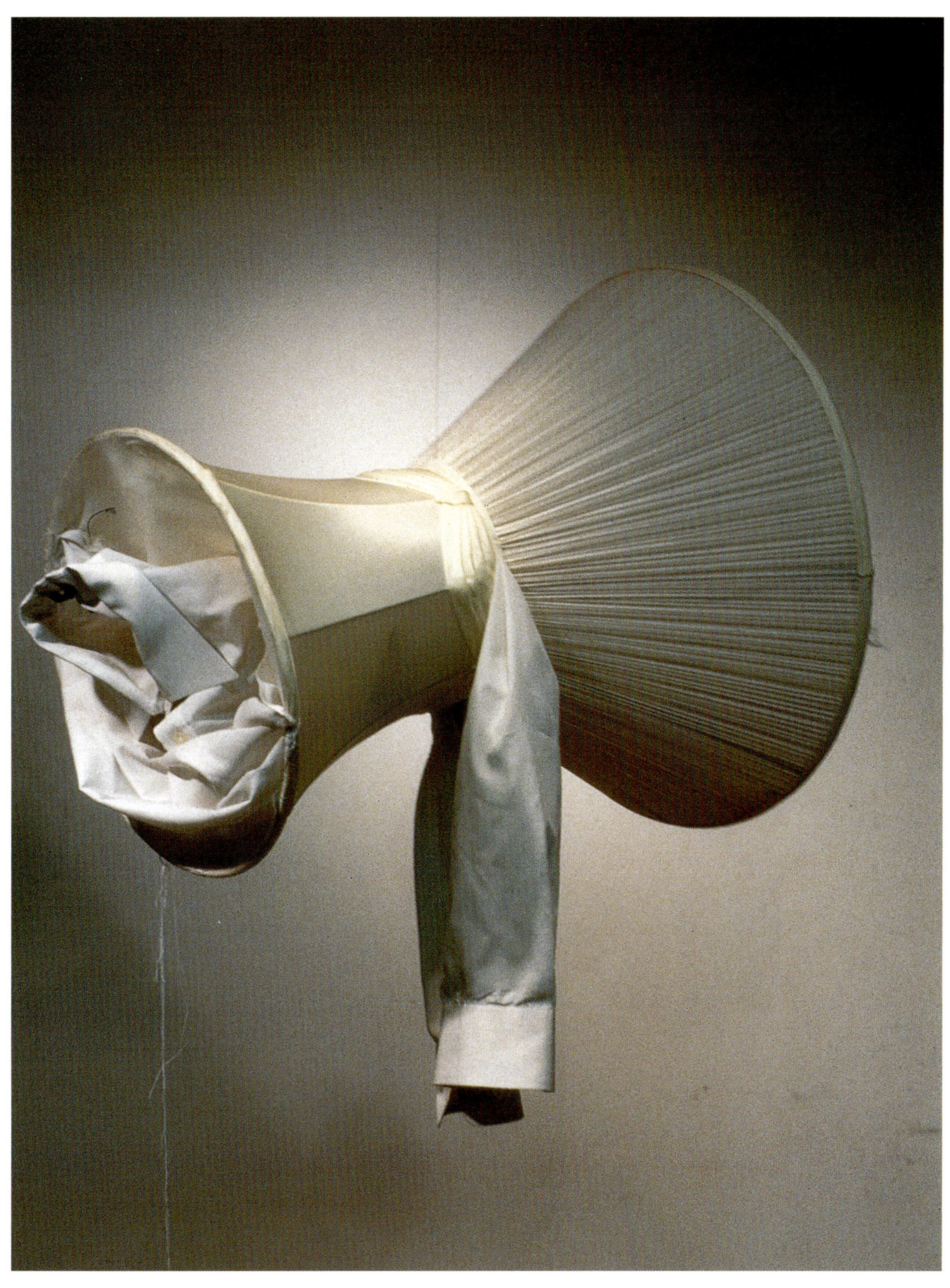

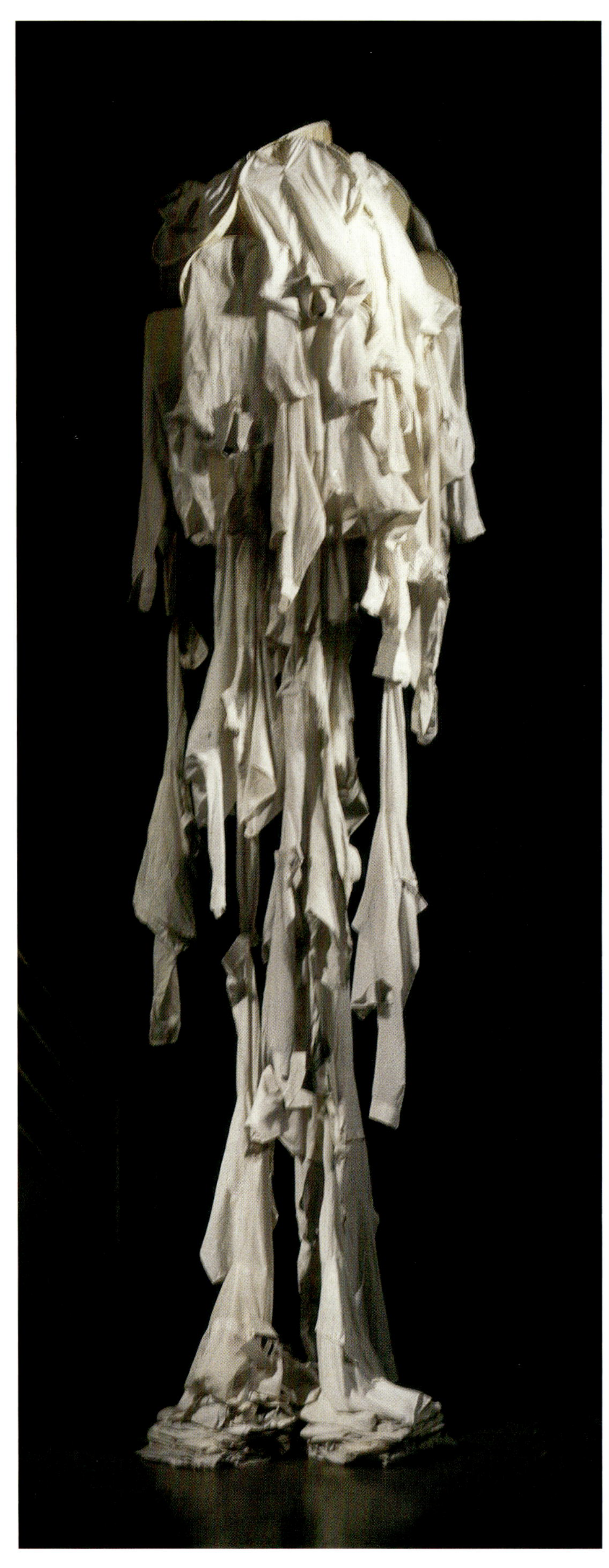

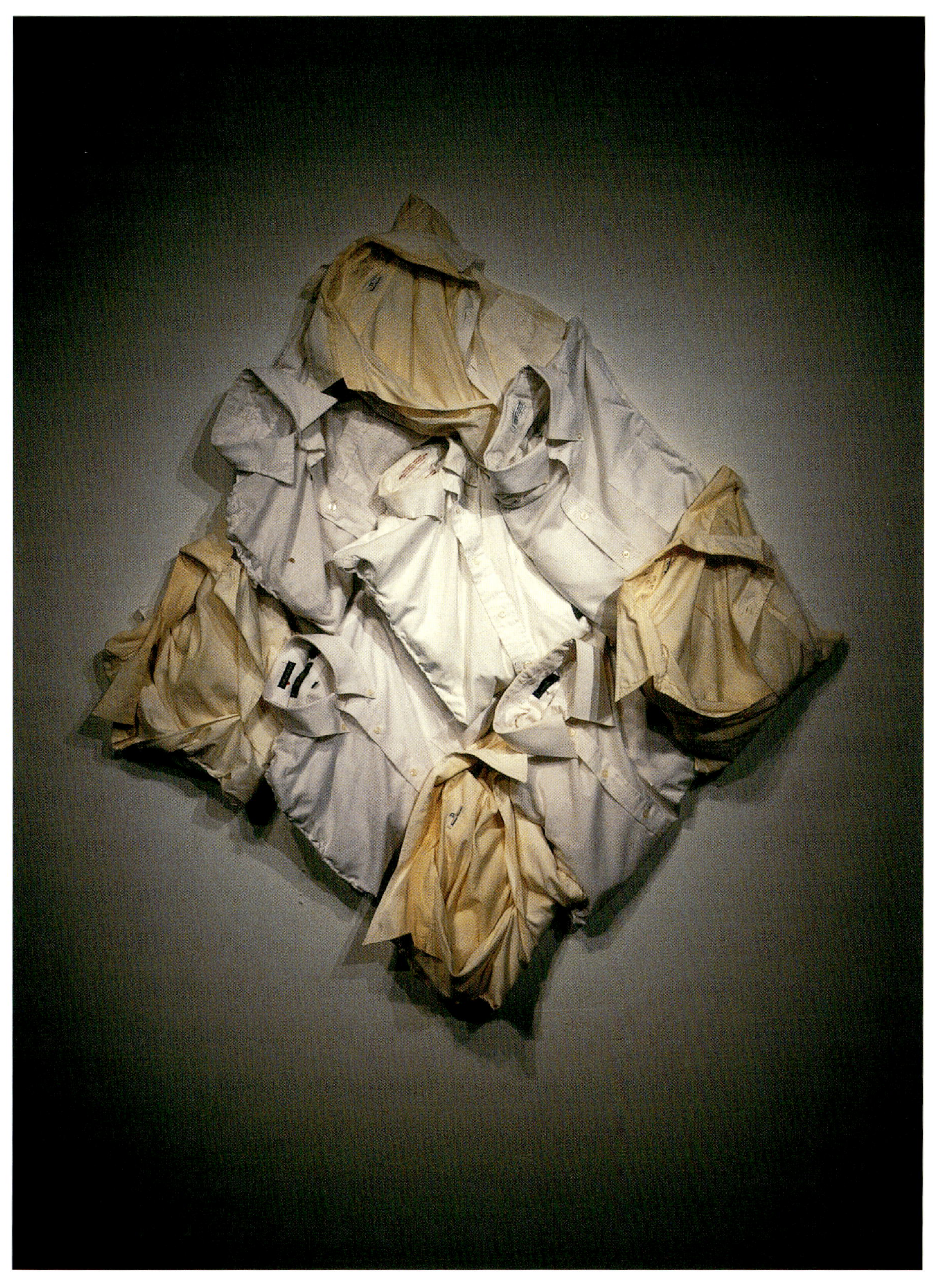

◀ PLATE 6 ***White***, *1994*

PLATE 7 ***Boogie Woogie***, *1995* ▶

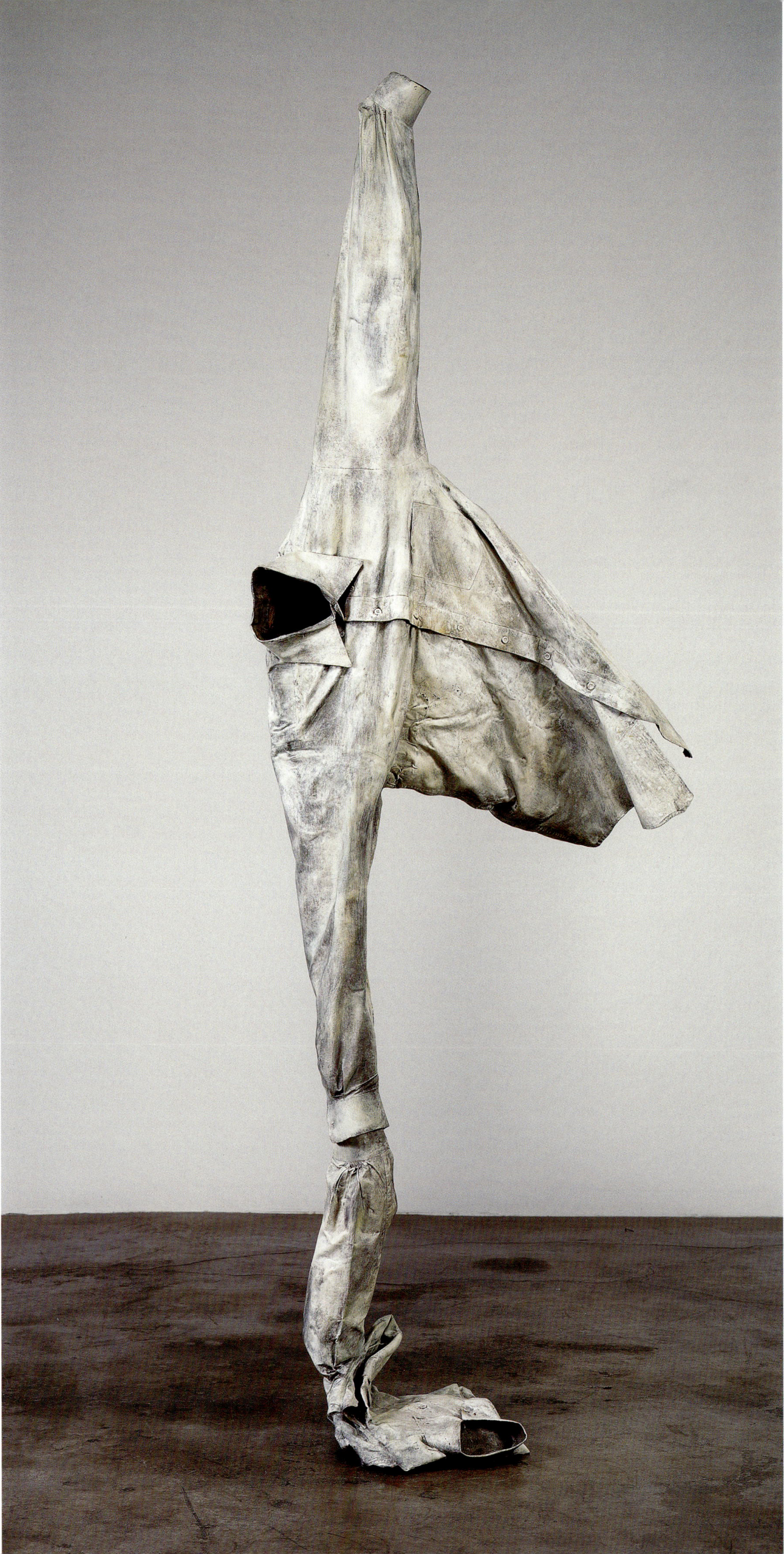

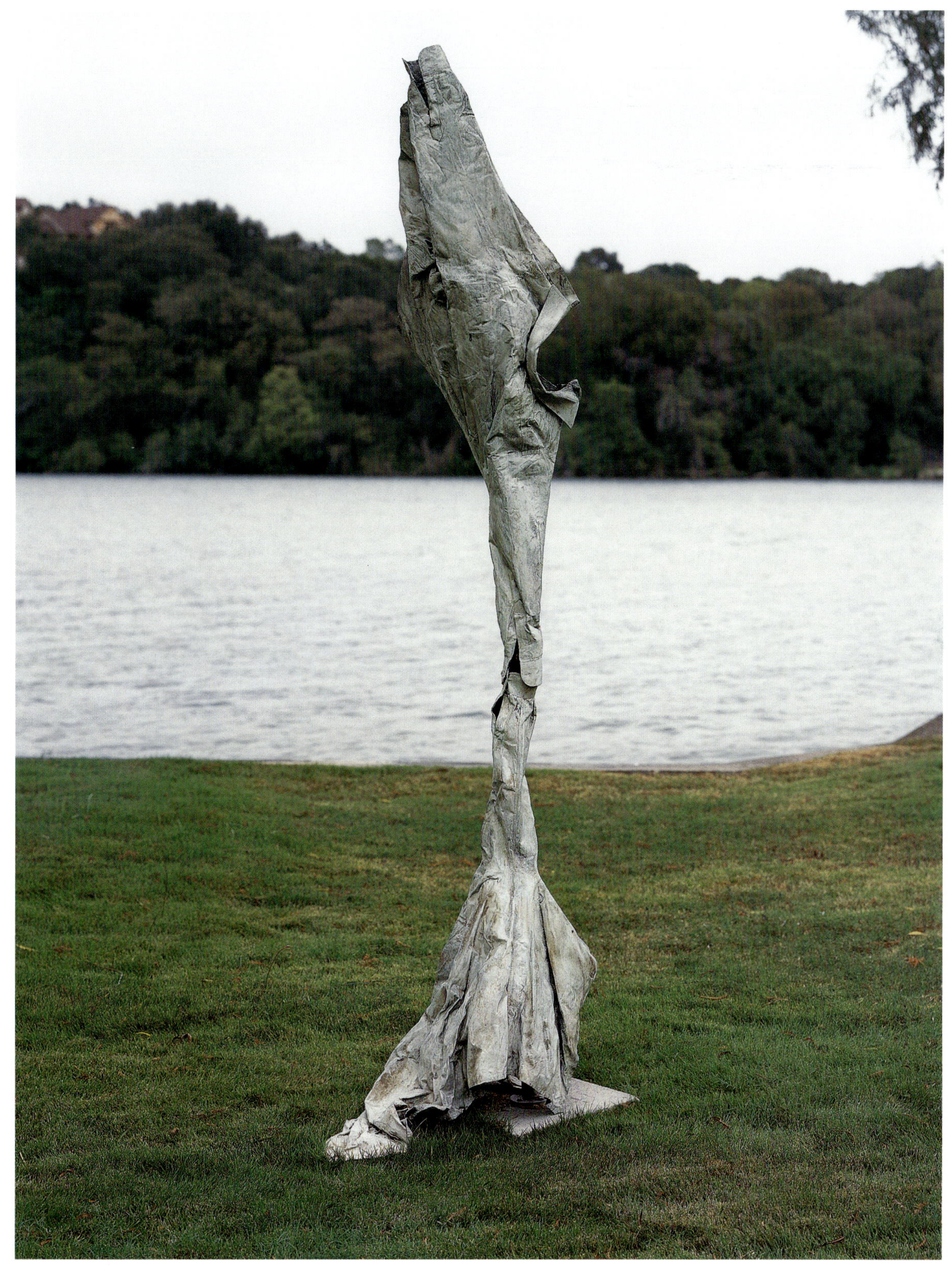

◀ PLATE 8 ***Laundered Pair**, 1996*

PLATE 9 ***Un-Laundered Pair**, 1996* ▶

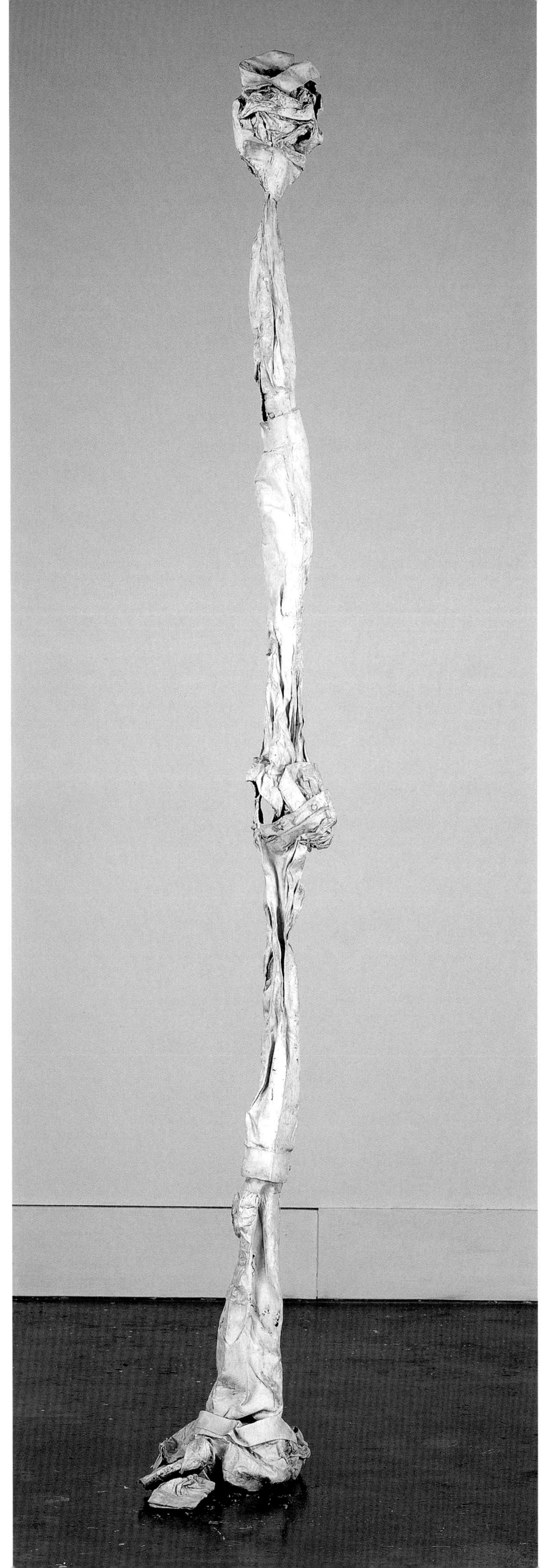

PLATE 10 ***Three***, *1996*

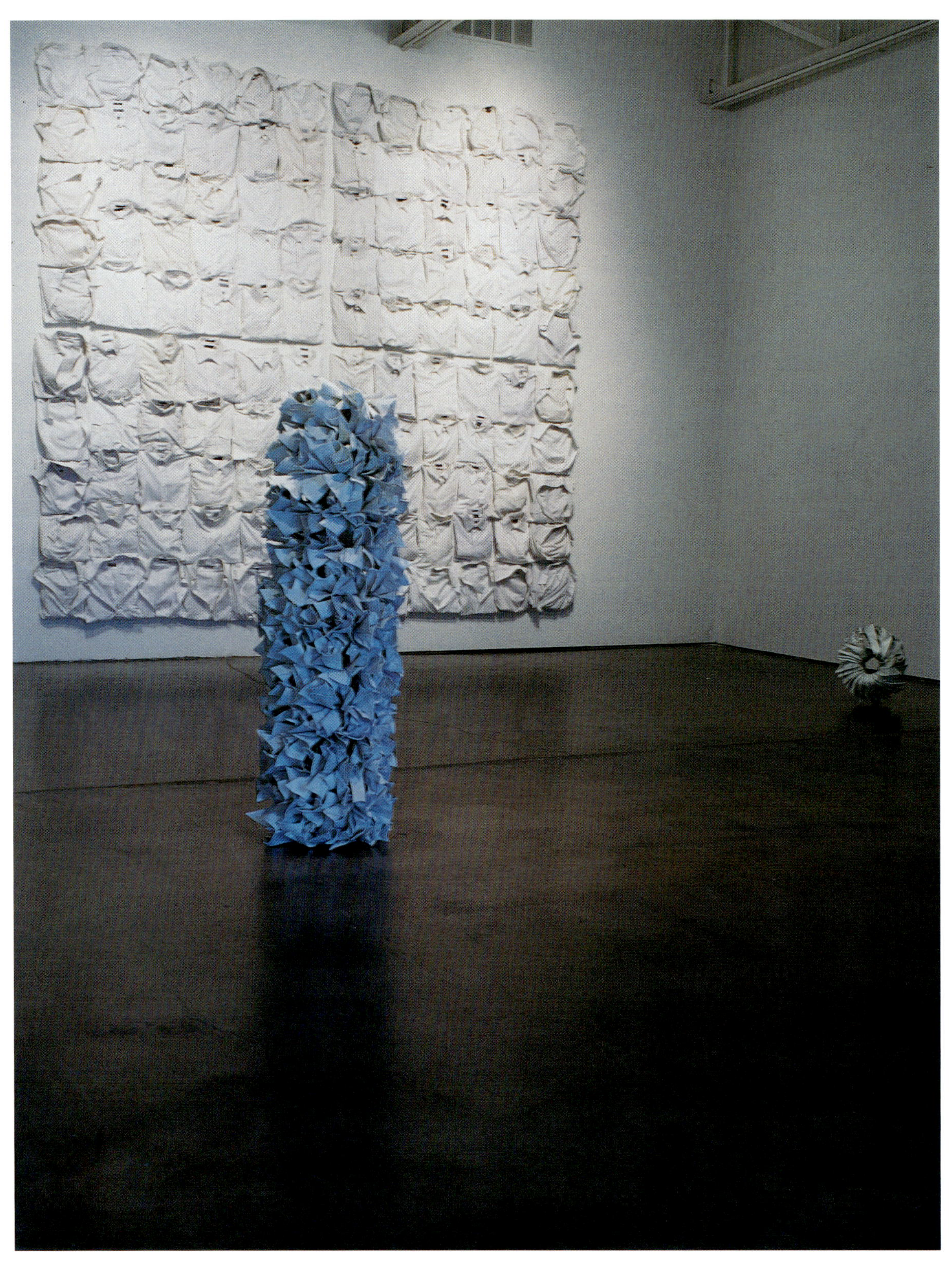

◀ PLATE 11 ***Corps Blanc***, *1995*

PLATE 12 ***February***, *1996* ▶

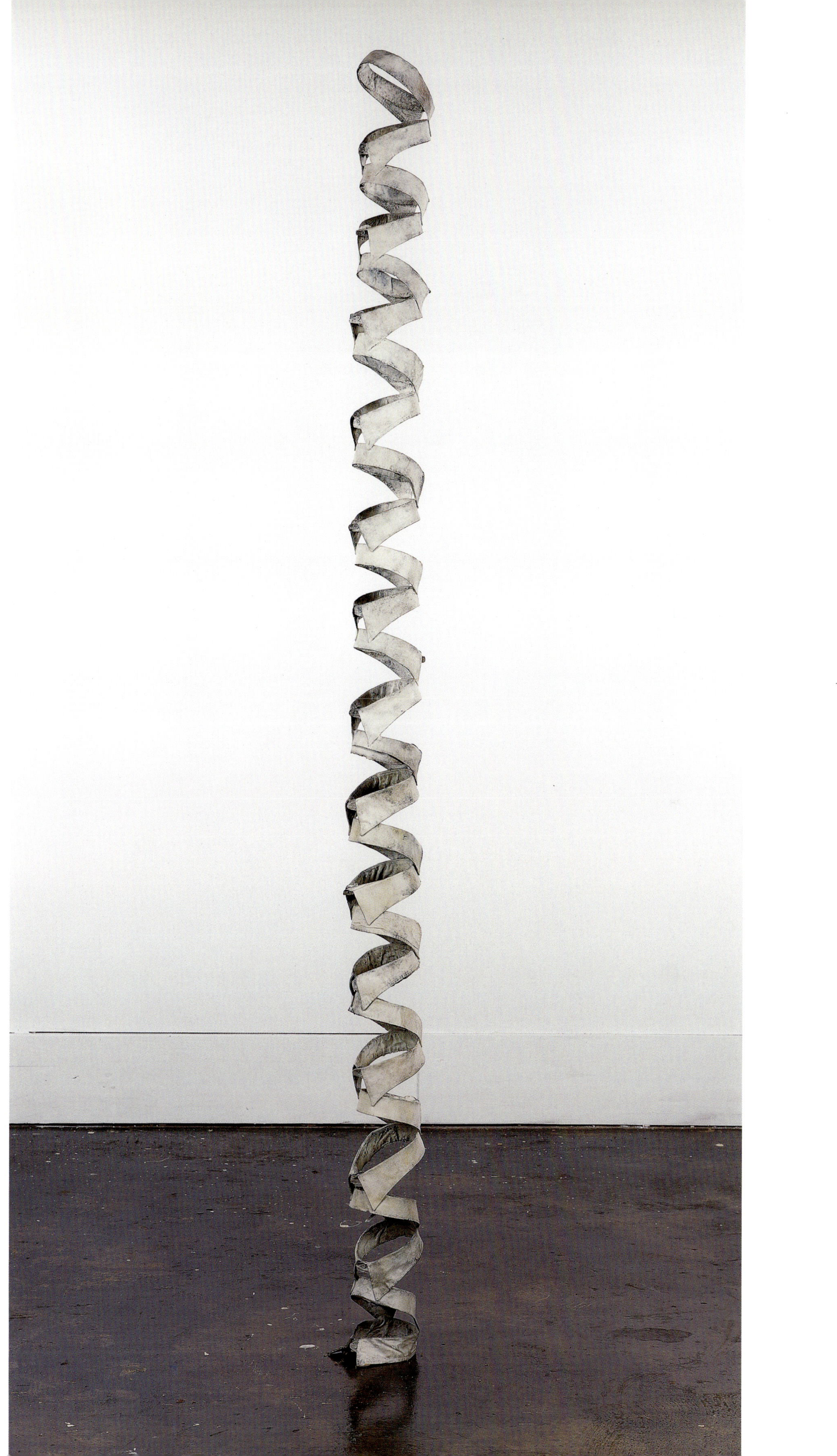

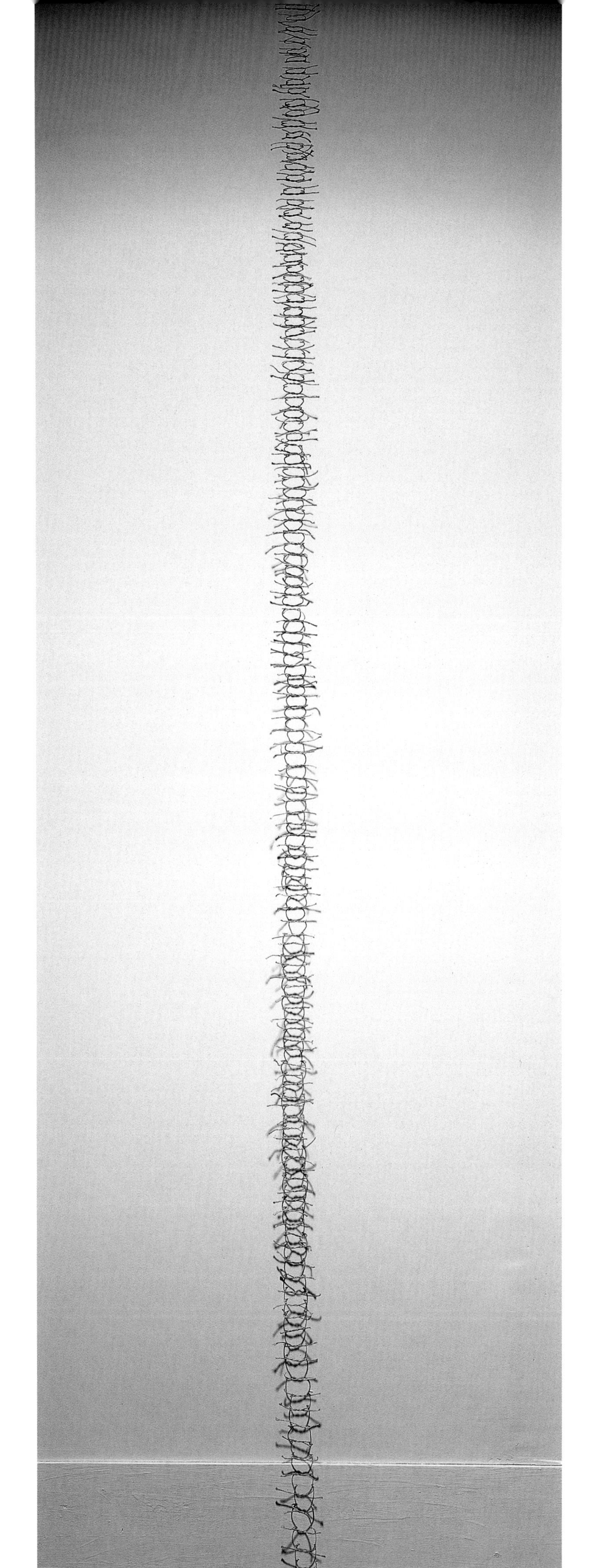

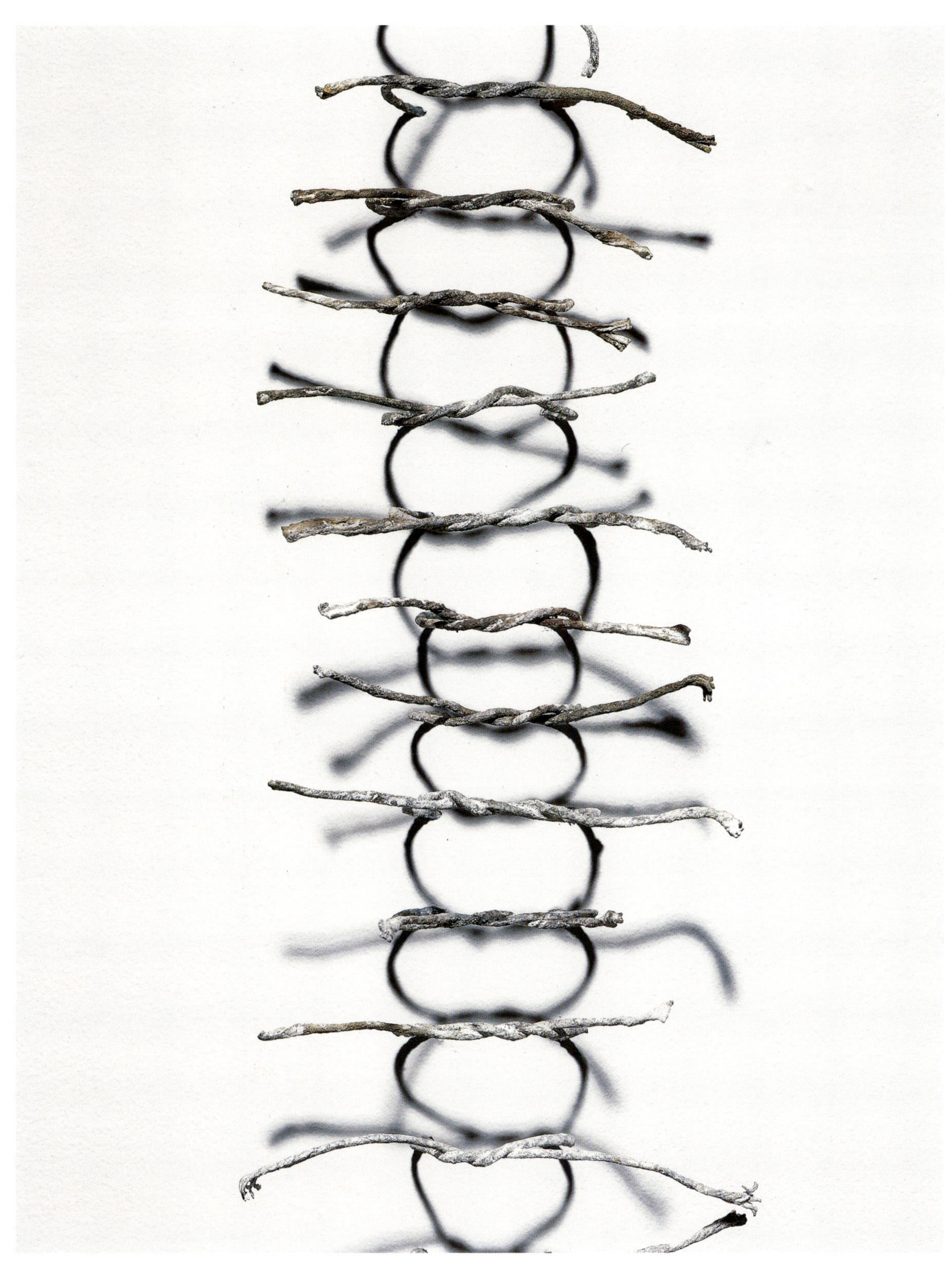

PLATE 14 **Seam (detail)**, *1995–96* ▶

◀ PLATE 13 **Seam**, *1995–96*

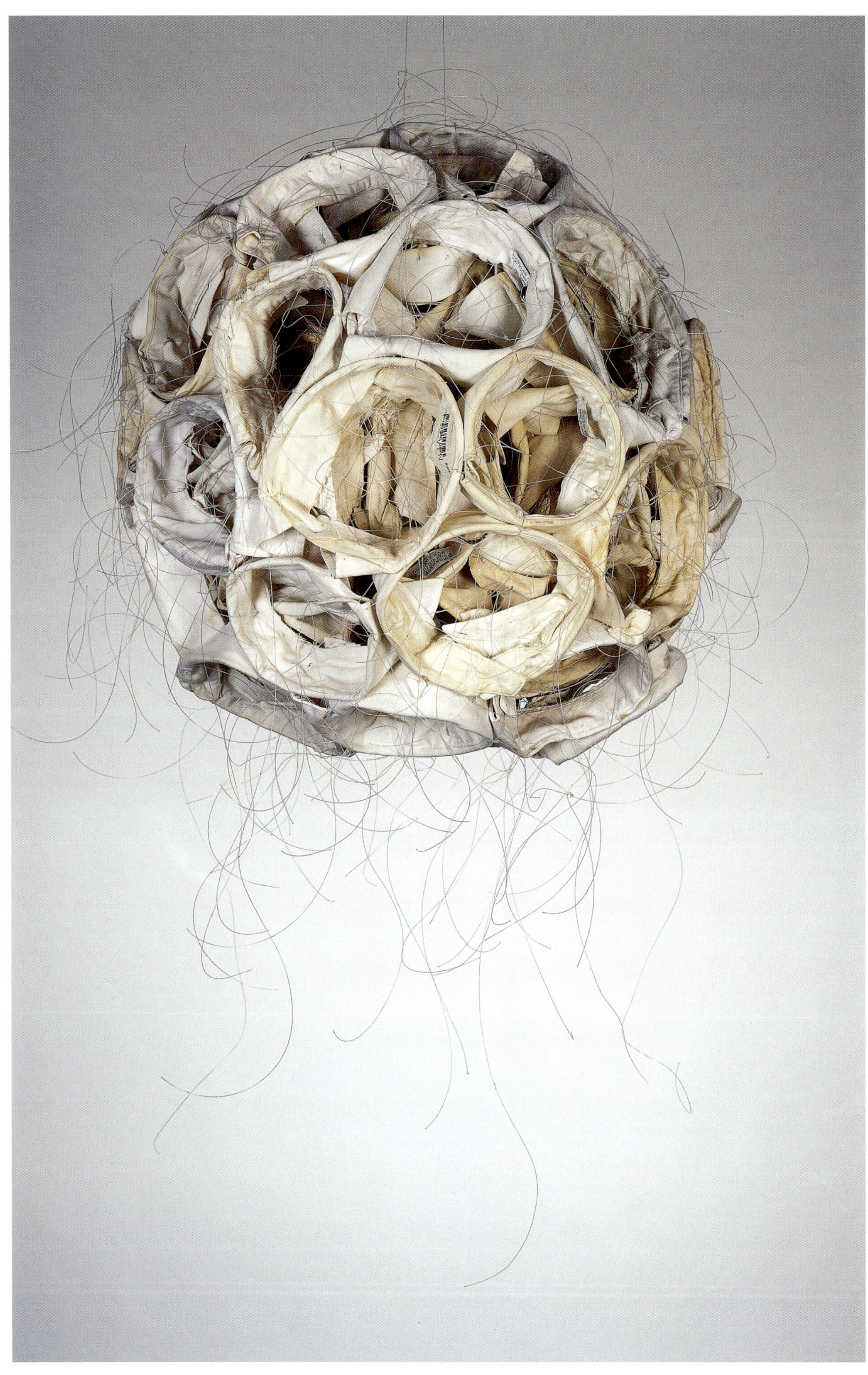

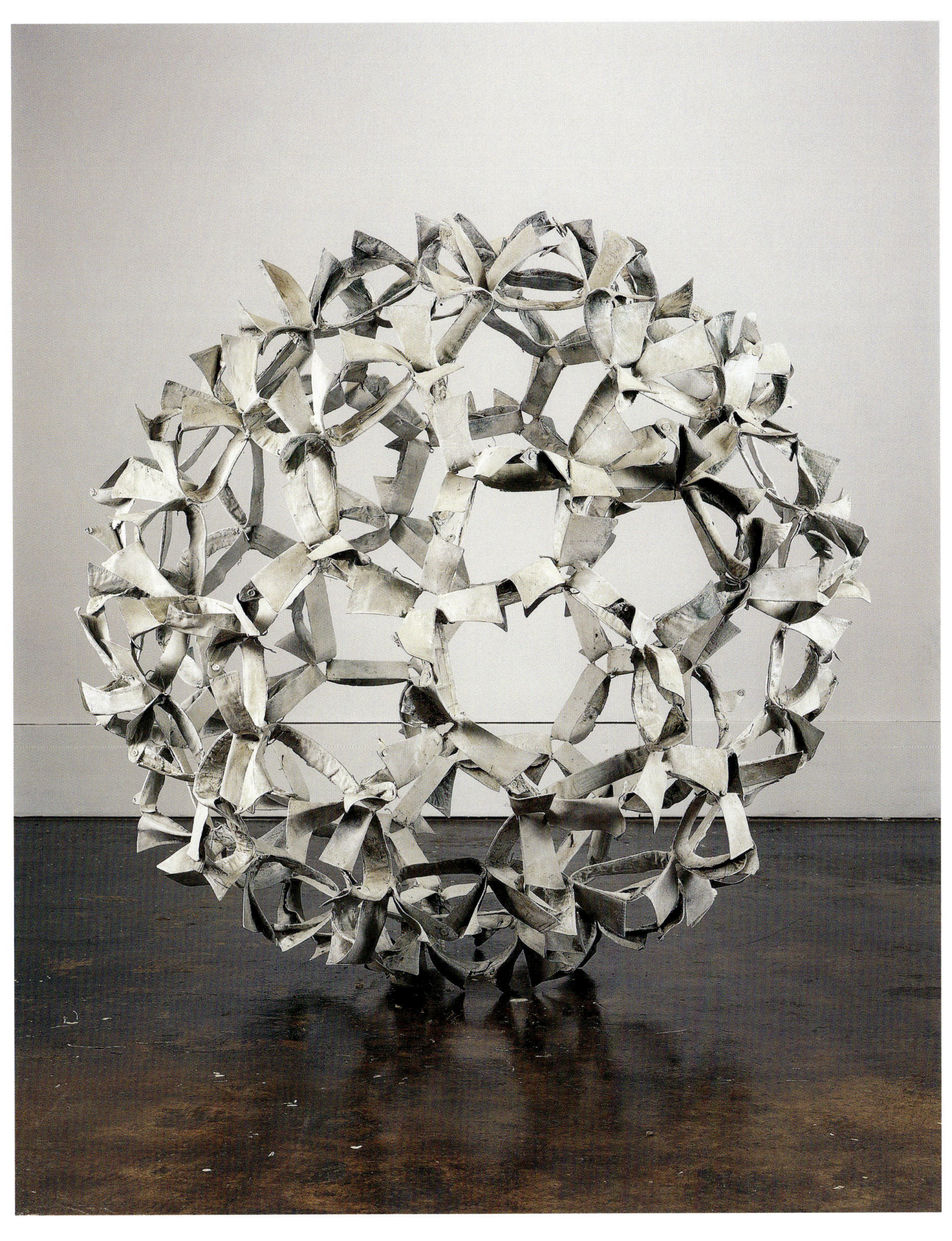

◂ PLATE 15 ***Moon***, *1998*

PLATE 16 ***Star***, *1997–98* ▸

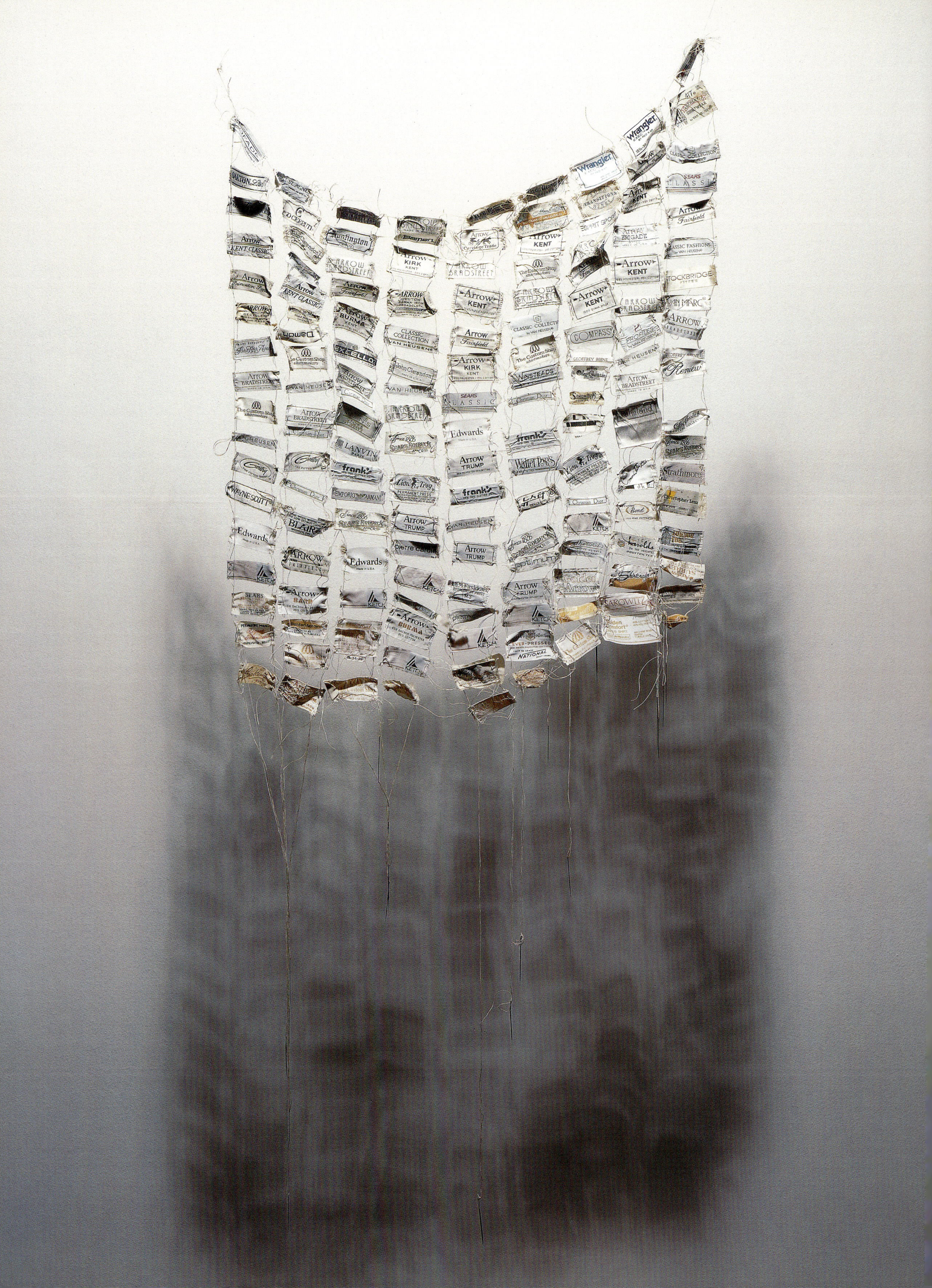
Wrangler
Wrangler
SEARS CLASSIC
Arrow Fairfield
Huntington
Arrow KENT CLASSIC
Arrow KENT
CLASSIC FASHIONS
STOCKBRIDGE
ARROW BRADSTREET
VAN MARC
CLASSIC COLLECTION VAN HEUSEN
COMPASS
The Custom Shop
EXCELLO
John Clarendon
WINSTEADS
Review
SEARS CLASSIC
Edwards
frank's
LANVIN
Arrow TRUMP
Strathmore
WAYNE SCOTT
EMPORIO ARMANI
BLAIR
Edwards
KETCH
Arrow BURMA
NATIONAL

JOSEPH HAVEL: THE ACTIVITY OF STILL OBJECTS

Alison de Lima Greene

In 1977 Rosalind Krauss published *Passages in Modern Sculpture*, a text that placed the advent of conceptual art and minimalism within the larger arc of historical modernism. She opened her discussion with the observation: "One of the striking aspects of modern sculpture is the way in which it manifests its makers' growing awareness that sculpture is a medium peculiarly located at the juncture between stillness and motion, time arrested and time passing. From this tension, which defines the very condition of sculpture, comes its enormous expressive power."[1] Krauss developed her thesis by assessing examples from Auguste Rodin and Medardo Rosso to Richard Serra, Michael Heizer, and Robert Smithson, concluding with an examination of *Hand Catching Lead* (1969), *Double Negative* (1969), and *Spiral Jetty* (1969–70): "With these images of passage, the transformation of sculpture—from a static, idealized medium to a temporal material one—that had begun with Rodin is fully achieved. In every case the image of passage serves to place both the viewer and artist before the work, and the world, in an attitude of primary humility in order to encounter the deep reciprocity between himself and it."[2]

Passages in Modern Sculpture arrived at turning a point in American art. Krauss articulated many of the concerns facing contemporary sculptors in an era that had seen the discipline expand to embrace performance, film, and earthworks, releasing the genre from the confines of object making. However, the book ended slyly with a coda that pointed in another liberating direction: an untitled Joel Shapiro from 1974 (New York, The Museum of Modern Art). Krauss offered no analysis of this icon of new figuration; rather, she chose to present Shapiro's pared-down image of a house supported by a simple L-shaped bar, cast in bronze, as a postscript, allowing the loaded reference to resonate with the reader. She then reinforced the associations stirred by Shapiro's work by quoting Marcel Proust's ruminations on lost time: "Somewhere beyond the reach of the intellect, and unmistakably present in some material object (or in the sensation which such an object arouses in us), though we have no idea which one it is. As for that object, it depends entirely on chance whether we come upon it before we die, or whether we never encounter it."[3]

Joseph Havel was coming of age during these years, and like many of his contemporaries, he

PLATE 17

developed his work within the complementary temporal frames of process and memory described by Krauss. Havel has investigated both the breadth of minimalist practice and the associative power of the object, delving into the concept of passage and drawing upon the history of art, literary conceits, and the mundane stuff of everyday existence. In 1997, Havel embarked on a series of works that came to enfold many of these concerns, and as these sculptures clarified into curtains in particular, Havel found a platform to powerfully express, as he has explained, "the activity of still objects." [4]

• • •

In 1977 Havel was in graduate school, studying drawing and ceramics at Pennsylvania State University. After making his home in Texas in 1979, he gradually shifted his attention to found materials and assemblage. Many of his early works embraced vernacular imagery, and he has pointed to Joan Miró's hybrid bronzes of the 1960s and 1970s, with their telling wit and lyrical eroticism, as immediate sources. [5] In 1987 he began to render selected pieces in bronze as well, working in collaboration with Harry Geffert and Ken King at Green Mountain Studio and Garden near Fort Worth. Geffert's and King's mastery of direct casting techniques enabled Havel to capture every nuance of surface and form, while the tensile strength of the metal permitted him to invest his constructions with a new dynamism. Direct casting further allowed Havel to refine his sense of poetic composition, and much as Lautréamont praised the chance encounter, Havel found beauty in unlikely junctions. [6] By the mid-1990s, however, he moved away from assemblage, with its surrealist and narrative overtones, and concentrated instead on imagery that conveyed more discrete information: men's shirts and collars, bedsheets, drapes, curtains, and shirt labels. Rather than building meaning out of juxtaposition, Havel turned his attention to the object itself, using reiteration or isolation to tease out fresh layers of significance. He pared down his compositions, at times highlighting only a single gesture or task; in a recent interview, he quoted John Berryman's *The Dream Songs*: "all nouns became verbs," to define his current approach to making sculpture.[7]

Fleece (1997; plate 17), among Havel's first label arrays, is a key transitional work. The used shirt labels, the evident stitchery, and the dangling needles that act as ballast look back to strategies Havel used in earlier assemblages, such as *Aura* (1995–96; plates 1 and 2). At the same time, *Fleece* also offers a preamble to the *Curtain* series, signaling an important shift toward pictorial concerns. Like a theatrical scrim, it commands our regard and defines an independent plane in space. [8] The center of the composition is dominated mostly by white labels, the lower edge mostly by gold, and the unitary progression of the rectangular segments gives *Fleece* the appearance of a minimalist lattice. Havel has stated:

The labels were selected for their color and formal fit in the grid, with the source for all of them being men's white shirts. (The collecting of the shirts was completely based on cost at Houston's Value Village, anything under $1). . . . After collecting the labels, I was essentially behaving as a formalist, trying to ignore the sociological information, as if it were neutral, and trying (and failing) to compose a modest transcendent grid, a Golden Fleece.

Indeed, Havel did not ignore other levels of information, and he opened up the modernist composition to a different frame of reference as well. The poignantly elegiac nature of the worn and displaced labels, and their suspended delicacy, evokes Jim Hodges's floral cascades of the mid-1990s (fig. 6). Constructed from silk flowers, with their symbolic baggage of beauty and transience, these profoundly tender memorials pay tribute to generations lost to AIDS. Hodges commented tellingly of these works: "For any viewer, these pieces function architecturally. They act like *real* curtains; they create a 'here' and a 'there.'" [9] Implicit in this statement is an acknowledgment of the curtain as a metaphor for the point of passage between life and death.

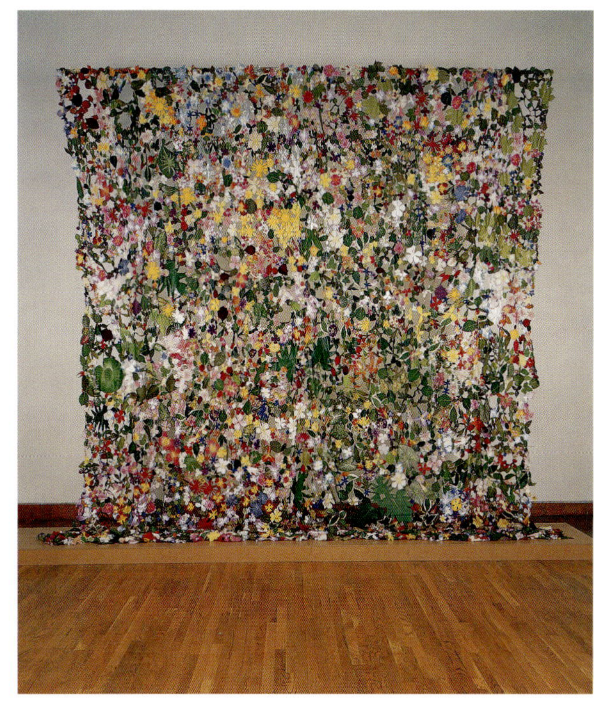

FIGURE 6

Havel's *Fleece* broadens and redirects Hodges's approach. An unassuming presence, it implies the precious frailty of life and of masculine identity through the very ordinariness of its materials. Yet its materiality is also the source of its power, for like Veronica's veil marked by the features of Christ, *Fleece* carries the identity, literally the DNA, of the men who once came into contact with these fabric fragments. The dimensions of the work (it measures less than two feet across) demand an intimate level of engagement from the viewer, who is invited to step up close and read the manufacturers' labels, each logo triggering other layers of association: Manhattan, Arrow, Arrow Kent, Men's Custom Shop, Oleg Cassini, Christian Dior, Harold's, Frank's. Seen in this context, the dangling needles and threads point not only to the painstaking nature of a work in process, but also to the possibility of adding even further lives and untold tales to this project.

FIGURE 7

The following year Havel embarked on several works that permitted him to revisit and expand upon the theme of the curtain, including a commission for the Audrey Jones Beck Building, then in the final planning stages for the Museum of Fine Arts, Houston. At the invitation of Peter C. Marzio and Gwendolyn H. Goffe, director and associate director of the MFAH, respectively, and of Rafael Moneo, architect, Havel was given free reign to propose two bronze reliefs to flank the bronze and glass doors of the Main Street entrance. Working drawings (figs. 7 and 8) document Havel's initial concept, which mimic, and even invert, the revelatory swagger of the drawn-back curtain embedded in the history of Western paintings, ranging from Raphael's reverent *Sistine Madonna* (c. 1514; Dresden, Gemäldegalerie) to Charles Willson Peale's declamatory self-portrait, *The Artist in His Museum* (1822; fig. 9).[10] However, as the project evolved, Havel moved toward a more linear measure; related drawings assumed the narrow austerity of Barnett Newman's zips, and the finished reliefs billow only slightly from the wall, their vertical folds creating a gentle, variegated rhythm.

FIGURE 8

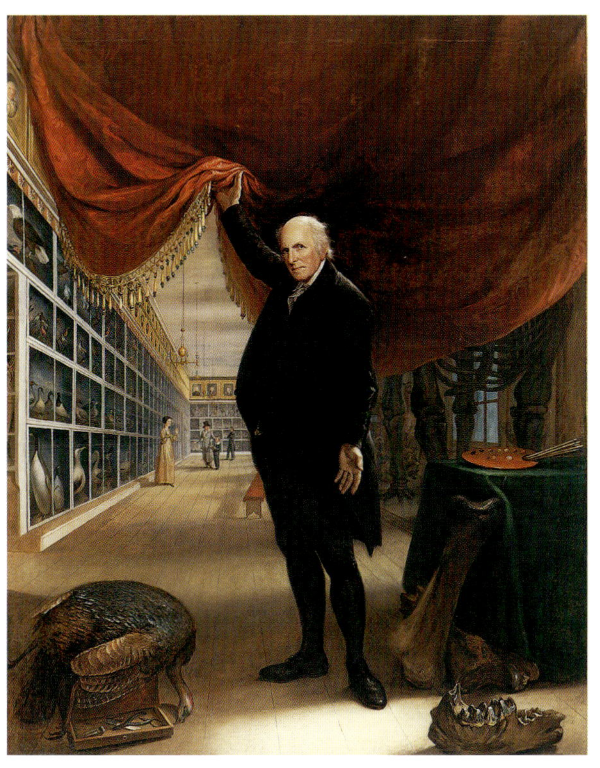

FIGURE 9

Curtain (1999; plates 28–30) was fabricated in several stages. Havel chose a rough-weave canvas-like muslin, which indirectly announced the painting collection that the Beck Building galleries would house. Working in his Houston studio, he attached the fabric to temporary support frames measured to the scale of the entrance, allowing for the degree of difference that would occur as the panels were cast. Then, with the assistance of Ken King, he infused the cloth with wax from the reverse surface so that the outer face would maintain its woven texture through the translation into bronze. [11] At this stage the material—now stiff—was shaped using a heat gun. As the wax softened in the heat, Havel could use gravity to define the cadence of the undulating cloth, with the bottom edges crimping slightly as they hit the ground. As he has recalled, "I had to work back from the composition until the composition wasn't imposed on it, but was more inherent in the form." At this stage the two panels were reinforced by another application of wax on the rear face and transported to Green Mountain Studio and Garden. There Harry Geffert, Havel, and King worked together to cut the panels into 177 segments, which were subsequently molded, cast, reassembled, welded, ground to remove casting marks, finished, sandblasted, and patinated a chalky white. [12] Stainless steel scaffolds were also fabricated to support the panels, and on June 11, 1999, *Curtain* was inserted into the façade of the Audrey Jones Beck Building, nine months before the building's inauguration. Each relief spans roughly 10 by 10 feet, is 14 inches deep, and weighs 1800 pounds, facts that are contradicted by the panels' airy delicacy within Moneo's chastely severe granite, limestone, bronze, and glass enclosure.

In the *Poetics of Space*, Gaston Bachelard defined the door as compounding images of "hesitation, temptation, desire, security, welcome and respect." [13] Much the same can be said of Havel's use of the curtain in the museum's entrance as a multivalent signifier. A visitor approaching the Audrey Jones Beck Building from Main Street rarely sees both panels at once; they are separated by a 30-foot expanse, and are best regarded as a pair from the sidewalk. From a distance they maintain the illusion of muslin, capable of being reconfigured by any gust of wind. *Curtain* meets the architectural frame with a certain restrained formality, but seen in conjunction with Moneo's use of bronze as a planar and structural element, Havel's panels assume a sense of complementary play. The panel on the left has folds concentrated in the center; the one on the right pushes the folds to either side. Up close the painterly surfaces of the slightly mottled patina introduce another level of action. Havel acknowledged: "I wanted *Curtain* to suggest things about drapery, but I also wanted to treat the panels very much like they were big abstract paintings or reliefs. I was interested in the fact that the building is going to hold Western European paintings, and that a lot of those paintings have areas of drapery in which there is movement and passage." [14]

At the same time, Havel also noted the more prosaic aspects of the curtain motif. Hanging curtains in a window is a way of humanizing and domesticating a space, and he has described his self-consciously gendered approach to the commission much as a girlfriend or sister might have once volunteered "I could make curtains" to a new homeowner. He explained further:

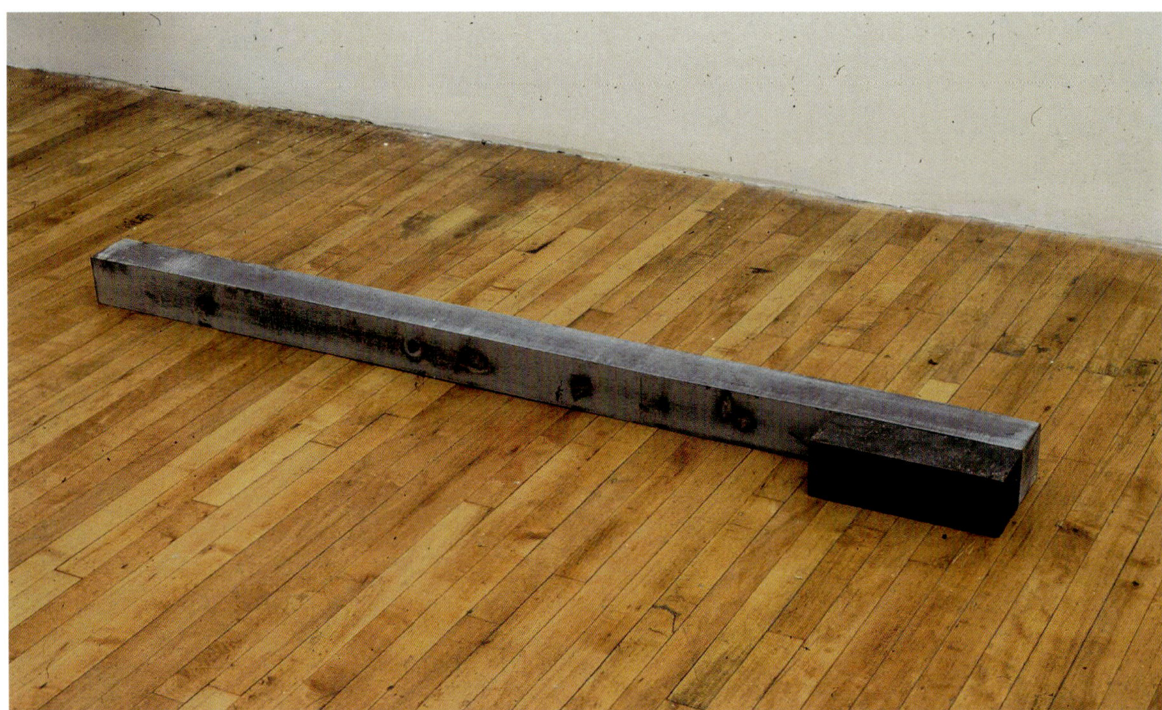

FIGURE 10

> *I wanted something that had grand implications, but which was a small intervention. In essence they echo some of the experiences you will have within the museum: they're about theater, they're about home, they're about being able to scale down the building, they have a little humor to them, they are abstract and formal and serious.* [15]

Havel realized many of these themes afresh in a related series of freestanding drape and curtain sculptures, also produced in 1999, most notably in *Curtains* (plate 25). Unlike the MFAH commission, where each panel complements the other with a tacit reserve, the two elements of *Curtains* engage one another with a sensual immediacy. While they remain separate entities, they are formed in tandem, leaning and bowing in the same direction, the skirt of one parting to welcome the skirt of the other. It is tempting to read the work as two figures—perhaps male and female—an interpretation that Havel permits to a degree. In a recent interview, he commented: "The body is always present, but the figure as subject matter is only present in some works. . . . The figure has been a dominant but not completely exclusive concern." [16]

Havel fabricated *Curtains* using the same method as the MFAH panels, also in collaboration with Green Mountain Studio and Garden. However, where the museum's drapes were shaped over a frame that mimicked the function of a curtain rod, the freestanding drapes were suspended from wires as the wax was applied; once cast in bronze, they appear to be magically supported by an invisible force. Illusion operates on other levels as well: the striated warp and weft of the fabric have been remarkably preserved, as have the tucked gathers at the top, directing the viewer's attention back to the original found material. Furthermore, while one curtain seems larger and more dominant than the other, they are actually made from a matching set, using the same amount of bronze, and occupying the same amount of physical space—one rising up, the other spilling across the floor. In so doing, Havel positions himself in the wake of such quantitative projects as Joel Shapiro's 1970 series, *Untitled: 75 LBS* (fig. 10). Shapiro described these works as being "about juxtaposition and density;" [17] each piece consisted of two sections made out of materials of differing mass (i.e. lead and magnesium), the volume of each section determined by its weight. In contrast, Havel conjures up the illusion of difference, while maintaining a quietly discernable balance.

Curtains, Drape (1999; plate 26), and *Table Cloth* (1999; plate 34) were first shown at the *Whitney Biennial 2000*, the first biennial to feature internet art. The only bronzes in the exhibition, they were installed with works by Ingrid Calame, Ghada Amer, and Richard Tuttle (plate 27). Calame's *b-b-b, rr-gR-UF! b-b-b*, 1999, a Mylar curtain stenciled with images of found stains and blots that flowed from wall to floor, offered a quirky parallel to Havel's imagery and appropriative method. Tuttle's *Rough Edges 1-12* series of 1999 presented a subtler analogue. As the catalogue noted: "Richard Tuttle has always been engaged in breaking down the barriers that have traditionally separated a work from its surrounding space and challenging the conventional distinctions between drawing, painting, and sculpture. His art has confounded two-and three-dimensionality and, by extension, the expected distinctions among art, illusion, and reality." [18] Although Havel's bronzes are materially distinct from Tuttle's example, his work assumes a similar illusionary and genre-bending presence.

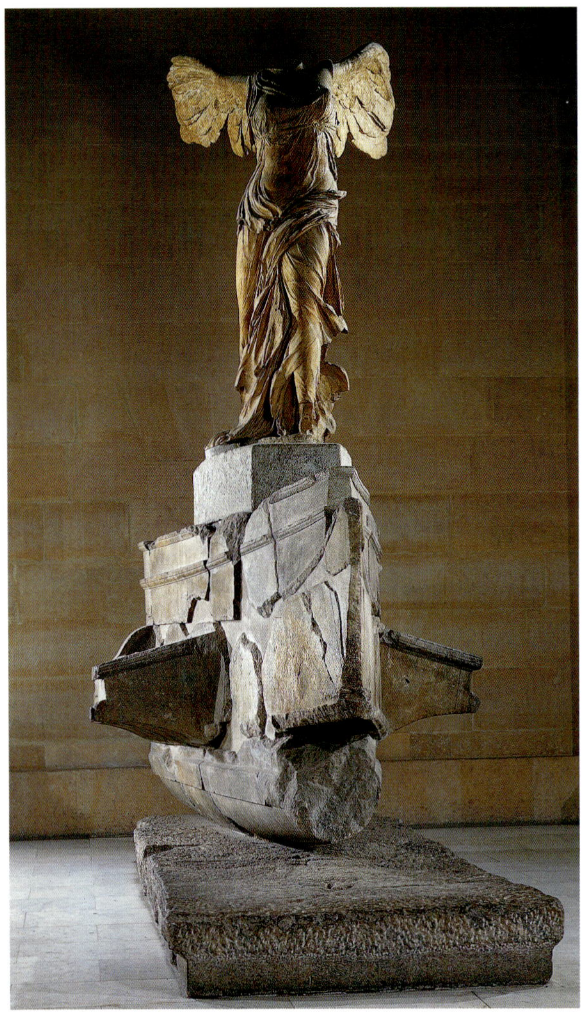

FIGURE 11

In 2000 Havel moved into a more spacious studio in Houston, adjacent to a new foundry established by Ken King. There, with the assistance of King, David Medina, Ketria Bastion-Scott, and Woody Golden, he engaged in a second series of bronze drapes and curtains, as well as works in other media, that took advantage of the soaring dimensions of the main working space. Exploiting the elasticity of bronze to liberate form from its actual weight, *Black Drape* (2002; plate 50) stretches over 14 feet high, while two works from 2004–5, *Twisted Curtain* (plate 65) and *Torn and Twisted Curtain* (plates 63 and 64), reach up to 16 feet. Typically sculptures that extend to such heights are created for public spaces, and these works self-consciously address this tradition. *Torn and Twisted Curtain* in particular assumes the dynamic beauty of the *Nike of Samothrace* (220–190 B.C.; fig. 11), its elaborately wrapped and twisted folds, as well as its V-shaped composition, indirectly referencing the arrested motion and triumphant authority of this masterpiece of Hellenistic art. More than the earlier curtain sculptures, *Torn and Twisted Curtain* also evokes the abstract flourishes of drapery that punctuate mannerist and baroque paintings (fig. 12), and Havel has observed: "Unlike the figure, drapes have no, or few, conventions. . . . They can defy gravity, or turn into clouds." [19]

Torn and Twisted Curtain was conceived for the exhibition *Joseph Havel: A Decade of Sculpture 1996–2006*, and it responds to the scale and measure of the 20-foot sheer curtains that encircle the Ludwig Mies van der Rohe galleries in the Upper Brown Pavilion of the MFAH's Caroline Wiess Law Building. Like the 1999 *Curtains*, it is made up of two elements of equal weight, yet in this instance the equilibrium is disguised—the densely twisted and knotted "foot" of the sculpture is cast from a curtain that is the mate of the upper "sail." Much as Shapiro had once matched magnesium and lead, Havel here uses compression to counterbalance the open expanse of the material that swings up from the sculpture's core.

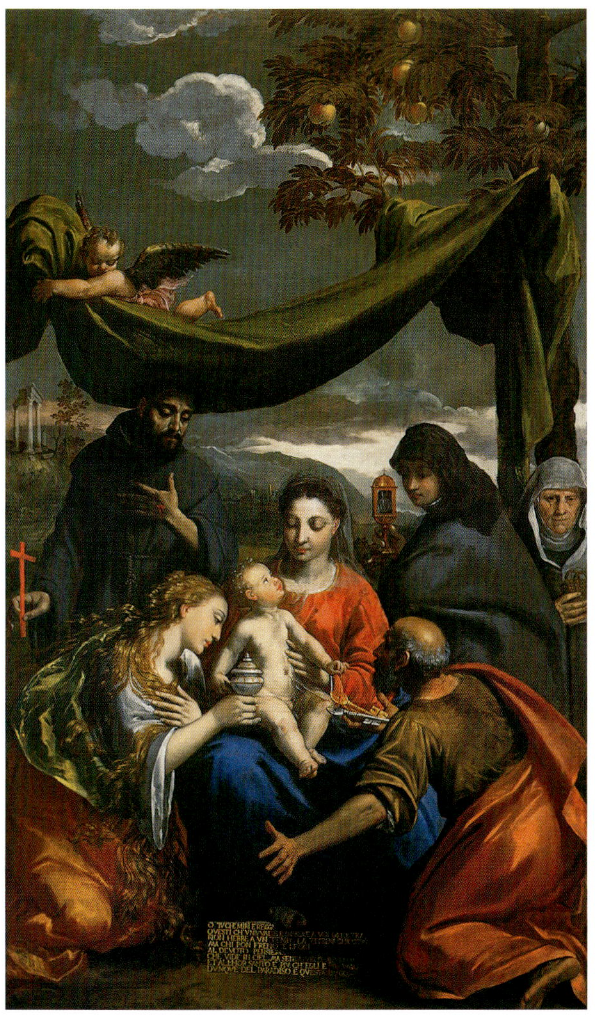

FIGURE 12

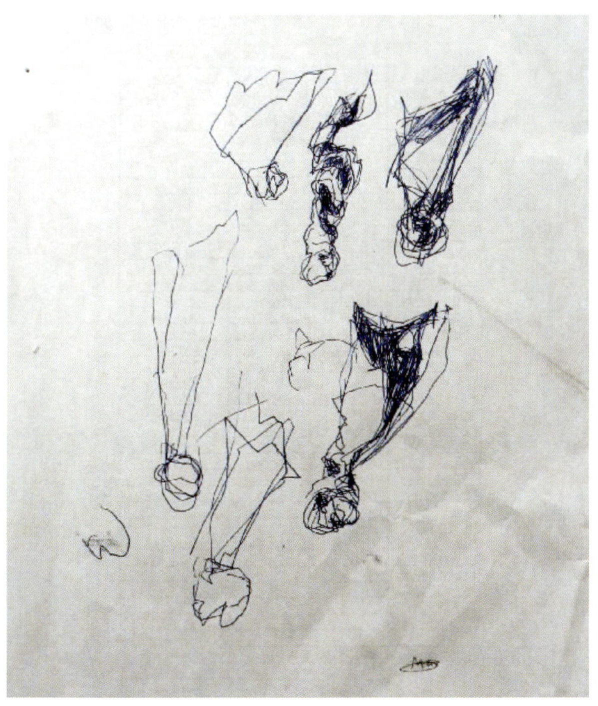

FIGURE 13

Havel spent more than a year and a half refining this composition before moving into the casting phase. Using a pair of heavy silk curtains, again found at Houston's Value Village, he hung the material from two points, the gathers cascading asymmetrically down one side. Preliminary sketches show the fabric ascending like an ecstatic whirlwind (fig. 13), but once the material was infused with wax, the vertical thrust became secondary to twists, tears, pulls, and even single threads. Havel has confessed to indulging himself in the amount of incident he created in the modeling of the surface: he stitched the fabric and formed the drapes and folds with an unusual degree of improvisatory freedom, "leaving my handwriting all over it." Indeed, although vastly different in scale and materials, *Torn and Twisted Curtain* returns to the informal handmade grace of *Fleece*. At the same time, the density of information preserved through the bronze-casting process is staggering, while the overall freedom of the composition instills awe. Havel has commented: "I thought about all the effort, all the heat, all the energy—all the calories—that go into transforming something into bronze. I wanted you to be able to feel the calories, to feel the transformation in the final piece." [20]

Fallen Reich brings the curtain series to a close. Like *Torn and Twisted Curtain*, it was conceived for the present exhibition and specifically addresses the museum's

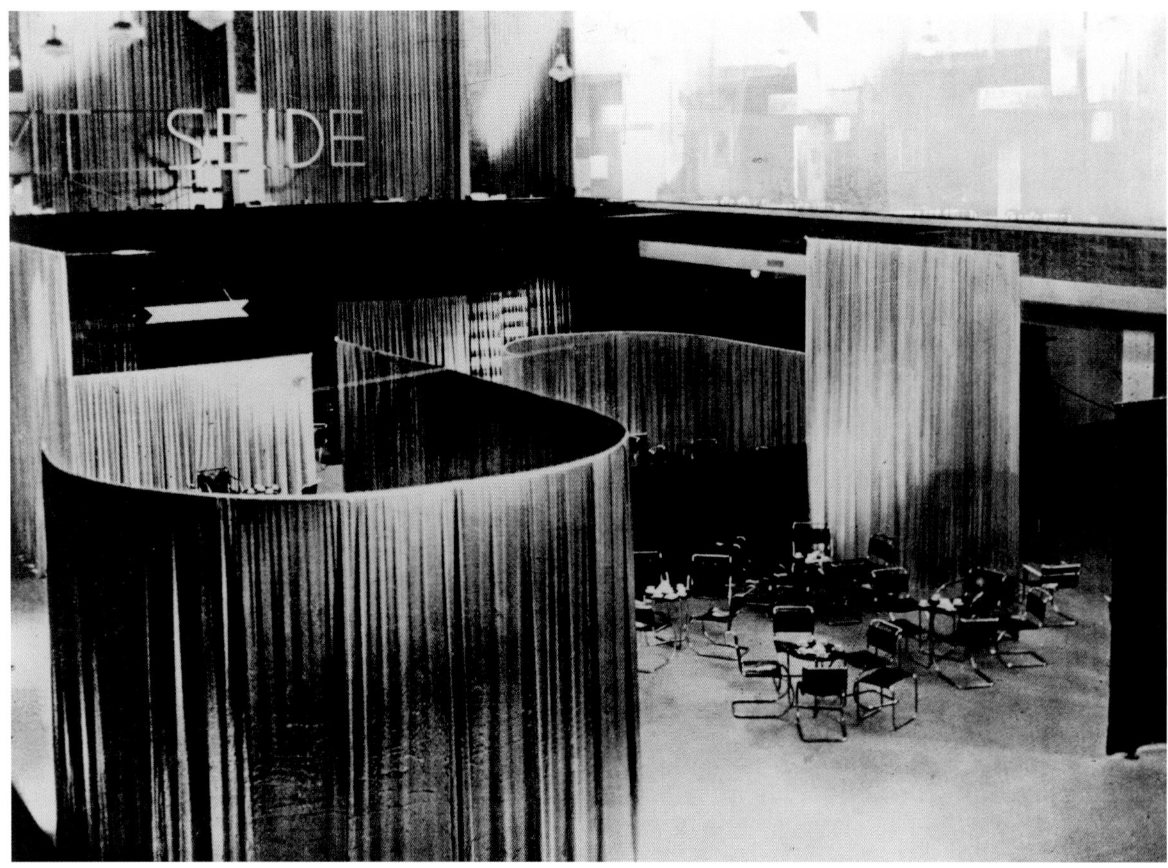

FIGURE 14

Mies van der Rohe galleries. However, rather than being a self-sufficient object, or a sympathetic commission reinforcing the MFAH's program, it is a site-specific intervention, using the architectural history of the institution to define Havel's rapport (and battle) with modernism.[21] The title pays homage to Lilly Reich (1885–1947), Mies's partner in the 1920s and 1930s, whose creative role in their relationship has only recently come to light. A brilliant textile designer, she also collaborated with Mies in furniture design and exhibition display, creating curtains for such celebrated projects as the 1927 *Velvet and Silk Café* (fig. 14).[22] The title of Havel's installation also suggests the end of modernism's reign and the fracture of culture engendered in the postmodern era.

Still a work in progress at the time of this writing, *Fallen Reich* will disrupt the line of curtains that enclose the perimeter of Mies's pavilion (fig. 15). Branching off from the main rail, Havel's curtain will slice 50 feet into the gallery, ultimately sending waves of fabric onto the floor. Not only will it present a lush counterpart to the rigor of Mies's architecture, but it also will challenge the masculine authority of many of Havel's own sculptures. Havel has described the installation:

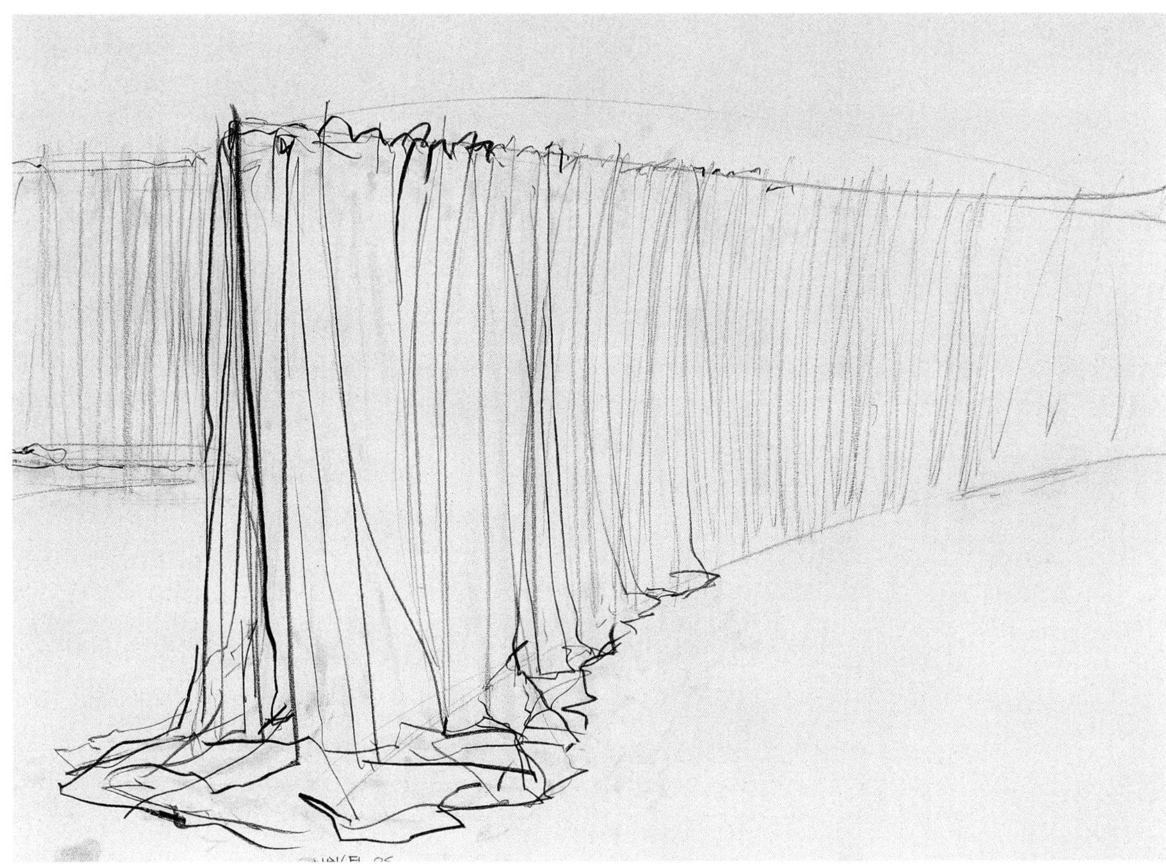

FIGURE 15

> *In some ways it follows along the lines of the* Seam *works (1995–96; plates 13 and 14), which announce that the thing being seen cannot be separated from the condition it is seen in; this is specifically true in a museum setting. Conditioning of all sorts comes with our entrance to the museum and tempers our response to an object. Also, modernist spaces, which affect neutrality ("form follows function"), project authority through their formal convictions.*
>
> *I wanted to play with an inversion of what I usually do, pulling something out of its previous place in domestic life and transforming it through the fabrication process. Here I am starting with the idea and making curtains that yearn to function in both worlds, potentially failing in either, I guess. They are neither functional nor capable of being read independently.*

In the final analysis, the image of the curtain cannot be separated from its role on the stage; indeed, one of Western culture's first modern theaters was The Curtain, which opened in London in 1577. For Havel, the curtain retains its essential theatricality, and in his work of the past decade it has served both as an indicator of the creative act and as a veiled self-portrait. Much as Rosalind Krauss demanded an attitude of primary humility from artist and viewer in her definition of passage in modern sculpture, Havel brings to this project a complex self-awareness, ambition, and poetic imagination. He then goes forward with the rueful consciousness of Samuel Beckett: "perhaps they have said me already, perhaps they have carried me to the threshold of my story, before the door that opens on my story, that would surprise me, if it opens, it will be I, it will be the silence, where I am, I don't know, in the silence you don't know, you must go on, I can't go on, I'll go on." [23]

NOTES

1 Rosalind Krauss, *Passages in Modern Sculpture* (New York: The Viking Press, 1977), 5.

2 Ibid., 282.

3 Marcel Proust, *Swann's Way*, 1912; trans. C.K. Scott-Moncreiff, quoted by Krauss, *Passages in Modern Sculpture*, 287. Krauss did address Shapiro's work more directly in the context of postmodernism in her subsequent essay, "Sculpture in an Expanded Field," *October* 8 (Spring 1979): 30–44.

4 Unless otherwise noted, quotations from the artist are taken from a series of conversations with the author between April and August 2005.

5 Havel was profoundly impressed by an exhibition of Joan Miró's sculpture at the Walker Art Center in 1971, and Miró remained a touchstone for Havel for many years thereafter. He has also acknowledged presentations of Alberto Giacometti and Claes Oldenburg at the Walker as additional formative influences during his high-school and college years in Minneapolis.

6 For example, Havel's *Exhaling Pearls*, 1993 (The Museum of Fine Arts, Houston) improbably unites industrial cable and Japanese lanterns, much as Lautréamont celebrated "The chance encounter of a sewing machine and an umbrella on a dissecting table." Isidore Ducasse, Comte de Lautréamont, *Les Chants de Maldoror*, Paris, 1868, quoted by William S. Rubin, *Dada, Surrealism, and Their Heritage* (New York: The Museum of Modern Art, 1968), 19.

7 Unpublished segment of "Non-Places: An Interview with Joe Havel," kindly provided by Marisa C. Sánchez. The phrase is taken from Chapter VII, no. 368, of Berryman's *The Dream Songs* (New York: Farrar, Straus, and Giroux, 1969), 390.

8 See Kathi Norklun, "Landscape: The Pastoral to the Urban," *The Woodstock Times*, August 7, 1997: "*Fleece* consists of a small curtain of manufacturers' labels taken from the necks of old shirts; the delicately and unevenly strung labels are suspended away from the wall, creating a second pattern by their shadow."

9 Jim Hodges, quoted by Dana Friis-Hansen, *Outbound: Passages from the 90's* (Houston: Contemporary Arts Museum, Houston, 2000), 47.

10 For a detailed overview of the symbolism of the pulled-back curtain, see Johann Konrad Eberlein, "The Curtain in Raphael's *Sistine Madonna*," *The Art Bulletin* 65, no. 1 (March 1983): 61–77, and John F. Moffitt, "Rembrandt, Revelation, and Calvin's Curtains," *Gazette des Beaux-Arts* 113, no. 4 (April 1989): 175–86. In Western painting, the curtain acted not only as a framing device but also as a metaphor for revelation, enabling the viewer to perceive and "enter" the pictorial realm.

11 Joseph Havel, unpublished interview with Jennie King, February 11, 1999. MFAH Archives, The Museum of Fine Arts, Houston.

12 The direct casting process ensures that each bronze is unique as the molds are destroyed after firing.

13 Gaston Bachelard, *La Poétique de l'espace*, Paris, 1957, trans. Maria Jolas, *The Poetics of Space* (Boston: Beacon Press, 1994): 224.

14 Joseph Havel, unpublished interview with Jennie King.

15 Ibid.

16 Joseph Havel, interviewed by Marisa C. Sánchez, "Non-Places: An Interview with Joe Havel," *ArtLies* 44 (Fall 2004): 41.

17 Joel Shapiro, interviewed by Lewis Kachur, 1988. Archives of American Art, Smithsonian Oral History Project, http://www.aaa.si.edu/oralhist/shapir88.htm.

18 Maxwell L. Anderson et al. *Whitney Biennial 2000* (New York: Whitney Museum of American Art, 2000), 209.

19 Joseph Havel, unpublished interview with Jennie King.

20 Although this statement referred to a somewhat earlier piece, Havel has affirmed that a similar intent applies to *Torn and Twisted Curtain*. See Michael Ennis, "Joseph Havel: Art that Confounds Expectations," *Texas Monthly* 28, no. 9 (September 2000), 226.

21 Like the earlier *Curtain* at the entrance of the MFAH's Audrey Jones Beck Building, *Fallen Reich* essentially domesticates the Mies galleries, and Havel has acknowledged: "I am attracted to the simplicity of the gesture of moving into a space and putting up personalized drapery. The act is very male in the grandiosity of the gesture, while remaining an activity socially assigned to the female, softening and decorating the space, making it both private and public. This is made even more poignant by the fact that the museum has been my home for fourteen years."

22 See Matilda McQuaid and Magdalena Droste, *Lilly Reich: Designer and Architect* (New York: The Museum of Modern Art, 1996). Havel was unaware of Reich's work when planning this installation, and the original title of this work was *Crashed for Mies*. On learning of Reich's curtain designs from this author, however, he readily embraced the broader frame of reference.

23 Samuel Beckett, *Malloy, Malone Dies, The Unnamable* (London: Calder & Boyars, 1959), 418.

Plate 17 ***Fleece***
1997
Shirt labels, thread, needles
29 x 21 inches
Collection of Dr. and Mrs. Bryan Perry, Dallas

Figure 6 *Jim Hodges*
Every Touch
1995
Silk fabric
14 x 16 feet
Philadelphia Museum of Art: Purchased with funds contributed by Mr. and Mrs. W. B. Dixon Stroud, 1995

Figure 7 *Joseph Havel*
Study for Curtain
March 1998
Graphite on paper
25 7/8 x 19 3/4 inches
The Museum of Fine Arts, Houston, gift of the artist, 2004.1516

Figure 8 *Joseph Havel*
Study for Curtain
March 1998
Graphite on paper
19 3/4 x 25 7/8 inches
The Museum of Fine Arts, Houston, gift of the artist, 2004.1518

Figure 9 *Charles Willson Peale*
The Artist in His Museum
1822
Oil on canvas
103 3/4 x 79 7/8 inches
Courtesy of the Philadelphia Academy of the Fine Arts, Philadelphia. Gift of Mrs. Sarah Harrison (The Joseph Harrison, Jr. Collection)

Figure 10 *Joel Shapiro*
Untitled; 75 LBS
1970
Magnesium and lead
4 x 73 1/4 x 8 inches
Courtesy Paula Cooper Gallery, New York

Figure 11 ***Nike of Samothrace***
220–190 B.C.
Marble
129 1/8 inches high
Paris, Musée du Louvre

Figure 12 *Lo Scarsellino*
The Virgin and Child with Saints Mary Magdalene, Peter, Clare, and Francis and an Abbess
c. 1600
Oil on canvas
110 7/8 x 63 5/8 inches
The Museum of Fine Arts, Houston, museum purchase with funds provided by the Agnes Cullen Arnold Endowment Fund, 97.118

Figure 13 ***Study for Torn and Twisted Curtain***
2005
Ballpoint pen on paper
11 x 8 1/2 inches
The Museum of Fine Arts, Houston, gift of the artist, 2005.428.

Figure 14 *Ludwig Mies van der Rohe, in collaboration with Lilly Reich*
Velvet and Silk Café*, Women's Fashion Exhibition, Berlin*
1927
The Museum of Modern Art, New York, gift of the artist

Figure 15 *Joseph Havel*
Study for Fallen Reich
2005
Graphite on paper
22 1/2 x 30 inches
Courtesy of the artist

Plate 18 ***Size***
1996
Shirt labels, pins
7 x 7x 1 inches
Collection of Louis and Margaret Skidmore

Plate 19 ***White Names***
1996
Shirt labels, pins
26 x 26 x 1 inches
Courtesy of the artist

Plate 20 ***Enough*** *(detail)*
1997
Shirt labels, pins
72 x 72 x 1 inches
Collection of Mark and Edith Vanmoerkerke

Plate 21 ***New York Times, Arts, May 31, 1998***
1998
Bronze with patina
5 x 15 x 23 inches
Courtesy of Dunn and Brown Contemporary

Plate 22 ***New York Times, Financial, June 7, 1998***
1998
Bronze with patina
5 x 15 x 23 inches
Collection of Nina and Michael Zilkha

Plate 23 ***New York Times, Arts, June 7, 1998***
1998
Bronze with patina
5 x 15 x 23 inches
Collection of Frances and Peter C. Marzio

Plate 24 ***Curtains*** *(version 1)*
1998
Bronze with patina
81 x 47 x 35 inches
Collection of Tim and Nancy Hanley

Plate 25 ***Curtains***
1999
Bronze with patina
104 x 24 x 26 inches
Collection of Toni and Jeff Beauchamp

Plate 26 ***Drape***
1999
Bronze with patina
119 x 56 x 56 inches
Collection, Modern Art Museum of Fort Worth, Museum purchase, Sid W. Richardson Foundation Endowment Fund

Plate 27 *Installation view of the* ***2000 Biennial Exhibition*** *(March 23–June 4, 2000) at the Whitney Museum of American Art, New York (left to right: Richard Tuttle,* ***Rough Edges 1–12****, 1999; Joseph Havel,* ***Curtains****, 1999; Ingrid Calame,* ***b-b-b, rr-gR-UF!, b-b-b****, 1999)*

Plates 28–30 ***Curtain***
1999
Bronze with patina
Each panel, 120 x 120 x 11 inches
The Museum of Fine Arts Houston, museum commission, gift of Ethel G. Carruth in memory of Allen H. Carruth, 2000.2.A,.B

Plate 31 ***Lost***
2000
Fabric shirt labels and steel pins
Dimensions variable
Courtesy of Devin Borden Hiram Butler Gallery

Plate 32 ***Lost*** *(detail)*
2000
Fabric shirt labels and steel pins
Dimensions variable
Courtesy of Devin Borden Hiram Butler Gallery

Plate 33 ***Bed Sheet***
2001
Fabric sheet and urethane resin
105 x 18 x 20 inches
Collection of Tim and Nancy Hanley

Plate 34 ***Table Cloth***
1999
Bronze with patina
77 1/2 x 11 x 12 inches
Collection of Blake Byrne

Plate 35 ***Veil II***
1999
Graphite and oil on paper
120 x 42 1/2 inches
Collection of Leslie Field

Plate 36 ***Veil IV***
2000
Oil and graphite on paper
120 x 42 1/2 inches
Collection of Leslie Field

Plate 37 ***Veil VI***
2000
Oil and graphite on paper
120 x 42 1/2 inches
The Museum of Fine Arts, Houston, gift of Leslie and Jack S. Blanton, Jr.; Robert Card, M.D. and Karol Kreymer; Louise and Robert Jamail; Inez Winston Reymond; and Debra and Joel Ruby

Plate 38 ***Veil IX***
2000
Oil and graphite on paper
120 x 42 1/2 inches
Collection of The Spires

Plate 39 ***Silk Drape***
2000
Bronze with patina
120 x 33 x 28 inches
Collection of the Sheldon Memorial Art Gallery, University of Nebraska, Lincoln

Plate 40 *Installation view of* ***Daydream Nation***
at Galerie Gabrielle Maubrie
2001
(left to right: ***Lost****, 2001;* ***Bed Sheet****, 2001;* ***Lust****, 2001)*

Plate 41 ***Lost*** *(detail)*
2001
Shirt labels and thread
120 x 48 x 48 inches (dimensions variable)
Collection of Lester Marks

Plate 42 ***Lust*** *(detail)*
2001
Shirt labels and thread
120 x 48 x 48 inches (dimensions variable)
Collection of Lester Marks

Plate 43 ***Fading Desire***
2002
Fabric shirt labels and steel pins
Two squares, each 144 x 144 x 2 inches
Courtesy of Galerie Gabrielle Maubrie

Plate 44 ***Fading Desire*** *(detail)*
2002
Fabric shirt labels and steel pins
Two squares, each 144 x 144 x 2 inches
Courtesy of Galerie Gabrielle Maubrie

Plate 45 ***Fading Desire*** *(detail)*
2002
Fabric shirt labels and steel pins
Two squares, each 144 x 144 x 2 inches
Courtesy of Galerie Gabrielle Maubrie

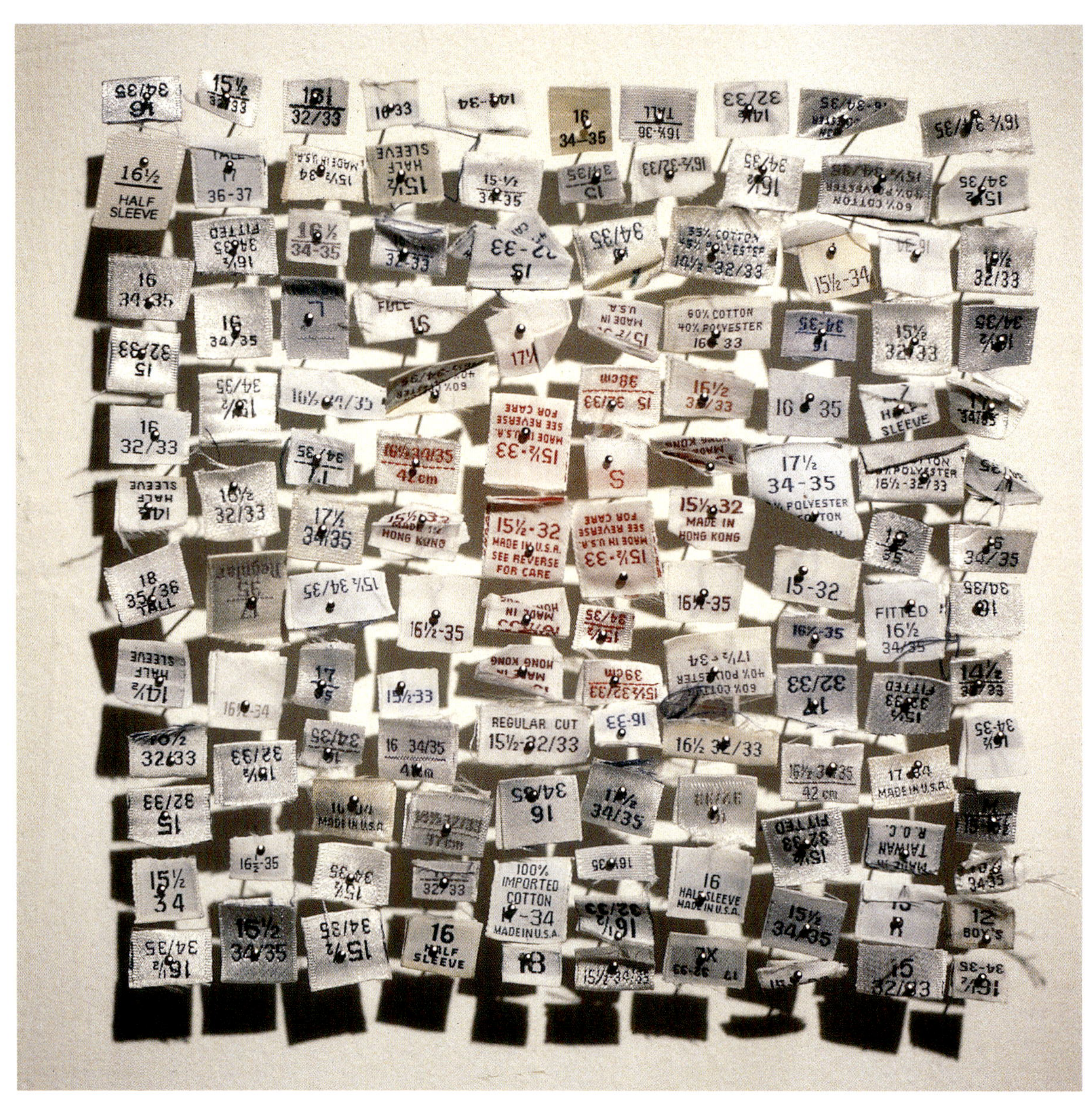

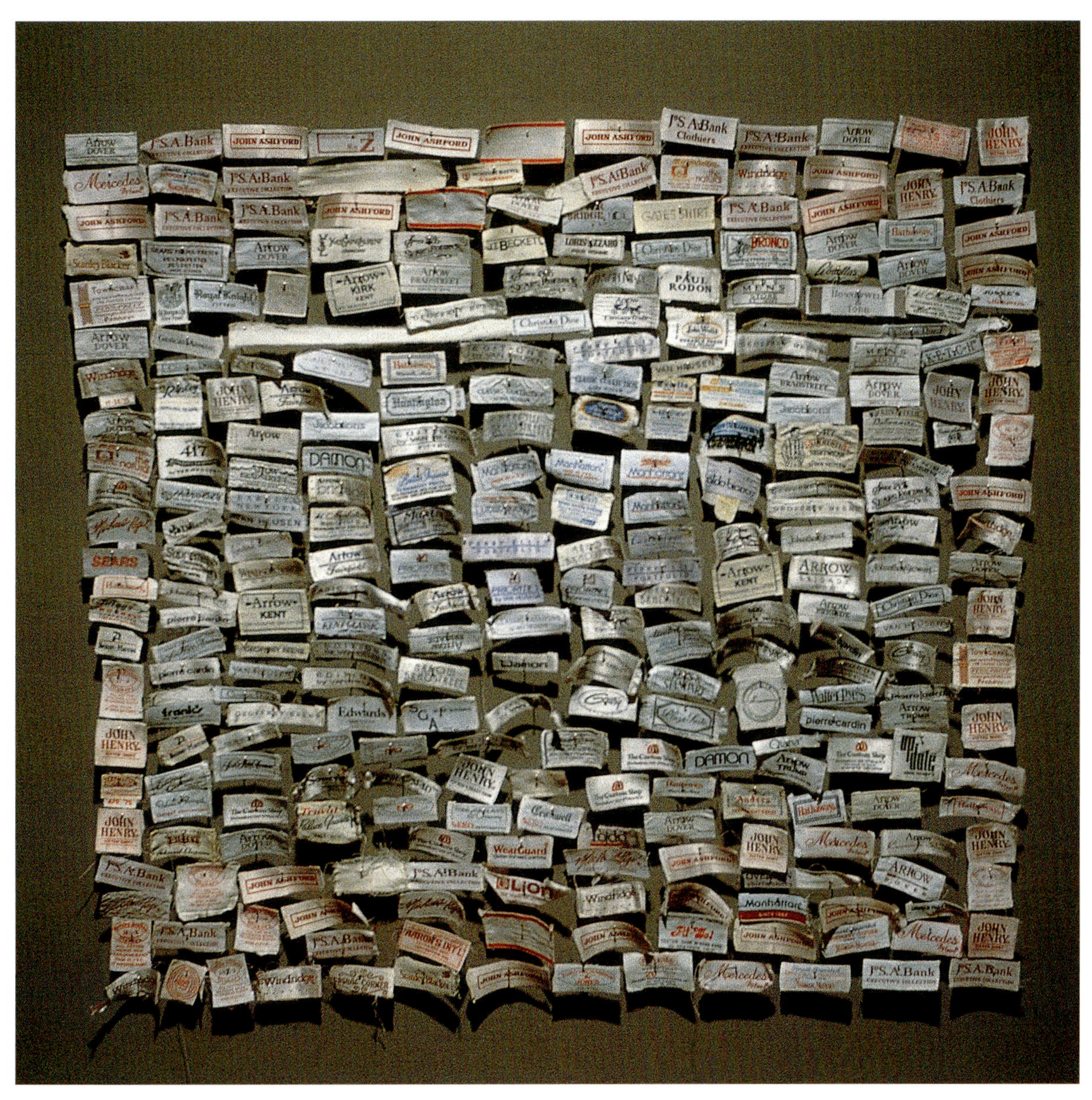

◂ PLATE 18 ***Size***, *1996*

PLATE 19 ***White Names***, *1996* ▸

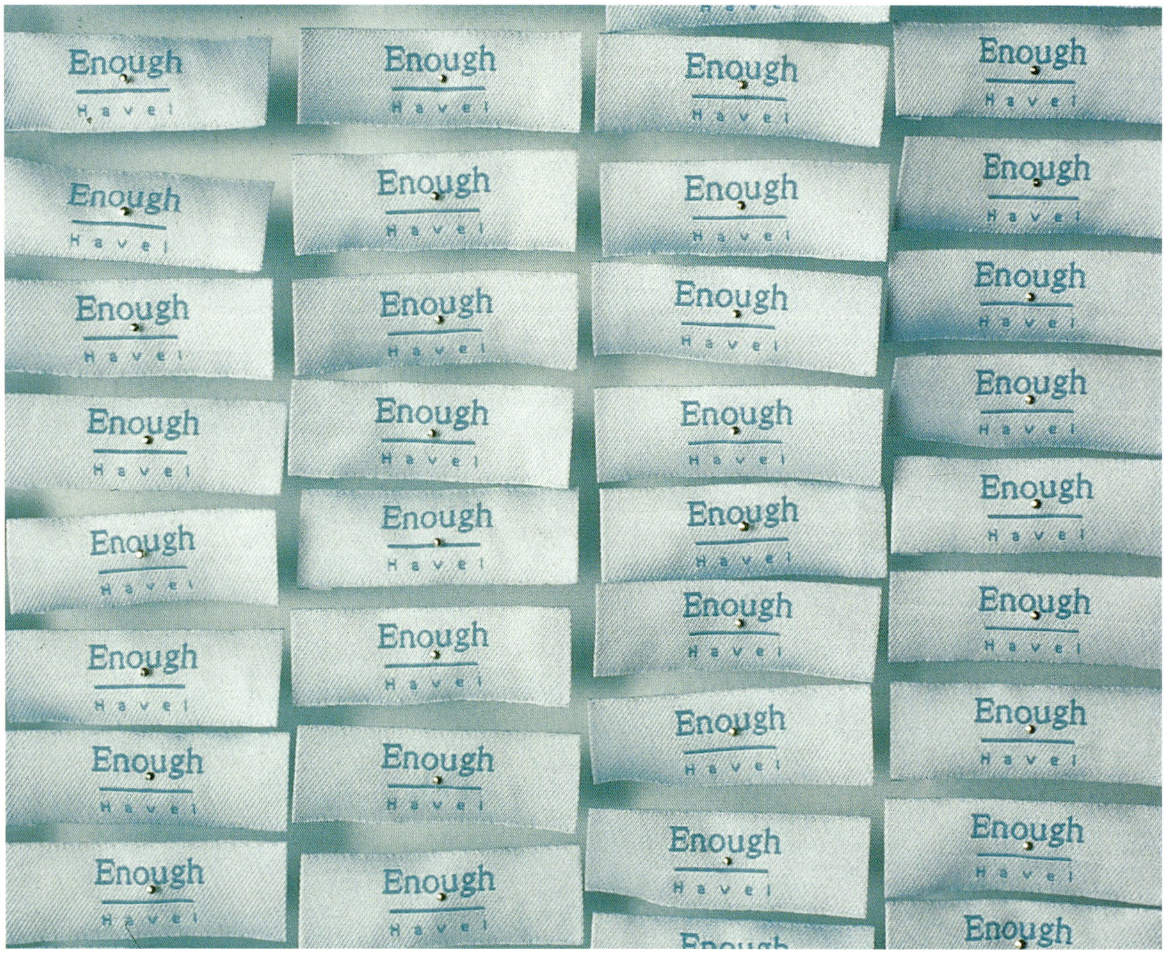

PLATE 20 ***Enough*** *(detail), 1997*

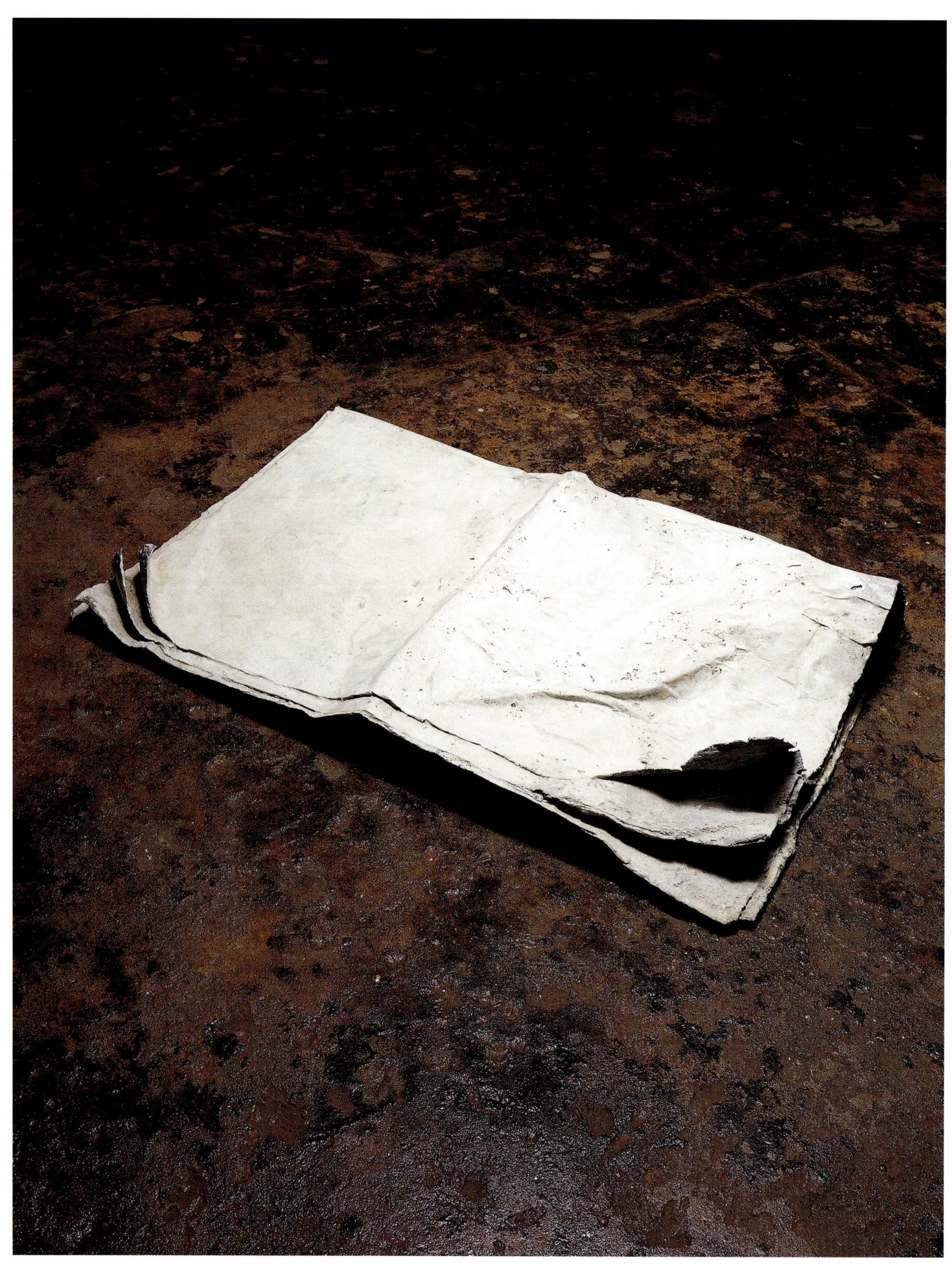

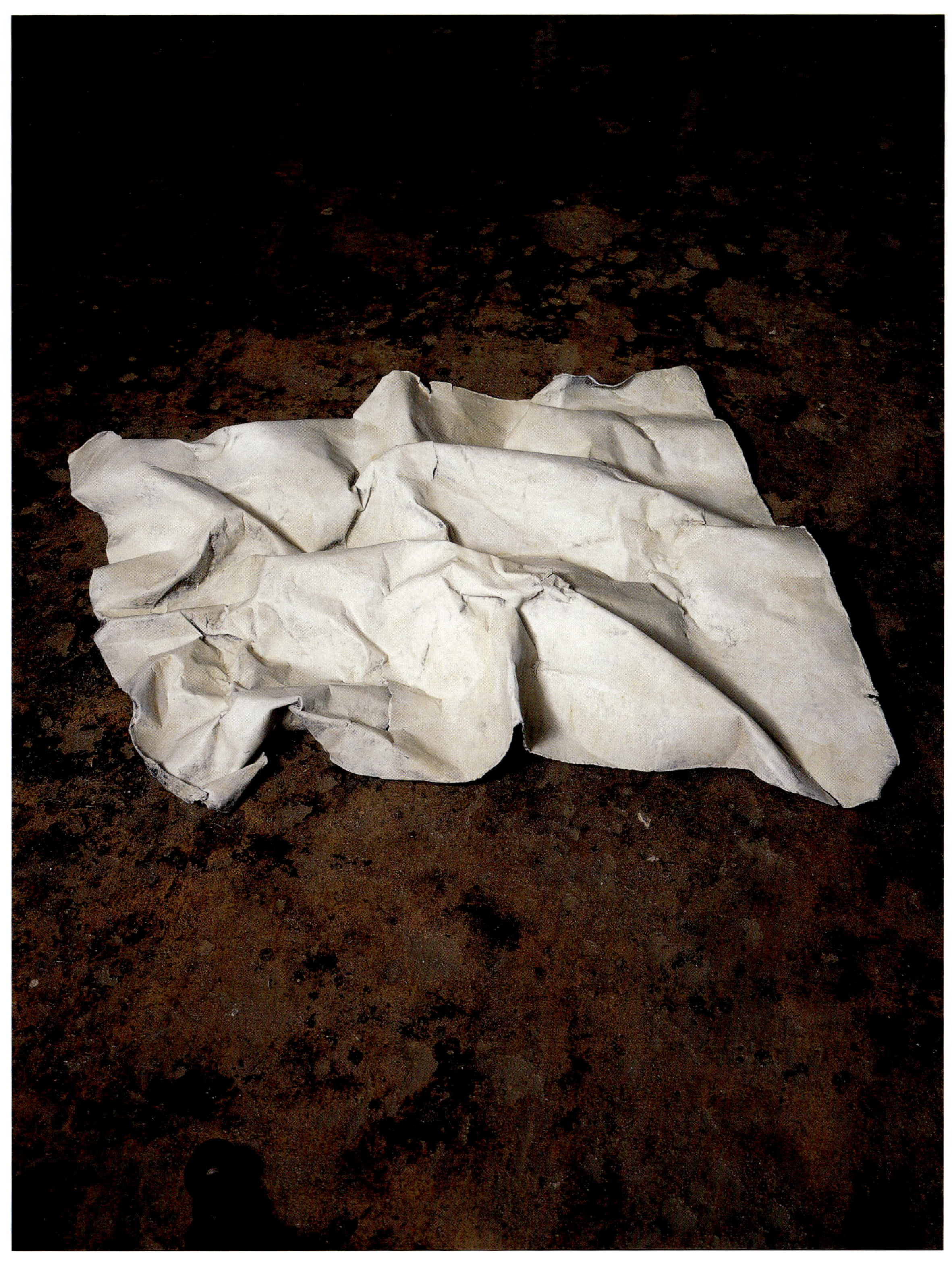

◀ PLATE 21 ***New York Times**, **Arts**, **May 31, 1998,*** *1998*

PLATE 22 ***New York Times**, **Financial**, **June 7, 1998,*** *1998* ▶

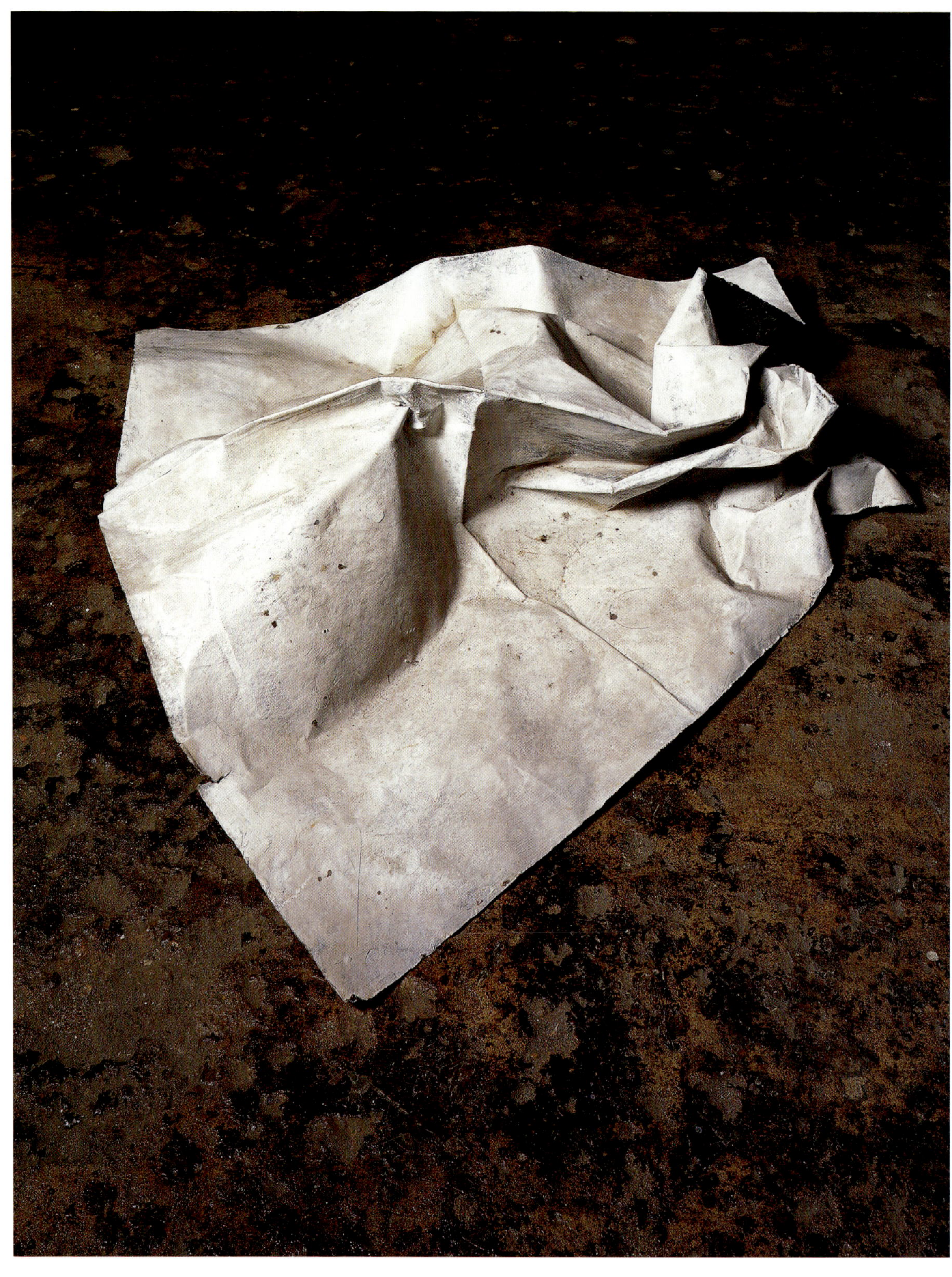

PLATE 23 ***New York Times, Arts, June 7, 1998,*** *1998*

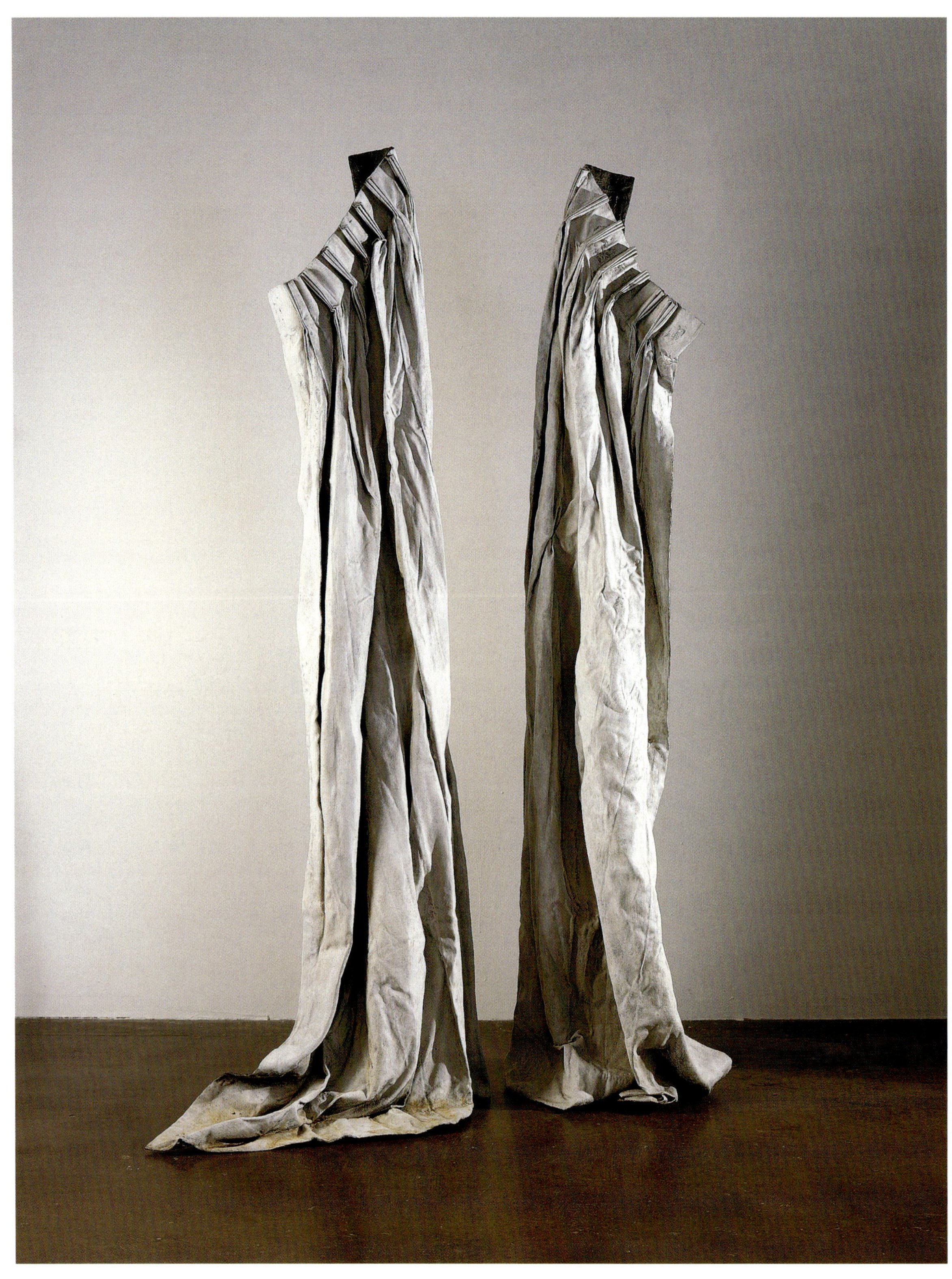

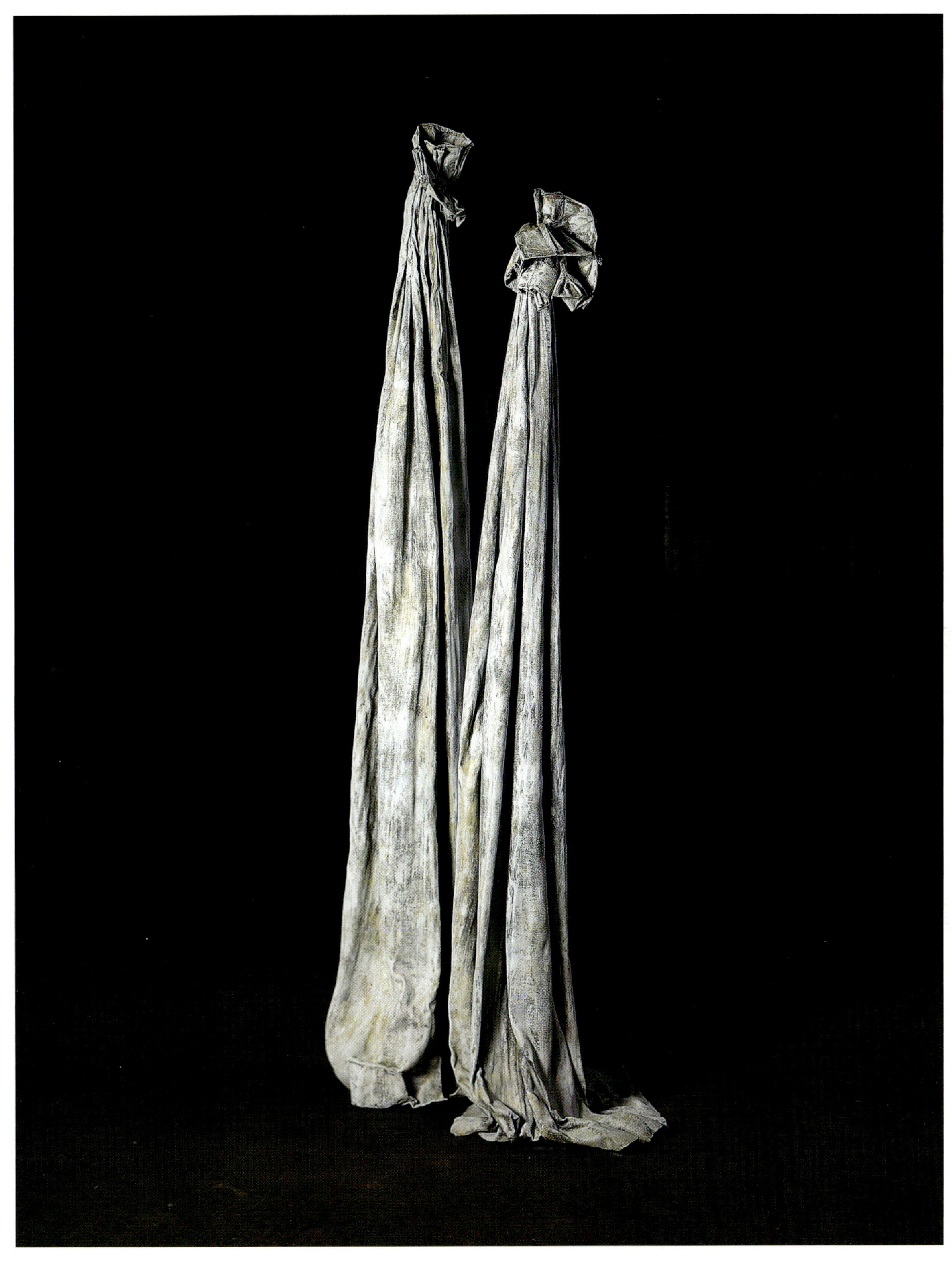

◂ PLATE 24 ***Curtains** (version 1), 1998*

PLATE 25 ***Curtains**, 1999* ▸

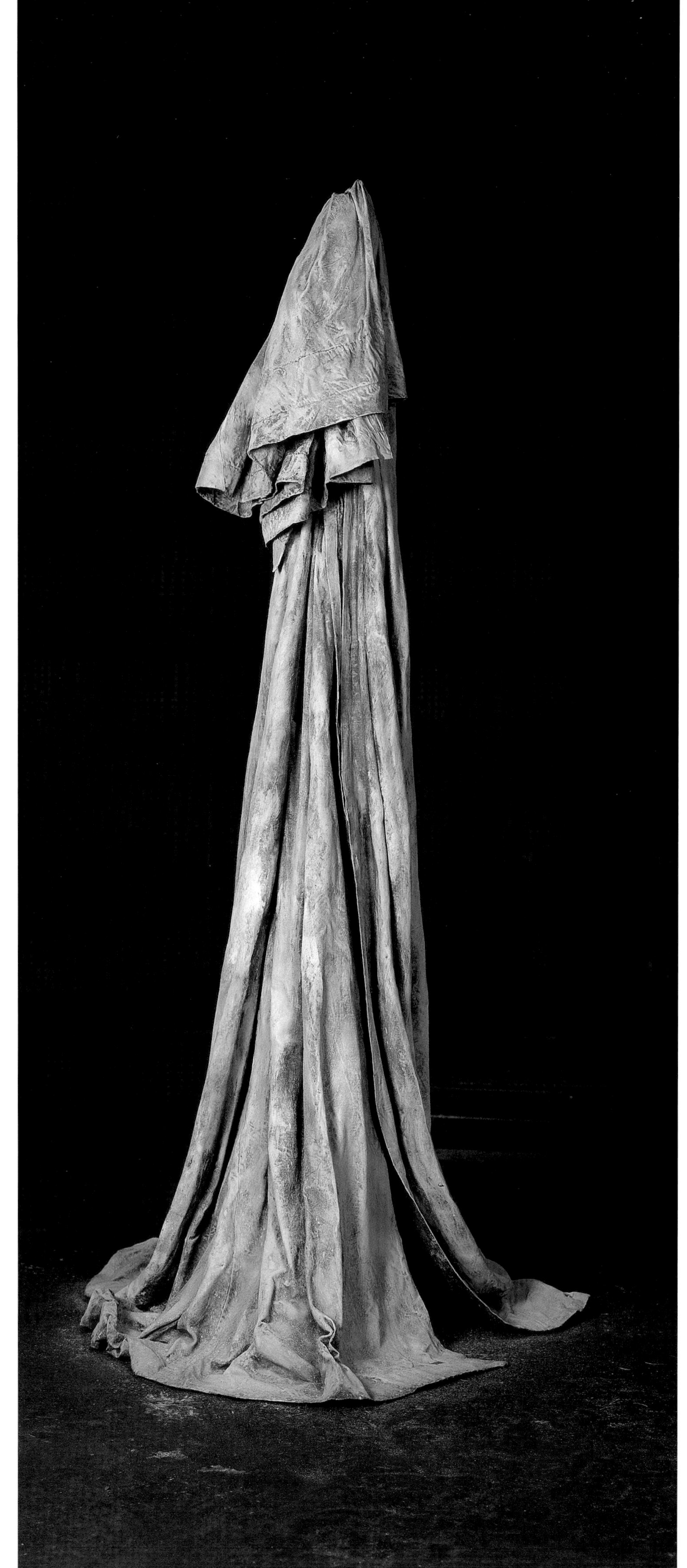

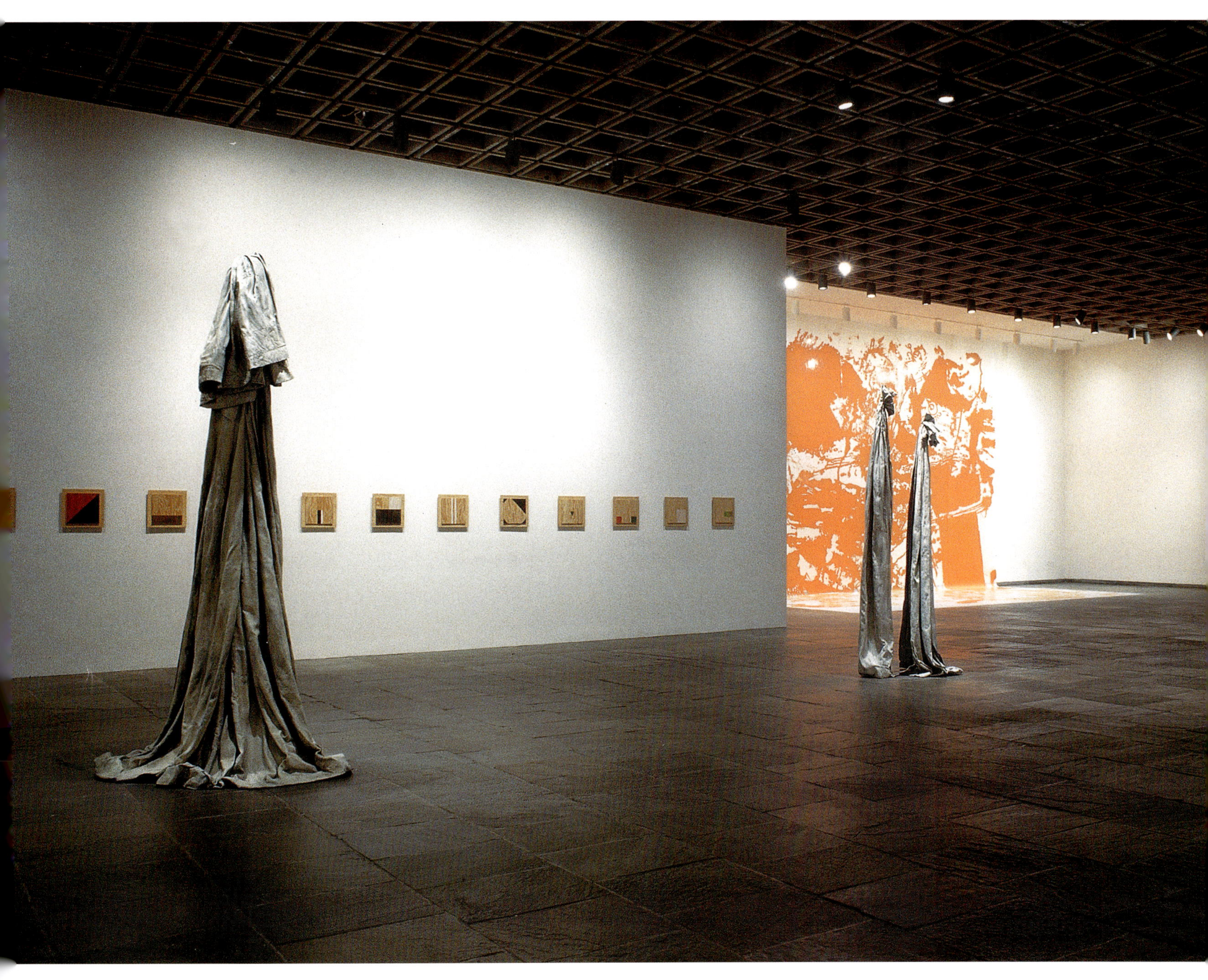

◀ PLATE 26 ***Drape**, 1999*

PLATE 27 *Installation view,* ***Whitney Biennial 2000*** ▶

PLATES 28–30 ***Curtain**, 1999*

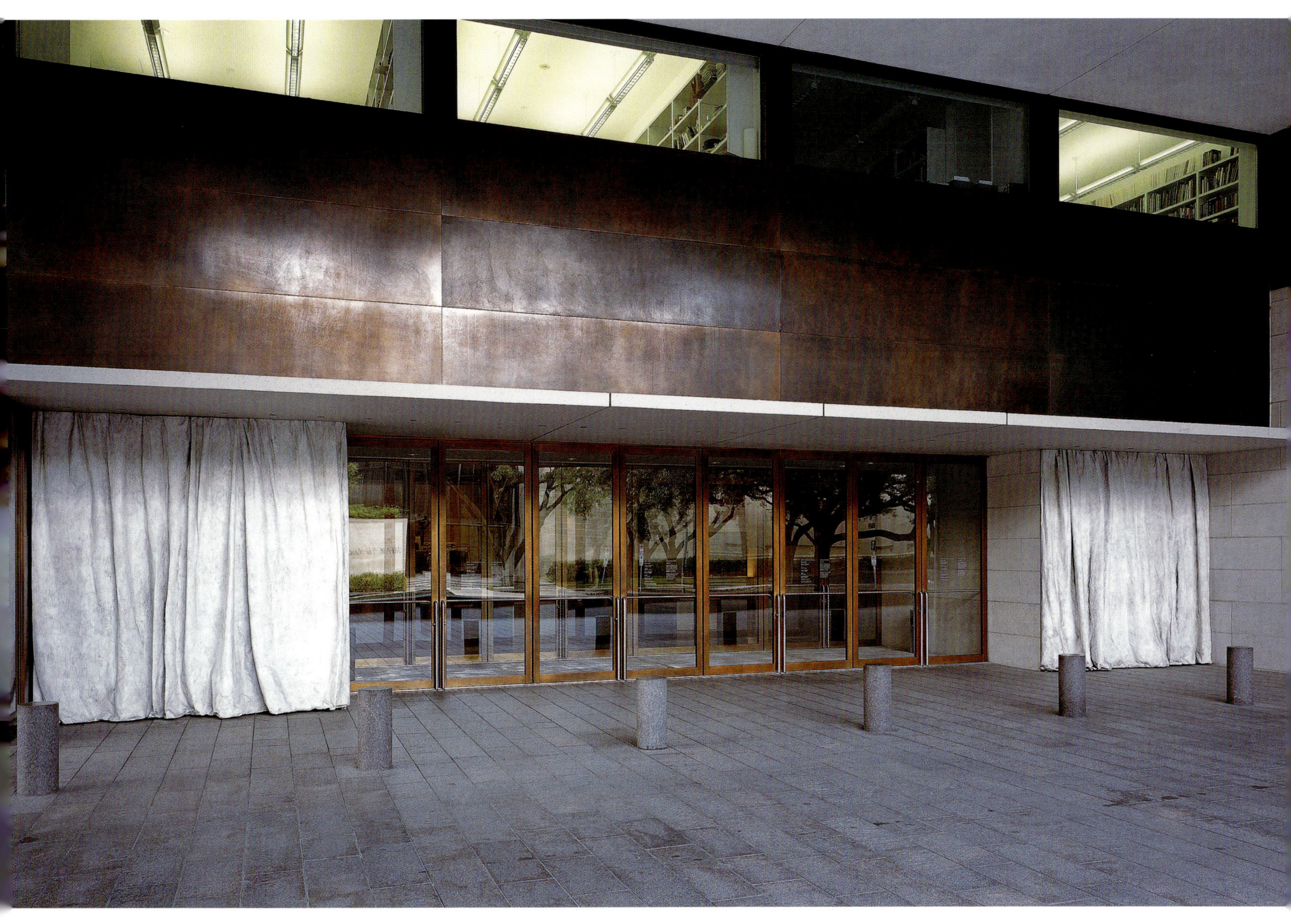

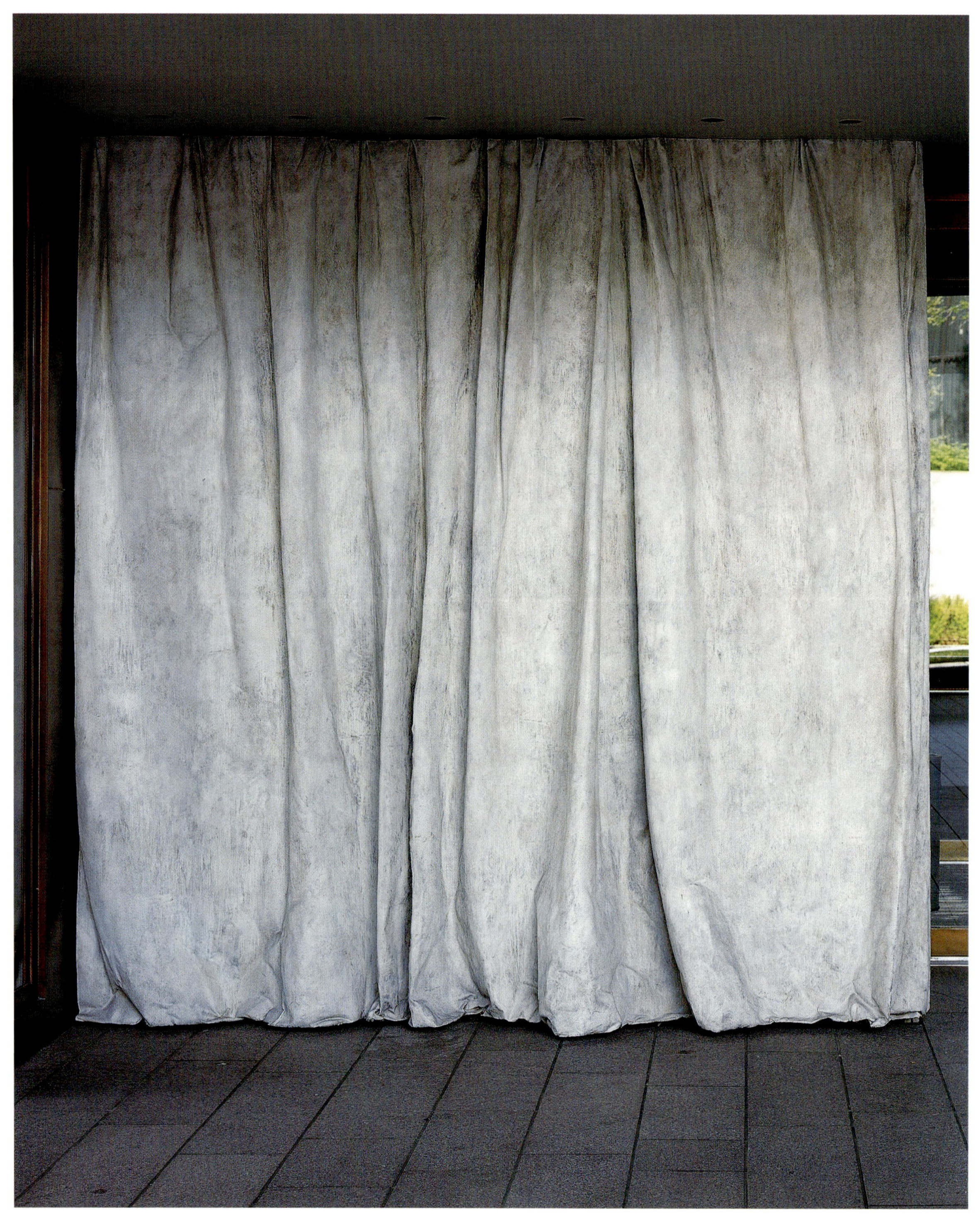

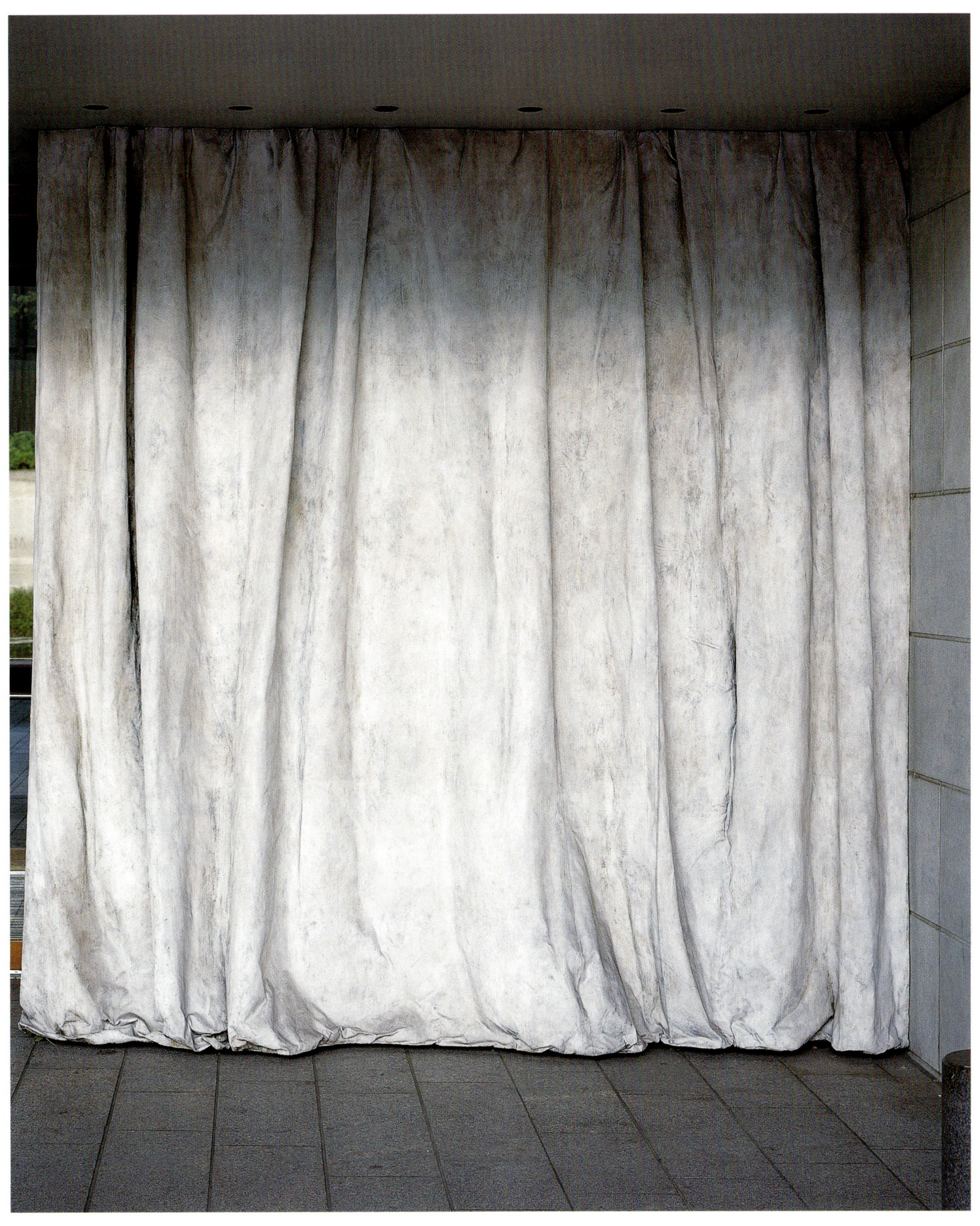

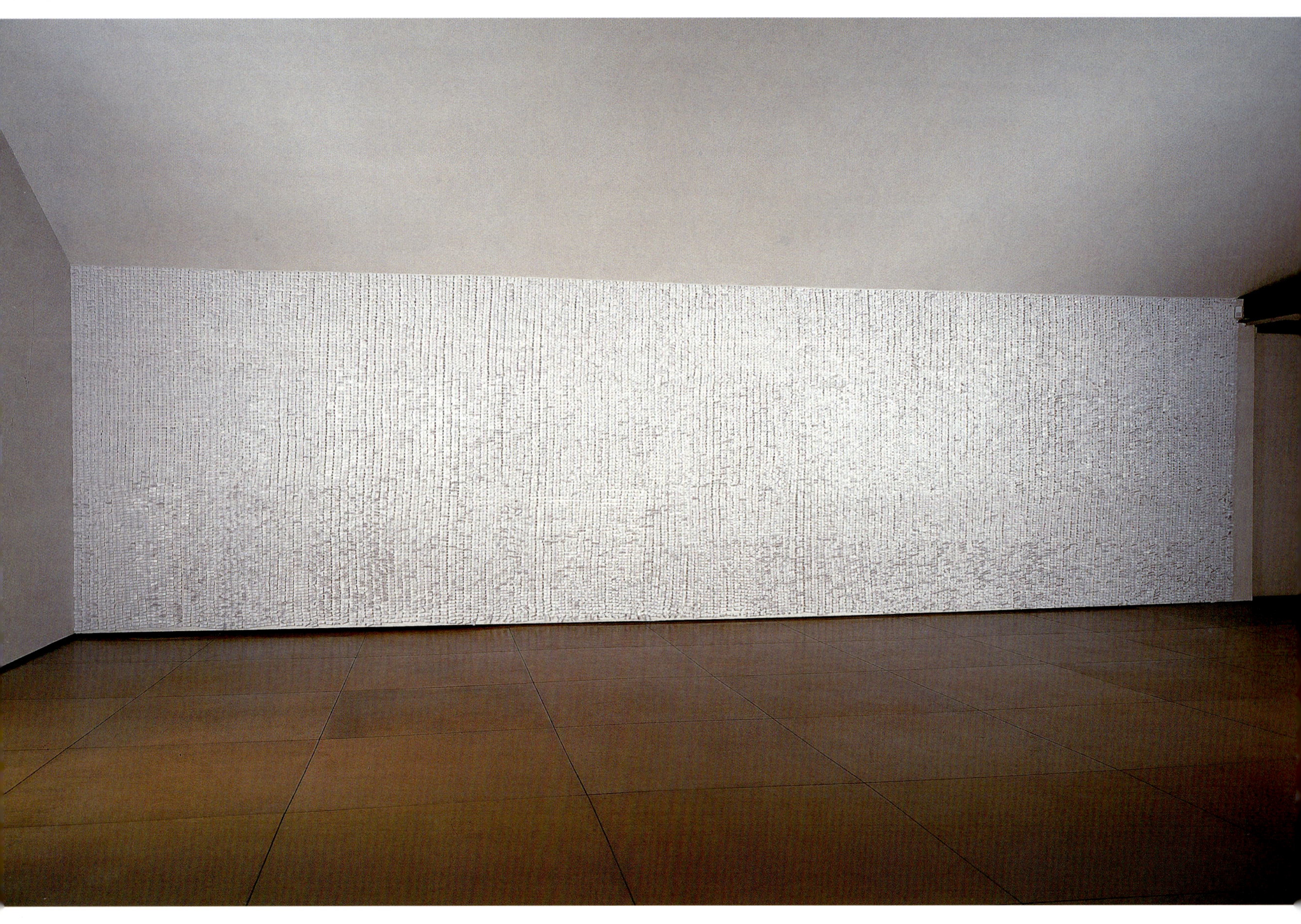

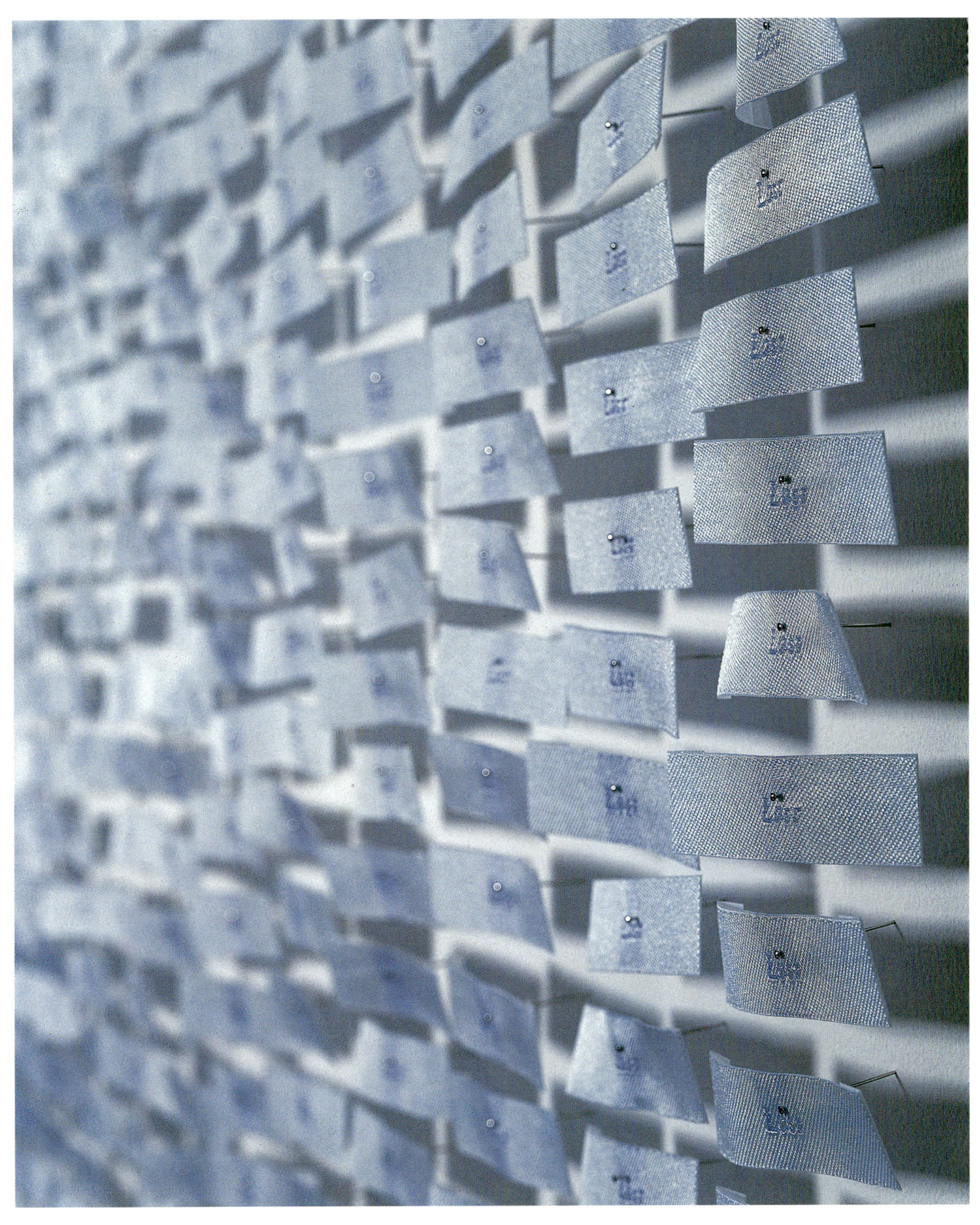

◀ PLATE 31 ***Lost**, 2000*

PLATE 32 ***Lost** (detail), 2000* ▶

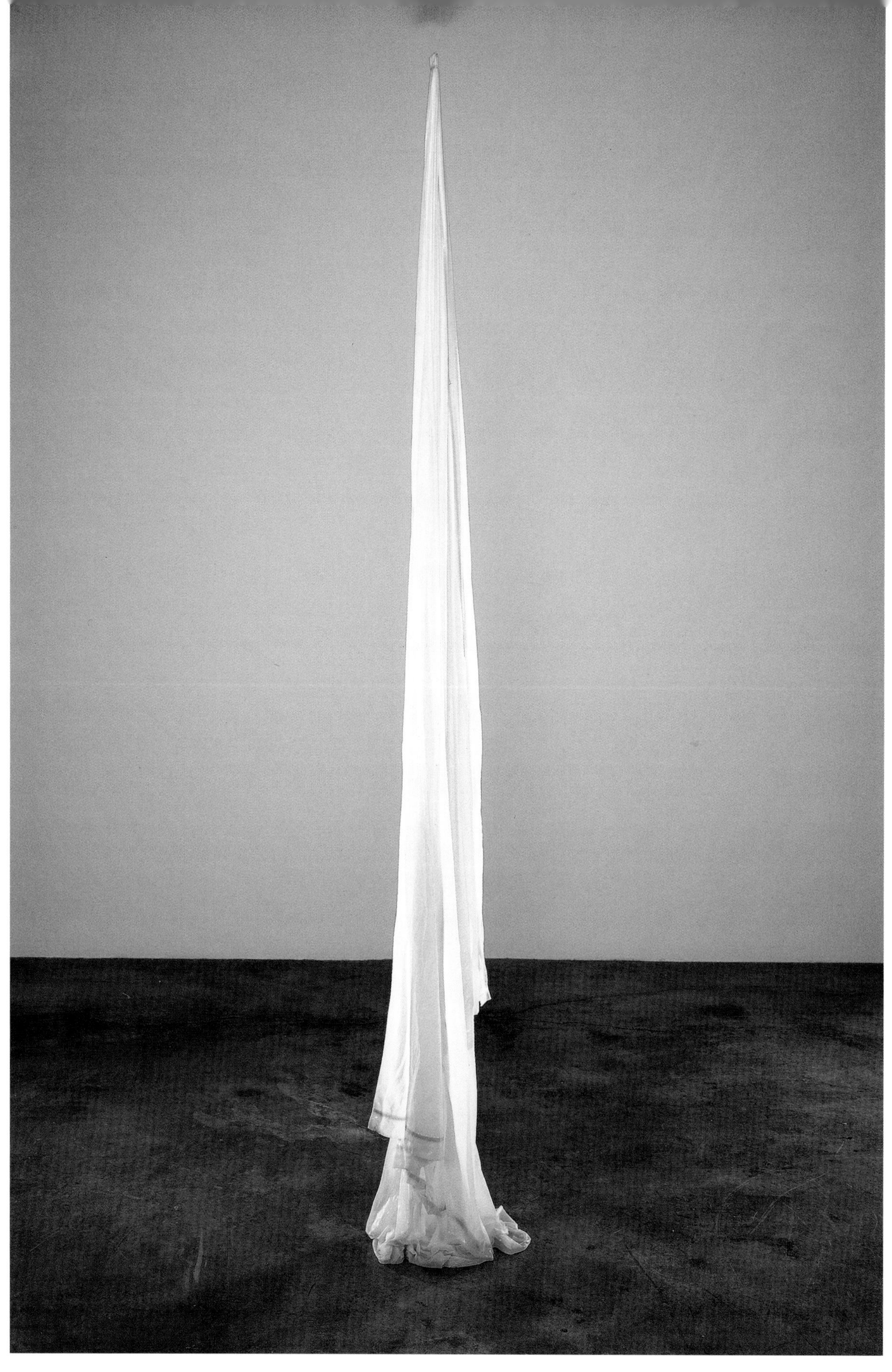

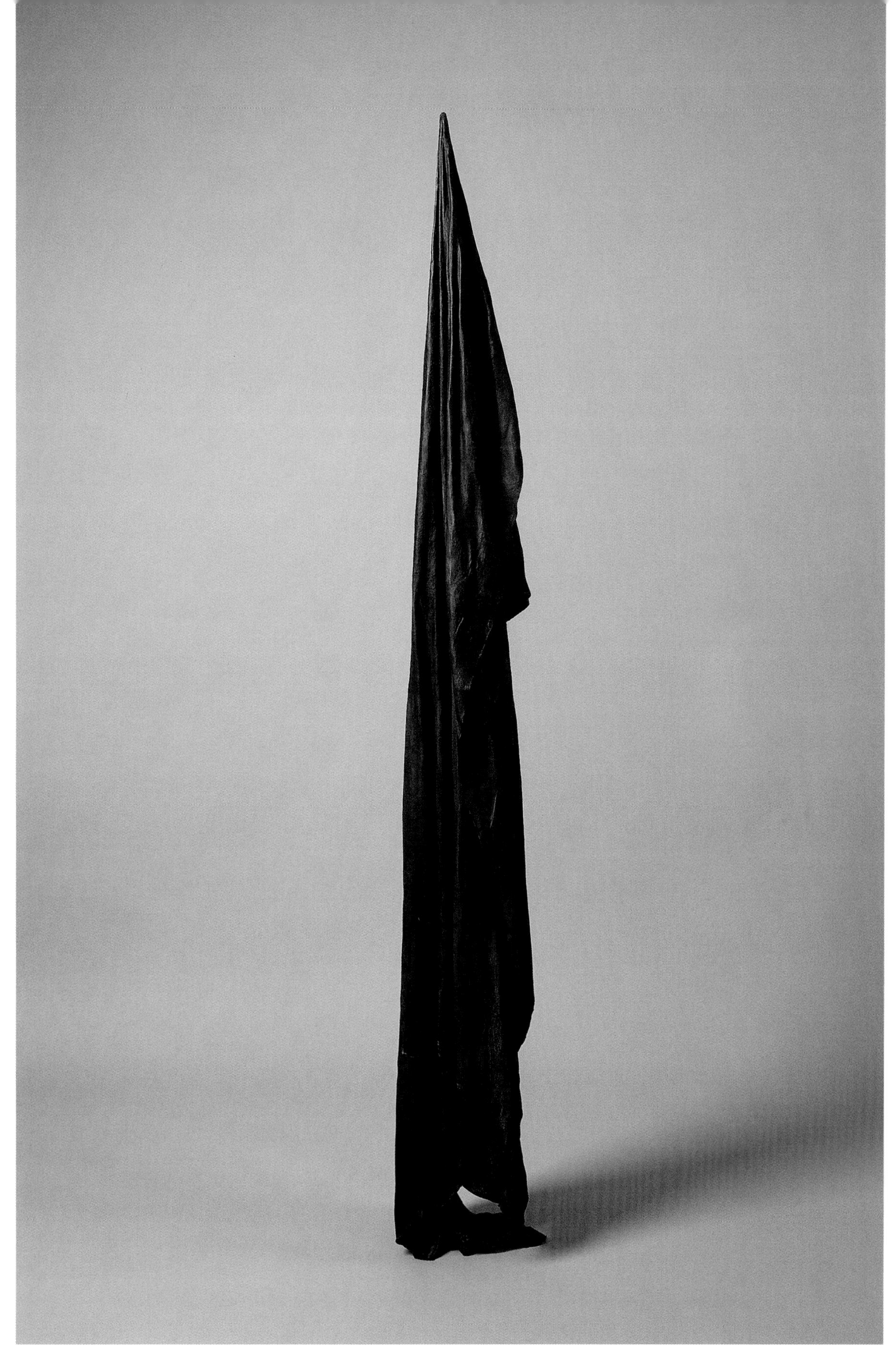

◀ PLATE 33 ***Bed Sheet***, *2001*

PLATE 34 ***Table Cloth***, *1999* ▶

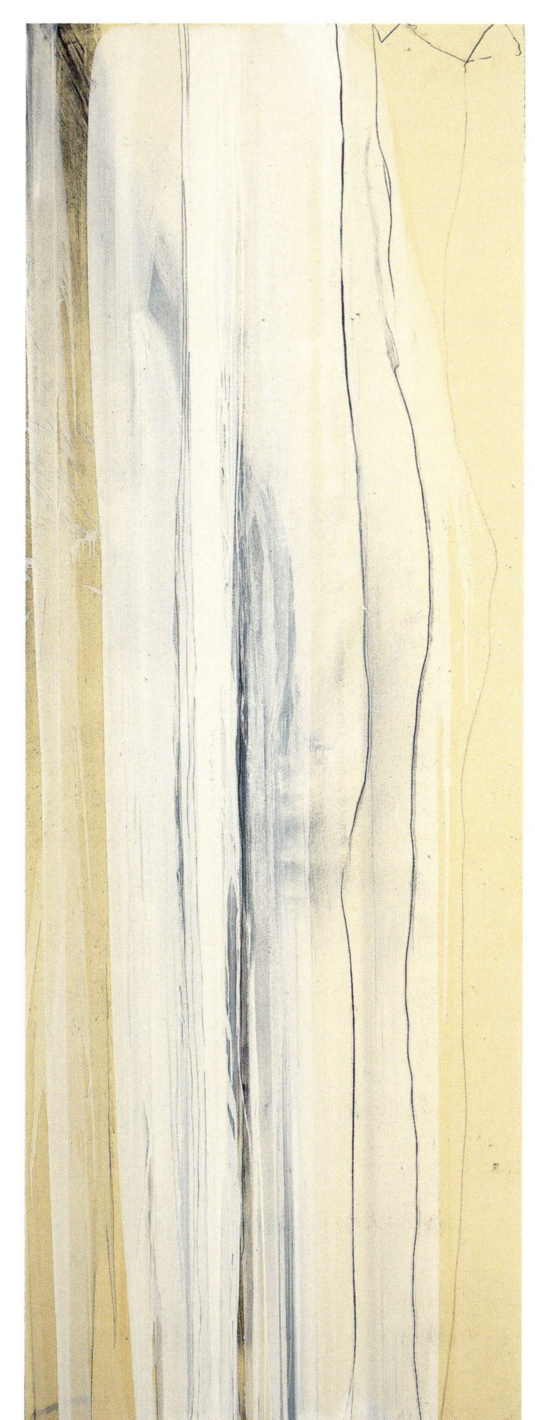

◀ PLATES 35/36 ***Veil II**, 1999;* ***Veil IV**, 2000*

PLATES 37/38 ***Veil VI**, 2000;* ***Veil IX**, 2000* ▶

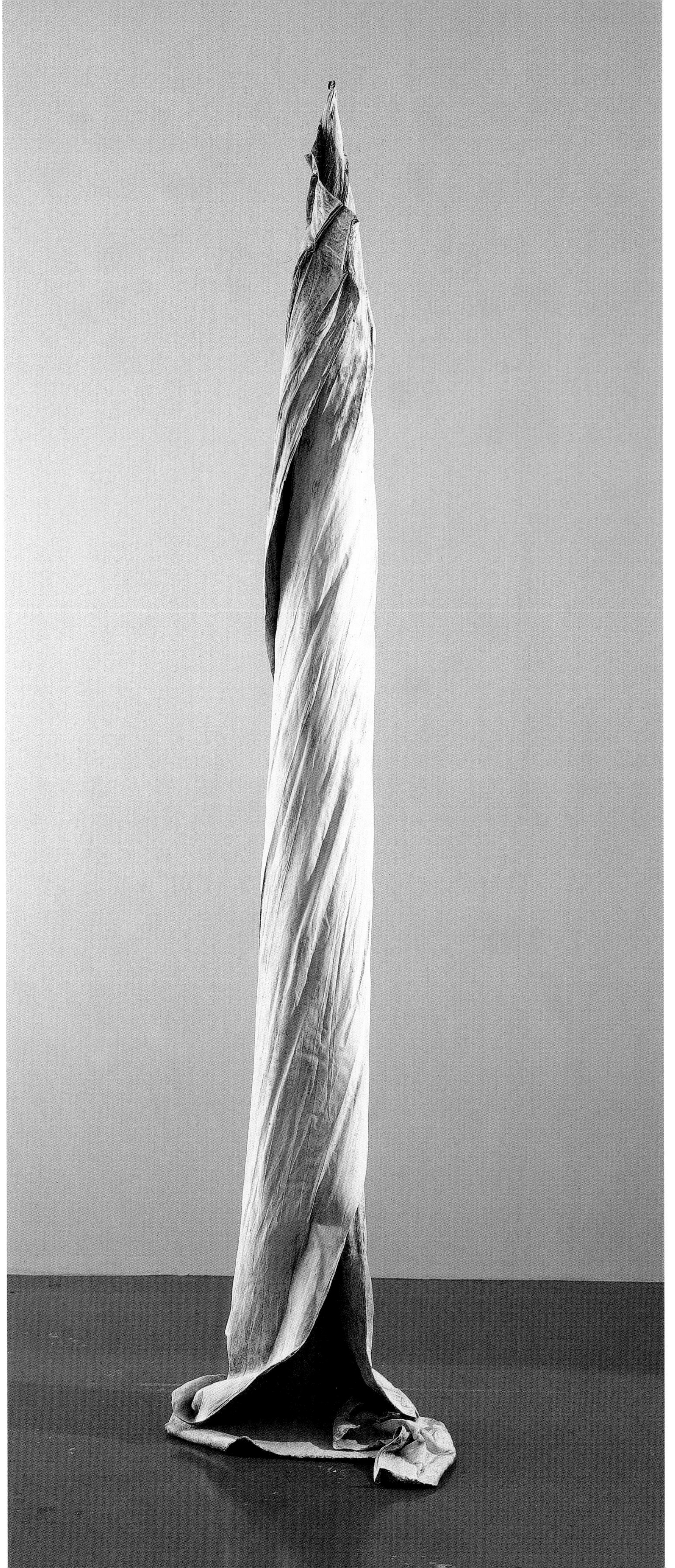

PLATE 39 ***Silk Drape***, *2000*

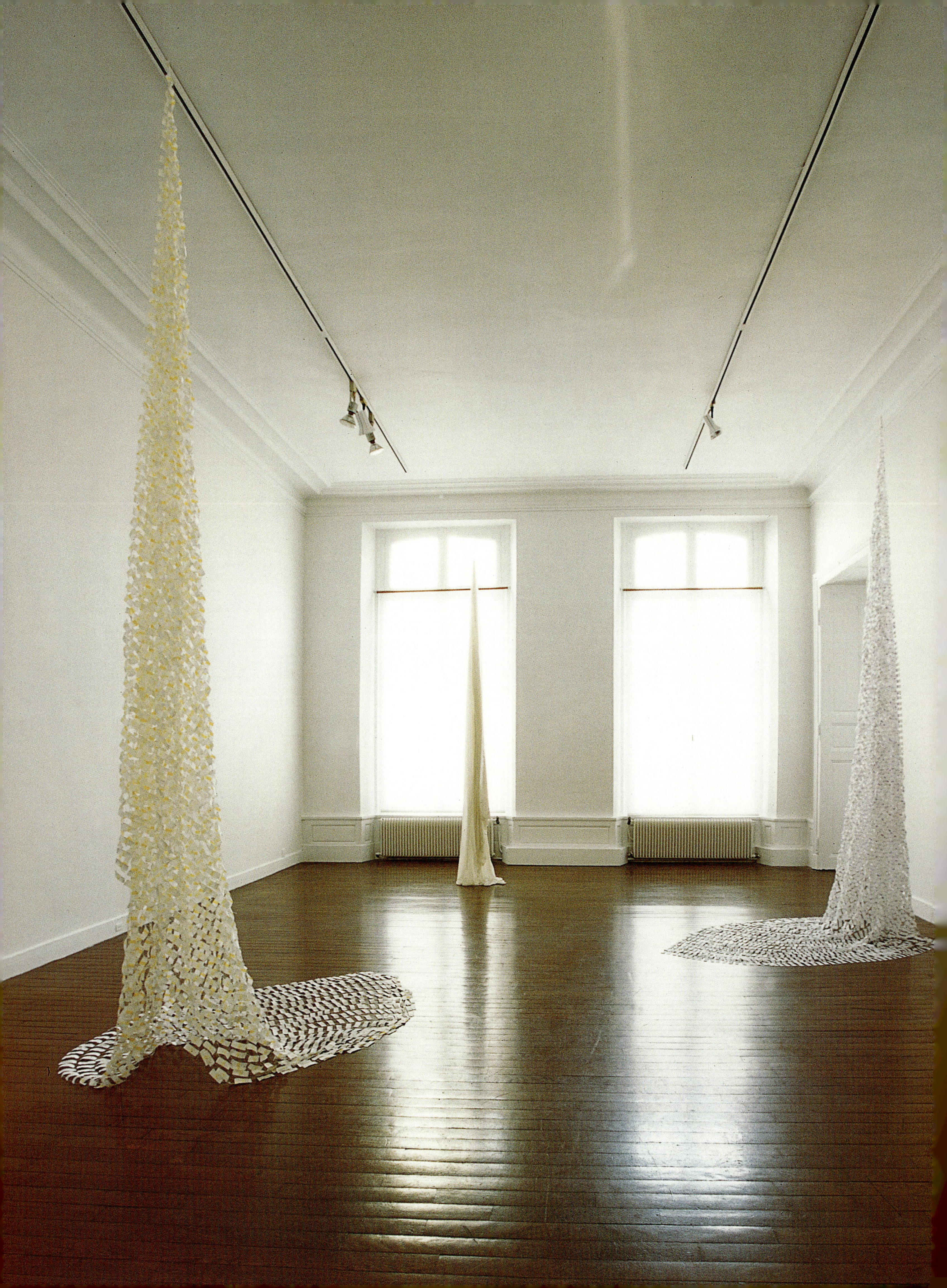

PLATE 40 *Installation view, **Daydream Nation**, 2001*

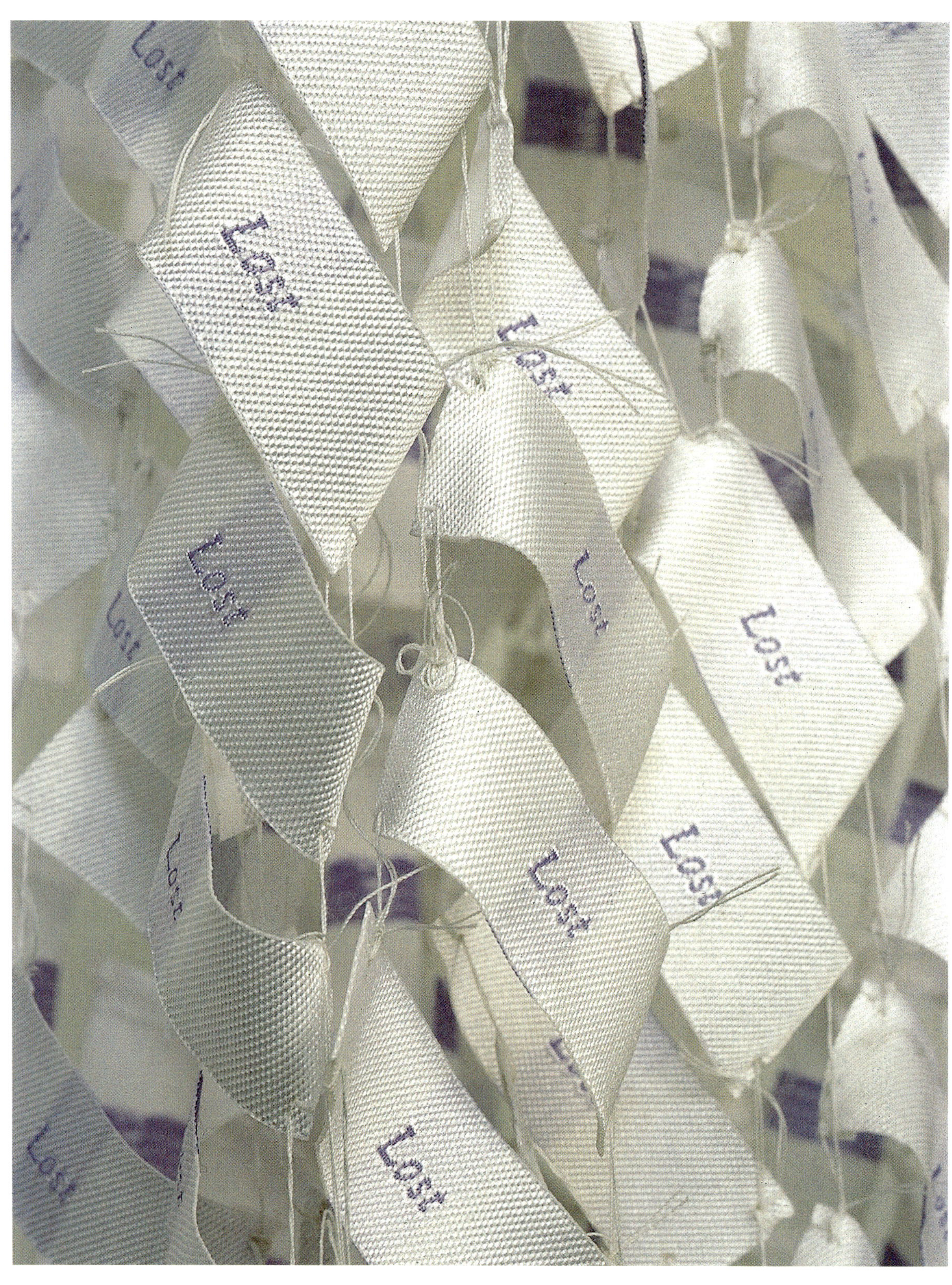
Lost
Lost
Lost
Lost
Lost
Lost
Lost
Lost
Lost
Lost
Lost

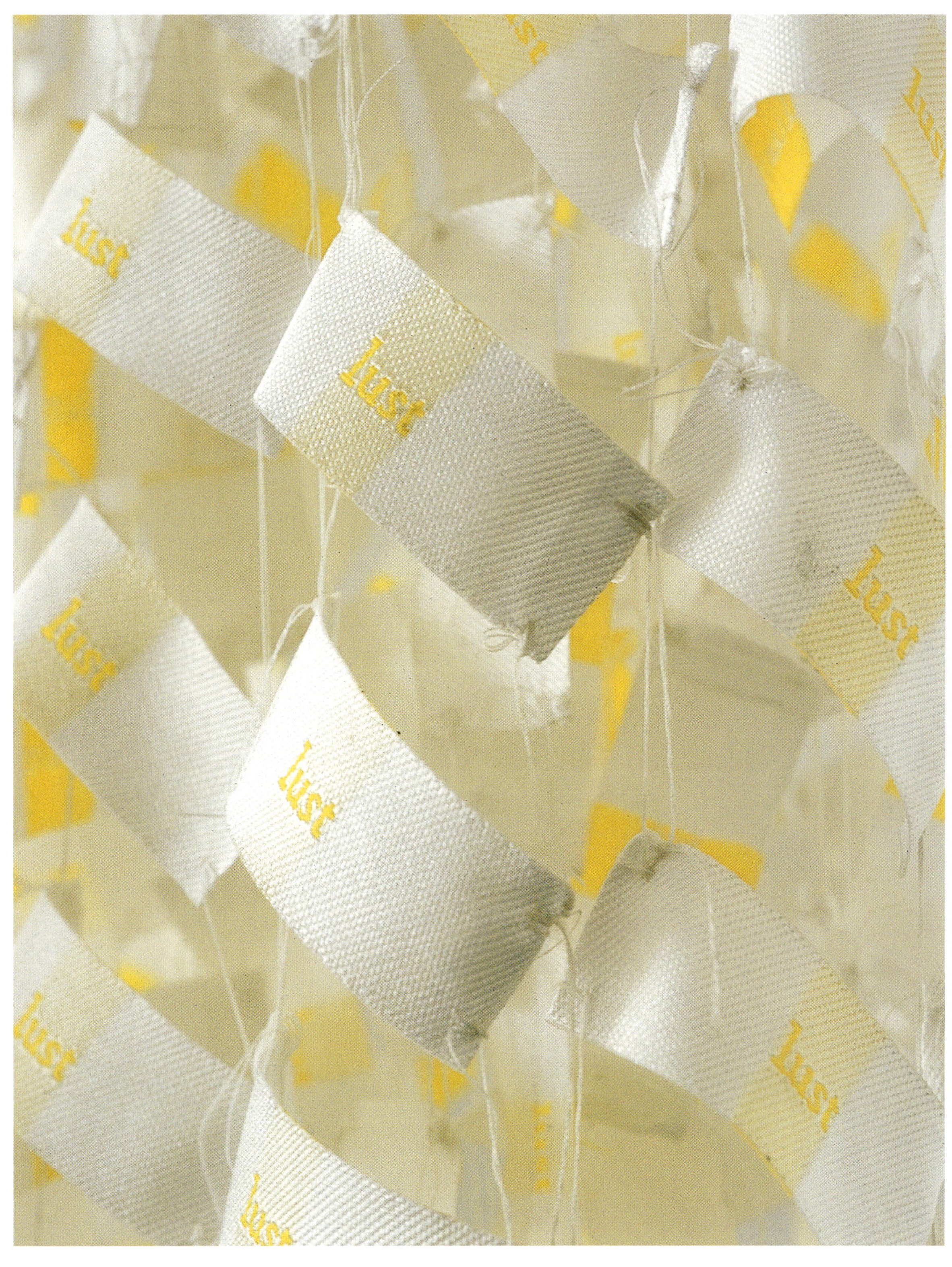

◄ PLATE 41 ***Lost*** *(detail), 2001*

PLATE 42 ***Lust*** *(detail), 2001* ►

PLATE 43 ***Fading Desire***, *2002*

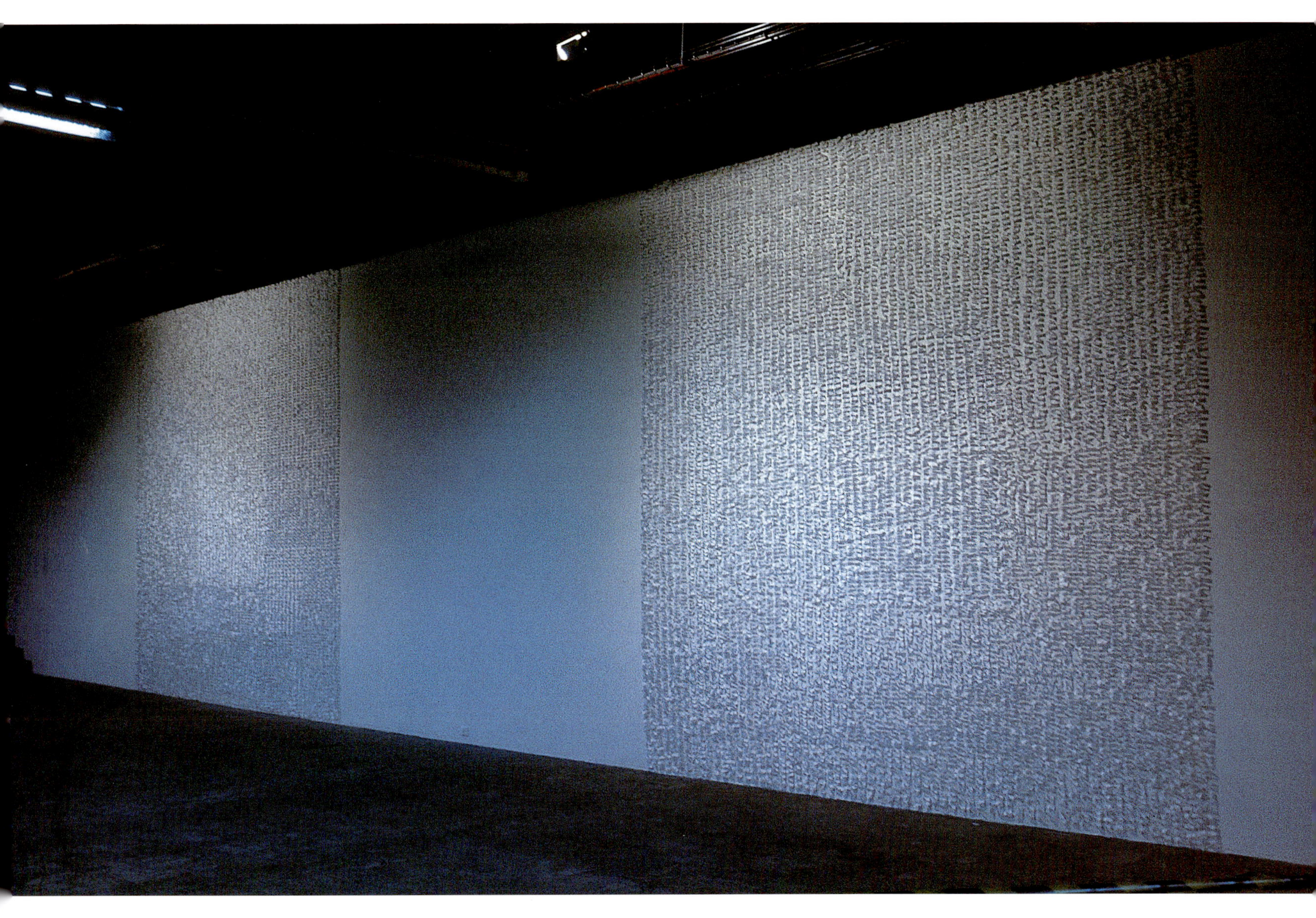

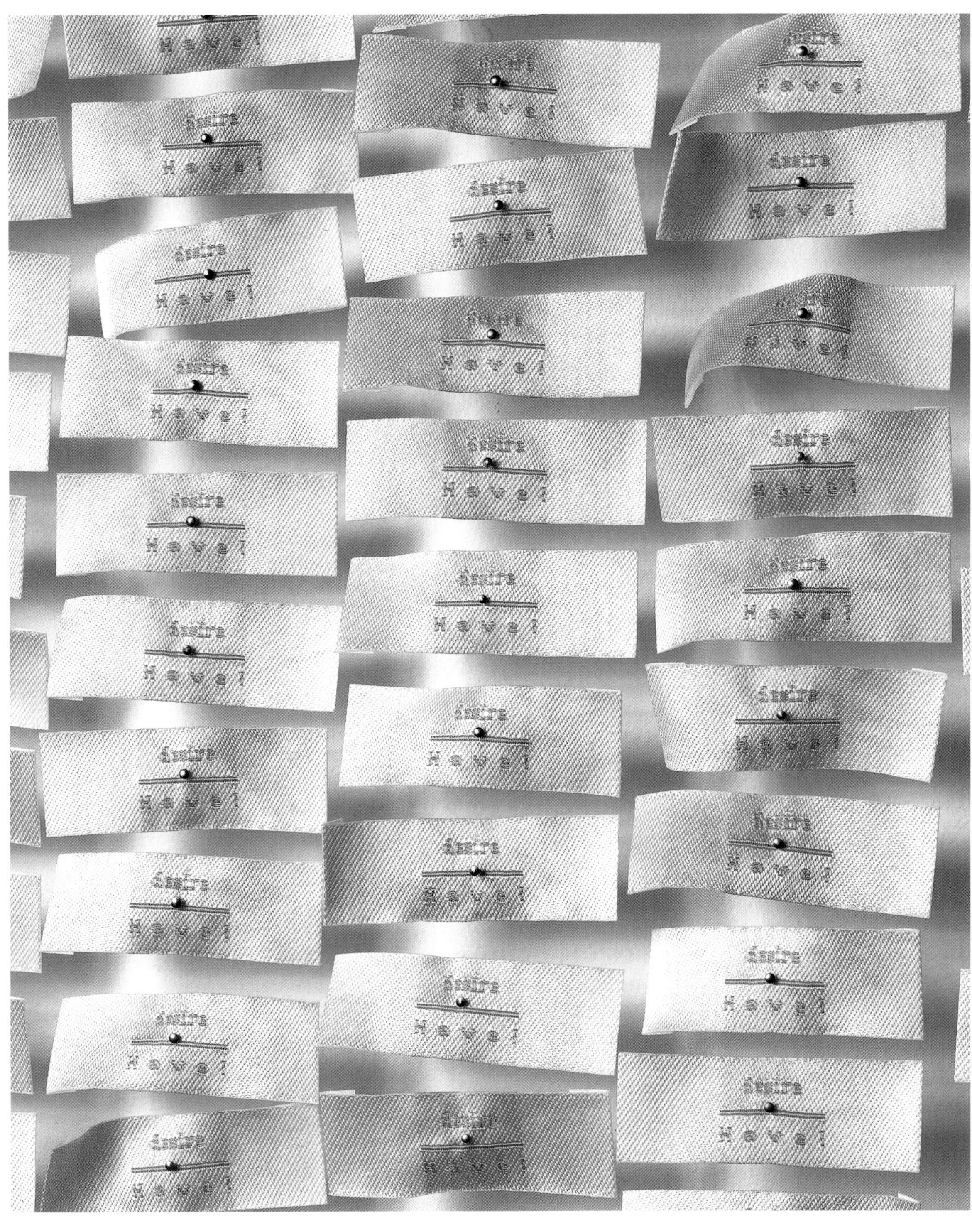

◄ PLATE 44 ***Fading Desire*** *(detail), 2002*

PLATE 45 ***Fading Desire*** *(detail), 2002* ►

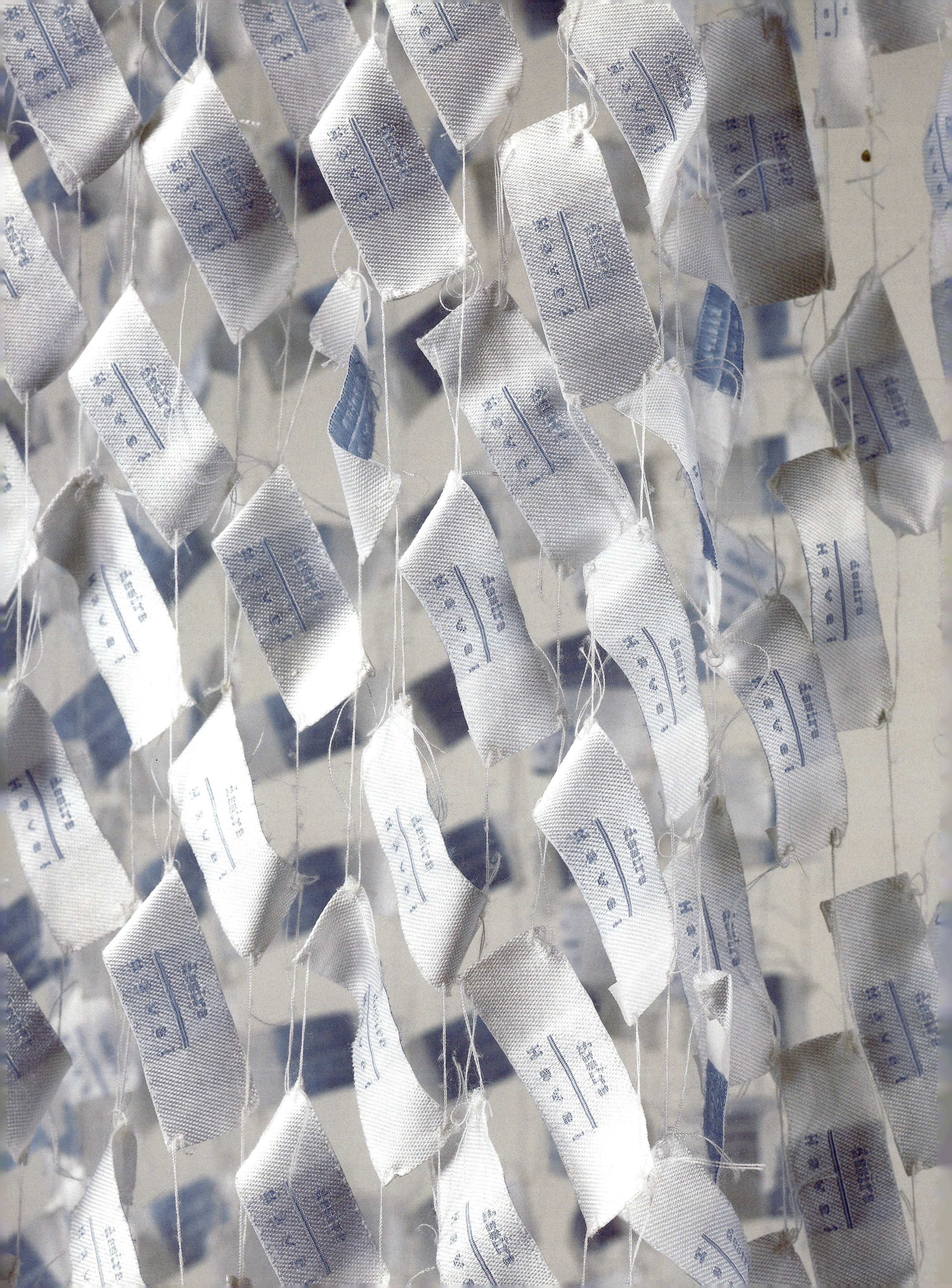

SPINELESS...JOSEPH HAVEL AND THE PRODUCTIVE EMBRACE OF FAILURE

Amelia Jones

"I was tired of making things that declared themselves too simply as art....
I wanted to make things that revealed themselves in more puzzling ways."
—*Joseph Havel* [1]

"You've got to be able to tear yourself apart and look at yourself objectively, but not be so distraught—because it always happens in public—that you can't make another gesture...Failure is part of what drives any good artist—the sense that you didn't get everything you wanted out of your work."
—*Joseph Havel* [2]

Engaging with Joseph Havel's work throws us backward as well as forward in time; allows us to linger between the narrative and the abstract, the domestic (and mundane) and the heroics of high art aesthetics; encourages us to dwell inside our own dreams, while propelling us outward into (art) history, the ideological spaces of gallery practice, and past aesthetic forms. Havel's objects hover between two realms, begging an unresolved tension that gets under our skin. Productively they instantiate the "failure...that drives any good artist," a failure accepted rather than disavowed or covered over with the icy theatrics of irony or a purist aesthetics obsessively foregrounding form alone. Profoundly unpretentious, they insist on being taken in multiple ways, potentially opening us to the possibility that art is nothing more (or less) than a materialization of the artist's struggle with the futility of making effective political and aesthetic interventions in a time in which politics and culture have turned into something we may no longer recognize.

Havel's work draws on the rich history of Western sculpture. Studiously he tweaks ways of making objects in space to send us catapulting back into memories of engaging monuments, installations, and things in vitrines. At the same time, his works spin us forward, suggesting what might be to come as we navigate increasingly complex networks of words, pixels, and brute things that continue to assault us from all angles. Havel's objects act as bridges between the past (our memories of the objects we've encountered, and the spaces and institutions in which we've encountered them) and what might be as our bodies and psyches change in response to new, networked, globalized ways of being in the world.

PLATE 46

Havel's works explore the tension in Euro-American sculptural traditions between *telling a story* (monuments, which encapsulate particular individual as well as national stories of heroism through the rendering of bodies on a large scale) and *producing an abstract spatial experience* (Richard Serra's metal slabs in space). Havel refuses to abandon the referential entirely, but rather than representing things or people through a realist aesthetic, he incorporates their materials and forms as the sculpture itself. He navigates between referent and sign (between the "thing"—say, a large curtain) and its symbolic or representational rendering, eschewing coming down on one side or another. Havel thus aligns himself with a long counter-history in human object-making traditions of lingering in the no-man's-land between signification and abstraction (from African fetishes, which terrified Europeans because of the claim that they *instantiated* rather than *represented* divinity; [3] to ancient to modern death masks, which both mark/mould the dead body's contours and symbolize the absent subject; to Marcel Duchamp's readymades, which are both functional objects and abstract sculptures; to Jasper Johns's Duchampian sculptural versions of a flashlight in the late 1950s).

Assaultive but also gentle and contemplative, Havel's objects—from twisted ropes of fabric yawning from floor to ceiling, to a span of stiffened shirt labels arranged in neat modernist grids and spreading across the floorboards—draw us into relation with them. Like minimalist artworks they demand that our bodies open outward, but also that the body/space relation is psychically registered such that our conception of ourselves in this particular space is mutated, if ever so slightly. They spark associations that move us in an outer direction (*"here I am, in this institutional gallery space, tiptoeing around the perimeter of this array of shirt labels, as if I were encountering the aggressive spatial politics of a Carl Andre")* but that also encourage us to dwell inward *("this reminds me of my Dad, who used to wear shirts with labels like this…")*.

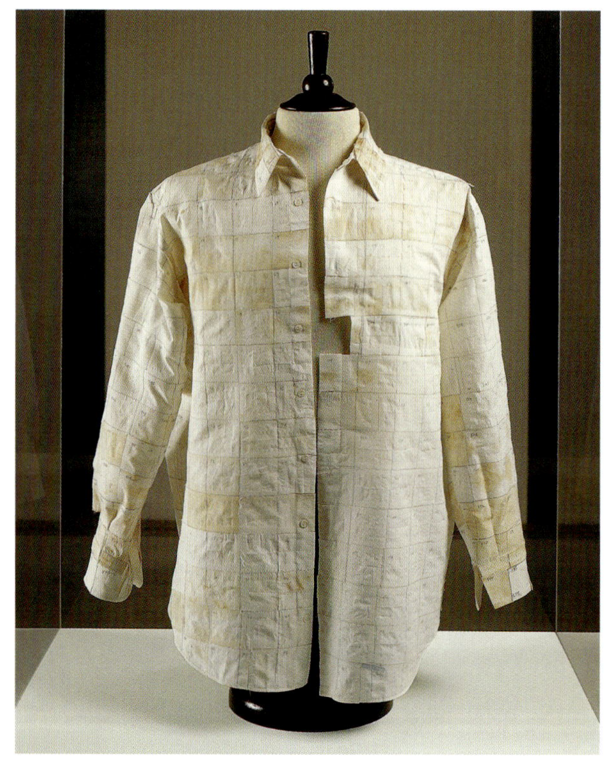

FIGURE 16

Treading these unresolved lines, marking these tensions between things, experiences, states of being, the works hover. The remainder of this essay will trace this hovering, linking each of Havel's works discussed here to a particular precedent in order to highlight the way in which Havel both dangles us in the past and catapults us into future possibilities.

Lost

Havel is obsessed with shirts. In *Laundered Pair* (1996; plate 8) a man's white shirt hangs in a rigor-mortis dance (frozen in space) like it's looking for a missing body. This surreal apparition reminds me of nothing more than Los Angeles-based artist Charles LaBelle's 2000 piece *Disappearer: Shirt That Passed Through My Body* (fig. 16), in which he reconstituted an actual shirt he had cut into pieces, wrapped in balloons that he swallowed and shit out the other end.[4] In Havel's case, the shirt wants to be transcendent—it looks like it wants to fly off, bodiless, into the ether but is held to earth by its bronzed commitment to masquerading as sculpture (the aesthetic, as it were, paradoxically drags it down to earth); in the case of LaBelle's *Disappearer*, the shirt is marked as unavoidably (literally: *viscerally*) tied to the human body. Marked by the stains of its journey through the artist's viscera (streaks of the stomach acids that made it through the pores of the balloons), the shirt is sewn back together in a Frankensteinian homage to the power of the human body to transform all that comes into contact with it.

In his 2000 installation piece *Lost* (plates 31 and 32), Havel arranges hundreds of fabric shirt labels into a loose grid formation, pinning them to the gallery wall. Fluttering like dead butterflies they seem ephemeral (lost in the mists of time) yet viscerally present. "Lost" means something has *already* gone, indicating a present and a future when that thing is *no longer around* and yet in which we are aware of its loss—and so a present and a future colored by the fact that it used to be manifest. They point backward (to what is gone—my dad's shirts; his body, inside them, making them smell of sweat, Bourbon, and cigars) and forward (to some universe where loss can be managed into a formatted regime of aesthetic contemplation).

One could argue that the controlling mechanisms of the aesthetic serve as one of the means by which we attempt to manage the inexorability of death, of the ultimate loss of the human body, here manifest only by the barest sign of one of its sartorial accoutrements—the label that points outward to the industrial/commercial matrix of its making (the company responsible for manufacturing the shirt) and potentially inward to the body that owned it (the kind of label, sewn on by one's mother before summer camp, that proclaims the wearer's name). But here, the labels only state "Lost."

What is lost? In addition to the body for which presumably the shirt was made, the relations of production through which mass-produced shirts are created, as well as through which "unique" objects called art are manufactured. While mass production hides its structures through seamless final products that gleam with desirable sleekness (desirable precisely because they hide their manufacture and thus promise perfection), artistic production and the apparatuses that subtend its value systems (art discourse, the art market, etc.) are made

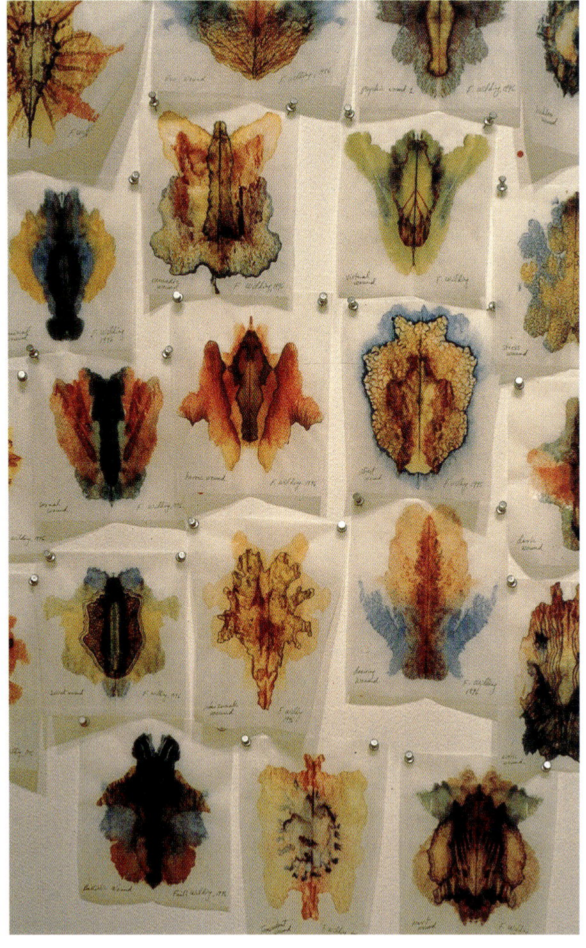

FIGURE 17

invisible by the discourse of the aesthetic. The philosophical belief system through which we insist that some objects are made by particular individuals who call themselves artists, and that these objects thus have a special (transcendental) status in the world—the aesthetic is in this sense alchemical; it turns objects back into subjects (or at least secures the objects as manifest material "facts" that point to the previous existence in time and space of the person who made them, the artist). In *Lost*, the artist is symbolized in one sense as the "lost" body of the person who wore the clothing that is no longer here...the lost body of the artist becomes a stand-in for the lost body we search for always, the lost body whose finding would secure our immortality by making real our fantasy of immersing ourselves in this *(m)other.*

Desire

The lost mother (the quintessential "other" within patriarchy, the desired complete union with whom is receding forever into the individual's past) is evoked with equal if not more dramatic passion in Faith Wilding's 1996 *Wall of Wounds* (fig. 17). Like Havel's *Lost,* the *Wall* consists of fluttering individual bits tacked tenuously to the gallery wall. But in Wilding's case, the individual pieces are approximately four- to five-inch-square pieces of tissue paper, marked by watercolor marks centered Rorschach-like along the central fold of the paper. Mirroring the infamous feminist central core images of the early 1970s (some of which were made by Wilding herself), the "wounds" are both gorgeous little "cunt" images and melancholic marks, symbols of damaged flesh—or, rather, they mark the sign of female genitalia as a sign of the woundedness and lack of all human existence.[5]

Havel's lost (m)other is less direct, but no less central to his project, which plays reiteratively with the boundaries (or lack thereof) between the self and other, the male and the female, the absent and the present body.

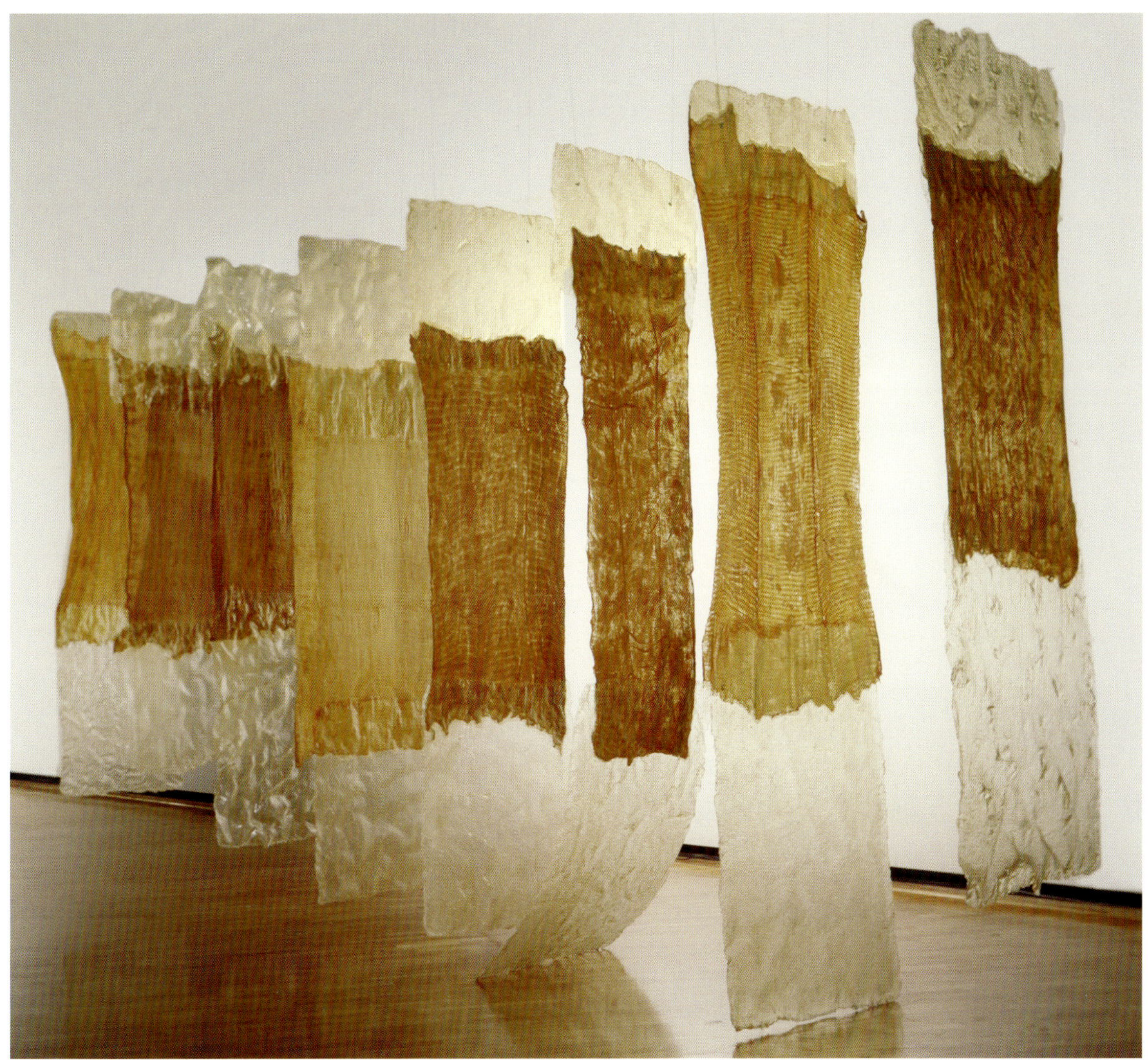

FIGURE 18

Joseph Havel is not afraid to embrace this lost feminine object (the subject of our dreams), or even to *inhabit* its body. In the 2003–4 piece *Desire* (plate 47)—a cascading wash of shirt labels tied tenuously together with thread, he produces a dangerously delicate (porous, permeable, palpating) counterpart to the macho folds of *Black Drape* (2002; plate 50). *Black Drape* might be seen as an updated version of the rigid phallic body of Rodin's *Balzac* (1897); in Havel's version, the body of the writer is evacuated and the drape itself (frozen in bronze) is forced to become the lost phallus literalized by this removal. If *Black Drape* is the Balzacian phallus, in parodic form, *Desire* is a renewed actualization of Bernini's ecstatic *St. Theresa* (c. 1650), whose orgasm seems displaced into the hurricane of fabric swirling around her body. Calmed into a falling slope of fabric labels in *Desire*, the storm of ecstasy dissolves into a waterfall of contentment and ephemerality.

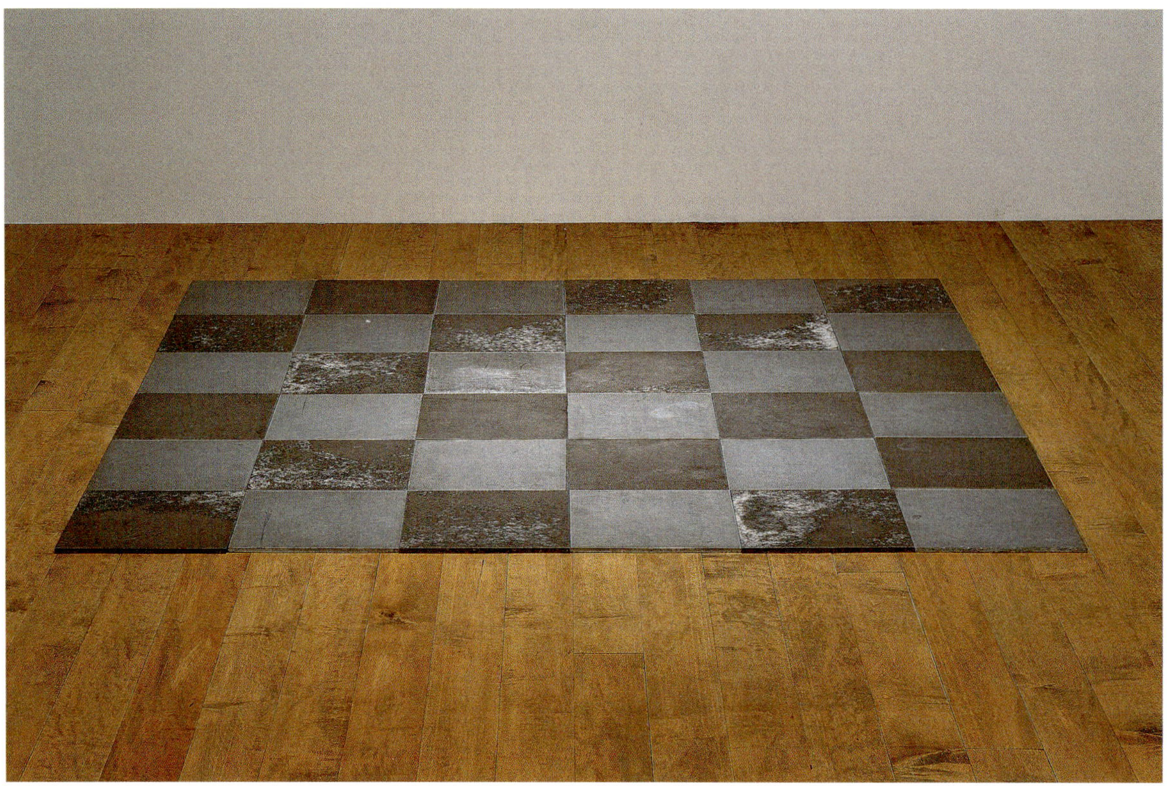

FIGURE 19

The tension between the "presence" of an object in space (one of the central defining aspects of conventional European sculpture, with the object most commonly referencing the human body) and the "absence" of this body marked by the holes and tenuousness of the sewn labels hanging in space, is palpable. While vaguely vertical in shape, the piece is first and foremost lacy and riddled with holes. The key point with *Desire*, however, is (for me) the "femininity" of this lost body. It's as if Havel wants the absence (the feminine orgasm itself?, which can never be rendered except via displacement) to override the weight of phallic presence mocked in *Black Drape*, and enacted originally in such an exaggerated way in the infamous Balzac (one of the versions of which unveiled the body of Balzac to show his striding form replete with fully visible penis, which merges into the pyramidal form supporting his rigorous body).

It's the same play between rigid and soft that characterizes all his drapery pieces—*Curtains* (1999; plate 25), with two curtains tied in a knot at the top and falling downward into pools on the floor—again, made rigid in bronze, belying the apparent flow of textiles drawn by gravity; or the equally rigid yet apparently "flowing" fabric forms in *Drape* (1999; plate 26), the closest of Havel's pieces to re-creating the fabrics of baroque sculptures, which in their languid or (as with *St. Theresa*) hysterically billowing appearance mimic the movements of the human form. In contrast, the unpredictability of human desire is more directly evoked in fabric pieces such as *Bed Sheet* (2001; plate 33), where the rigidity is melted into a more malleable and textured form (the fabric coated with urethane resin). Here, the bed sheet (already replete with sexual connotations) looks and feels almost like skin. Havel returns to the strategies of process art, perfected in pieces such as Eva Hesse's *Contingent* (1969; fig. 18), in which flaps of caucasian skin-colored flesh dangle across the gallery, human remains (post-flaying) as spider webs ready to brush across our faces in the most unsettling fashion.

At the same time, while Hesse's works avoid any direct reference to recognizable forms in everyday life or to the human body, Havel evokes the domestic (and thus the human activities within its spaces) directly—integrating bed sheets, curtains, and other household objects and fabrics into the works. Here, he extends the more recent traditions of assemblage, where everyday objects are put into the work. By directly courting reference to domesticity, too, Havel deploys a strategy developed in 1970s feminist art practice and embraces the feminine—those materials and tasks and ways of being conventionally excluded from modernist practice precisely because they throw its formalist closures into disarray.

With *Bed Sheet*, again, we are also thrown into chains of associations, artistic and otherwise—the cum- and sweat-tainted sheets, with stains reinforced by embroidery, displayed as abstract "paintings" by Charles LaBelle in the 1990s;[6] Rapunzel's long skein of locks (the climbing of which leads to consummation); the swaying sheets of waxed paper arranged, like Robert Morris's late 1960s felt pieces, by Lynn Aldrich (also based in L.A.) in the early 1990s; the handkerchief held by a magician under which magical tricks unfold, unseen. Or, by association with the title: Robert Rauschenberg's paint-stained *Bed* (1955; fig. 4) and Tracey Emin's 1999 *My Bed*, supposedly the "actual" thing, rumpled and covered with and surrounded by the detritus of a life well (or at least sexually actively) lived, from vodka bottles to condoms. *Bed Sheet*, however, typically of all Havel's work, doesn't let go of the formal simplicity of modernist sculpture. *Bed Sheet* seeks to take off, flying, into the air like Brancusi's 1919 *Bird in Space*, throwing its narrative connotations to the wind, as it were, but still letting them hover there, lightly, at the edges of our visual imaginary.

Bruised

Bruised, battered, and lying like a doormat ready to be trampled by disrespectful feet… Havel's *Bruised* (2004; plates 68 and 69) also evokes a myriad of artistic and mundane associations. Most obviously, it mimics (or mocks?) the formalist pretensions of Carl Andre's signature minimalist floor pieces from the late 1960s, such as the checkerboard 1969 *Magnesium-Zinc Plain* (fig. 19). While Andre's work is more or less aggressive, announcing its resistance to being touched or (God forbid) trodden on, Havel's more nuanced fabric surfaces in *Bruised* (composed again of fabric shirt labels, this time stacked in their small cardboard packing boxes) encourage more sensual encounters. As Andre asserts of his floor pieces, "[m]ost sculpture is priapic with the male organ in the air. In my work, Priapus is down on the floor. The engaged position is to run along the earth…"[7] While laying his work horizontally, then, Andre is still fixated on re-creating in sculptural form the phallic guarantee provided by "priapic" forms.

At the very least, in contrast, the textured—even apparently *bruised*—surface of *Bruised* seems malleable and open to (if not already marked by) the assaults of our gaze and physical presence. Notably, the "presence" of the author is referenced by the fact that Havel's name is printed on the labels, along with the word "bruised."[8] Havel becomes the name that authenticates the labels (as their "designer"?) and yet his "presence" actually once again emerges in dialectical tension with absence since the printed name only refers to him rather than confirming he is physically *there* (in fact, to the contrary, it makes us more aware than ever that presence is only ever a dream). Again, Havel takes some of the quintessential belief systems and forms of Euro-American sculptural traditions and makes them into something *other*—more equivocal, softer, more impressionable, and linked to the domestic or intimate pleasures of everyday life.

If Andre's work—made of magnesium and zinc—seems a paean not only to the masculine force of large-scale environmental sculpture but also to the heroic bodily labor associated with industrial production, Havel's *Bruised* submits itself to the more delicate imaginings of bodies whose flesh is marked by rough handling. The artwork itself becomes a metaphor for the human body—both potentially vulnerable to the harshness of unwanted encounters.

Spine(less)

The first piece I ever saw by Joseph Havel was *Spine* (1996; plate 3), a striking thirteen-foot-high "spine" of shirt collars. Phallic and porous—*Spine* has the attributes of the literal skeletal spine. The piece has the appearance of being a support yet also of potentially registering the slightest movement—of being both rigid and flexible. Quintessentially, Havel once again treads a series of thin lines between the everyday and the artistic (shirt collars and modernist sculpture); the hard and the soft; the inside and the outside; the corporeal and the fabricated; solid and permeable; present and absent.

Wandering again around the totem pole of *Spine*, I feel bodily memories returning me to earlier experiences of both "art" and "natural science" museums: *Spine* is like Brancusi's smaller versions of the mid-1930s *Endless Column*; it is also reminiscent of the slithering spinal columns of dinosaurs, painstakingly strung back together into a semblance of reanimated bodily movement in a natural history display. If, as Sigmund Freud suggested, civilization is precisely about the sublimation of base instincts into "higher" forms of cultural production (a sublimation he saw as paralleling the shift of apes, ambling horizontally across the jungle floor, into humans, standing vertically and so with maximum distance placed between sense organs and genital region), then Havel's *Spine* works to confuse these two supposedly opposed states of being. For Freud, there is a polar opposition between base instincts and civilized artistic creation ("[s]ublimation of instinct is an especially conspicuous feature of cultural development; it is what makes it possible for higher physical activities, scientific, artistic or ideological, to play such an important part in civilized life"), between the gross sexual self, which is epitomized by the menstruating female, and the superior figure of the sublimating artist ("women represent the interests of the family and of sexual life. The work of civilization has become increasingly the business of men, it confronts them with ever more difficult tasks and compels them to carry on instinctual sublimations of which women are little capable").[9]

In Freud's universe, which is the same early-twentieth-century European universe (more or less) occupied by Rodin's phallic *Balzac* (the sculptural materialization of the myths perpetrated in Freud's texts, which ultimately mesh the upright civilized artist inextricably with the body of the white European male) and Carl Andre's priapus, men are men (and artists) and women are "little capable" of transcending the reek of sexualized embodiment.

In Havel's universe, in contrast, the coexistence of vertical and horizontal, soft and hard, art and domesticity, the feminine and masculine (even, or perhaps especially, within one body or one form) are embraced. It is this kind of "spinelessness"—the deliberate embrace of failure (rather than the endless attempt to shore up divisions that no longer function, if they ever did, to secure a sense of each subject's role and position in the world)—that brings his practice into relevance as a nuanced and skilled negotiation of traditional and new sculptural forms and concepts that parallel and even welcome shifts in ways of being in the twenty-first century.

NOTES

1 Cited in Michael Ennis, "Joseph Havel: Art that Confounds Expectations," *Texas Monthly* 28, no. 9 (September 2000), 163.

2 Cited in Sam Houston, "The Man Behind the Curtain: Havel's Art Soars Above Its Origins," *Houston Lifestyles and Homes,* June 2001, 58.

3 On the Europeans' terror in relation to what they perceived the African fetish as representing, see William Pietz, "The Problem of the Fetish, I," *Res* 9 (Spring 1985): 5–17.

4 This piece is illustrated on LaBelle's Web site; see http://home.earthlink.net/~clabelle/exhibit/exhib_frame.html, under "Disappearer."

5 See Wilding's *Womb* (1971), reproduced in Amelia Jones, ed., *Sexual Politics: Judy Chicago's Dinner Party in Feminist Art History* (Berkeley: University of California Press, 1996), 14; and, on the *Wall of Wounds*, see Amelia Jones and Laura Meyer, *Feminist Directions 1970/1996*: *Robin Mitchell, Mira Schor, Faith Wilding, Nancy Youdelman* (Riverside, California: Jack and Marilyn Sweeney Art Gallery, UC Riverside, 1996).

6 See LaBelle's *I Can't Wait to Neglect You, I Can't Wait to Forget You*, 1996, illustrated on his web site (see note 4), under "University of Texas."

7 Anna Chave, "Minimalism and the Rhetoric of Power," *Arts Magazine* (January 1990): 45, 46.

8 Havel's name is also marked on the labels in *Desire*; as he has noted, "[t]he *Desire* label…carries my name which has a nice double play because it could be read as my desire or I suppose a request for others to desire me" (in an e-mail to the author, 7 July 2005). Indeed!

9 Sigmund Freud, *Civilization and Its Discontents* (1929–30), trans. James Strachey (New York: Norton & Company, 1961), 44, 50–51.

Plate 46 — ***Desire*** *(detail)*
2003–4
Fabric shirt labels and thread
195 x 56 x 56 inches
Courtesy of Devin Borden Hiram Butler Gallery

Figure 16 — *Charles LaBelle*
Disappearer: Shirt That Passed Through My Body
2000
Shirt and mending tape
72 x 32 1/2 x 24 1/2 inches

Figure 17 — *Faith Wilding*
Wall of Wounds
1996
Installation view and detail from the exhibition ***Feminist Directions*** *at the University of California, Riverside, 1996*
Watercolor and ink
100 6 x 6 inches

Figure 18 — *Eva Hesse*
Contingent
1969
Fiberglass and polyester resin, latex on cheesecloth
8 units, 114 to 168 x 36 to 48 inches
Collection of the National Gallery of Australia

Figure 19 — *Carl Andre*
Magnesium-Zinc Plain
1969
Magnesium and zinc
3/8 x 72 x 72 inches
Collection Museum of Contemporary Art San Diego
Museum Purchase with matching funds from the National Endowment for the Arts, 1974.4.1–36

Plate 47 — ***Desire***
2003–4
Fabric shirt labels and thread
195 x 56 x 56 inches
Courtesy of Devin Borden Hiram Butler Gallery

Plate 48 — ***Toy, Dream, Rest***
2003
Fabric shirt labels and thread
Dimensions variable
Courtesy of the artist

Plate 49 — ***Toy, Dream, Rest*** *(detail)*
2003
Fabric shirt labels and thread
Dimensions variable
Courtesy of the artist

Plate 50 — ***Black Drape***
2002
Bronze with patina
171 x 53 x 50 inches
Collection of Cornelia and Meredith Long

Plate 51 — ***Torn Flannel Duvet Cover***
2003
Bronze with patina
126 x 48 x 33 inches
Collection of Mr. and Mrs. Robert H. Dedman, Jr.

Plate 52 — ***Indian Fire***
2003
Fabric and urethane resin
92 x 38 x 34 inches
Courtesy of the Galerie Gabrielle Maubrie

Plate 53 — ***Kneel to Whisper in a Sow's Ear***
2004
Linen napkin and silk handkerchief
7 x 6 x 2 inches
Courtesy of the artist

Plate 54 — ***Meadow/Mountain/Idea***
2004
Handkerchief, paper, and glue
3 x 6 x 6 inches
Courtesy of the artist

Plate 55 — ***Heart of Froth***
2004
Handkerchief and yarn
5 x 4 x 4 inches
Courtesy of the artist

Plate 56 — ***To Bring***
2004
Bronze with patina
53 x 57 x 55 inches
The Barrett Collection, Dallas, Texas

Plate 57 — ***To Take***
2004
Bronze with patina
45 x 46 x 45 inches
Collection of Diane and Charles Cheatham

Plate 58–61 — ***Bed Sheet Bundles***
2004
Oil paint and graphite on vellum
Each 12 x 9 inches
Courtesy of the artist

Plate 62 *Exhibition: **To Bring/To Take**, Dunn and Brown Contempoary, Dallas*
2003

Plates 63–64 ***Torn and Twisted Curtain***
2004–5
Bronze with patina
192 x 53 x 22 inches
The Museum of Fine Arts, Houston, museum commission, gift of Nona and Richard Barrett, Nancy and Tim Hanley, Eliza Lovett Randall, Stanford and Joan Alexander Foundation, Claire and Doug Ankenman, Carol and Les Ballard, Toni and Jeff Beauchamp, Blake Byrne, Sara Dodd-Spickelmier and Keith Spickelmier, Kay and Al Ebert, Sam Gorman, Diana and Russell Hawkins, Janet and Paul Hobby, Karen and Eric Pulaski, Alice C. Simkins, Emily and Alton Steiner, Herbert C. Wells, Isabel B. and Wallace S. Wilson, Jill and Dunham Jewett, Karol Howard and George Morton, Jan Diesel, and Randee and Howard Berman, 2005.1051.

Plate 65 ***Twisted Curtain***
2004–5
Bronze with patina
198 x 25 x 18 inches
Courtesy of the artist

Plate 66 ***Lost and Lust***
2004
Fabric shirt labels and cardboard
1 x 120 x 120 inches
Collection of Stedelijk Museum voor Actuele Kunst (S.M.A.K.), Ghent, Belgium

Plate 67 ***Lost and Lust*** (detail)
2004
Fabric shirt labels and cardboard
1 x 120 x 120 inches
Collection of Stedelijk Museum voor Actuele Kunst (S.M.A.K.), Ghent, Belgium

Plate 68 ***Bruised***
2004
Fabric shirt labels and cardboard
1 x 132 x 132 inches
Courtesy of Dunn and Brown Contemporary

Plate 69 ***Bruised** (detail)*
2004
Fabric shirt labels and cardboard
1 x 132 x 132 inches
Courtesy of Dunn and Brown Contemporary

Plate 70 ***Wash***
2004–5
Bronze with patina
105 x 103 x 23 inches
Courtesy of the artist

Plate 71 ***Wash** (detail)*
2004–5
Bronze with patina
105 x 103 x 23 inches
Courtesy of the artist

Plates 72–73 ***Bed Sheet Drawings***
2005
Oil paint, ink and graphite on vellum
16 x 10 inches
Courtesy of the artist

PLATE 47 ***Desire**, 2003–4*

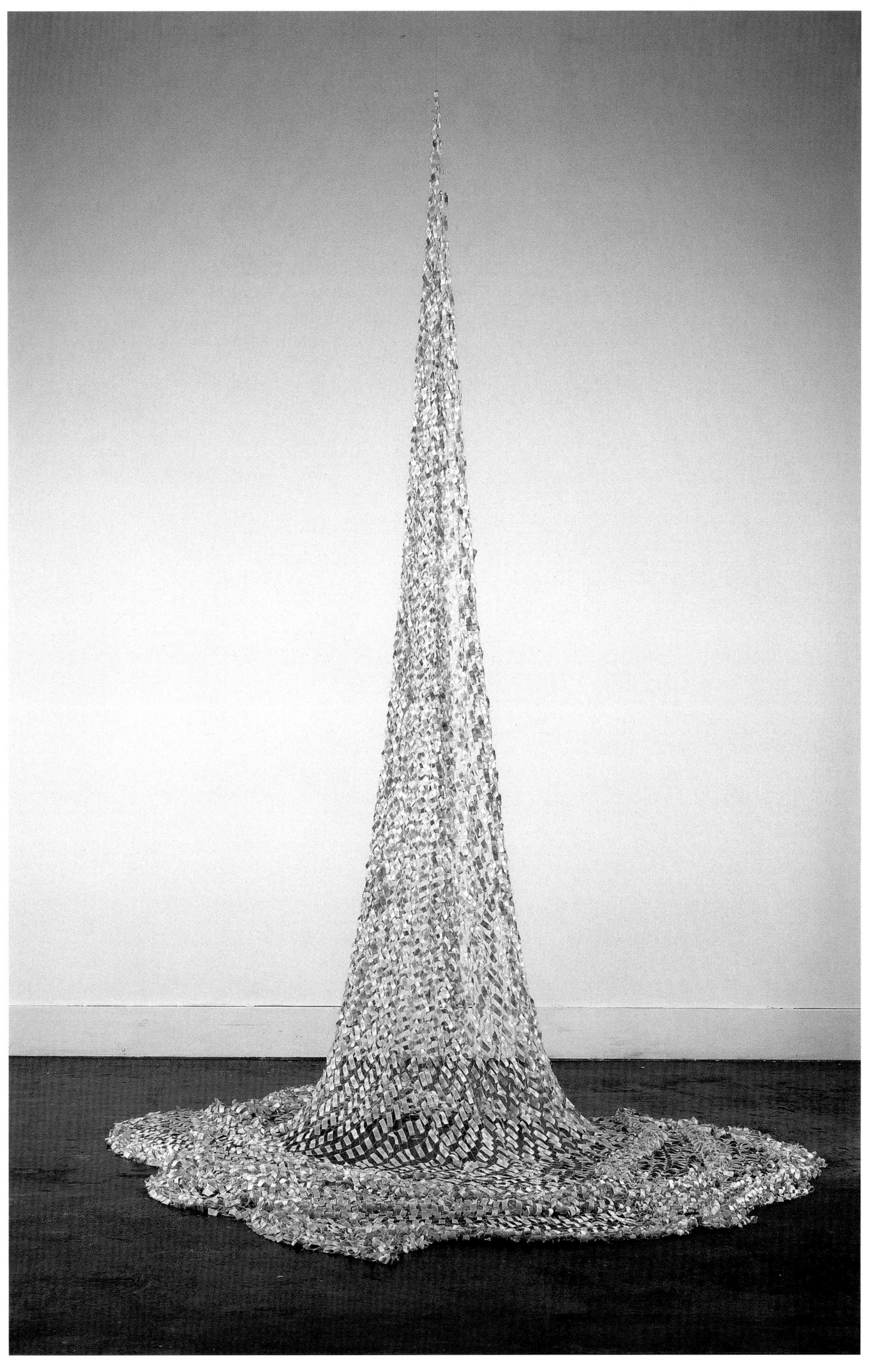

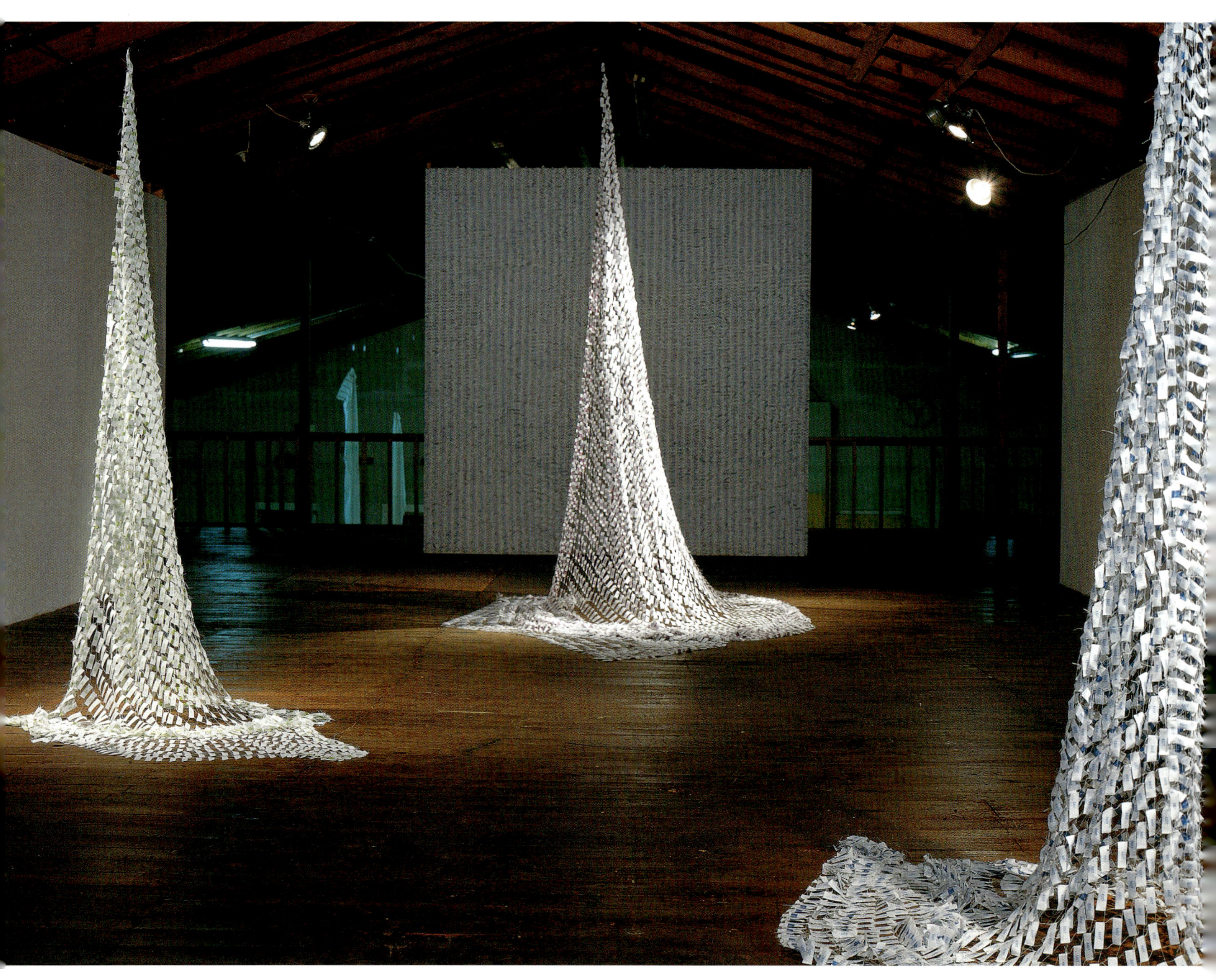

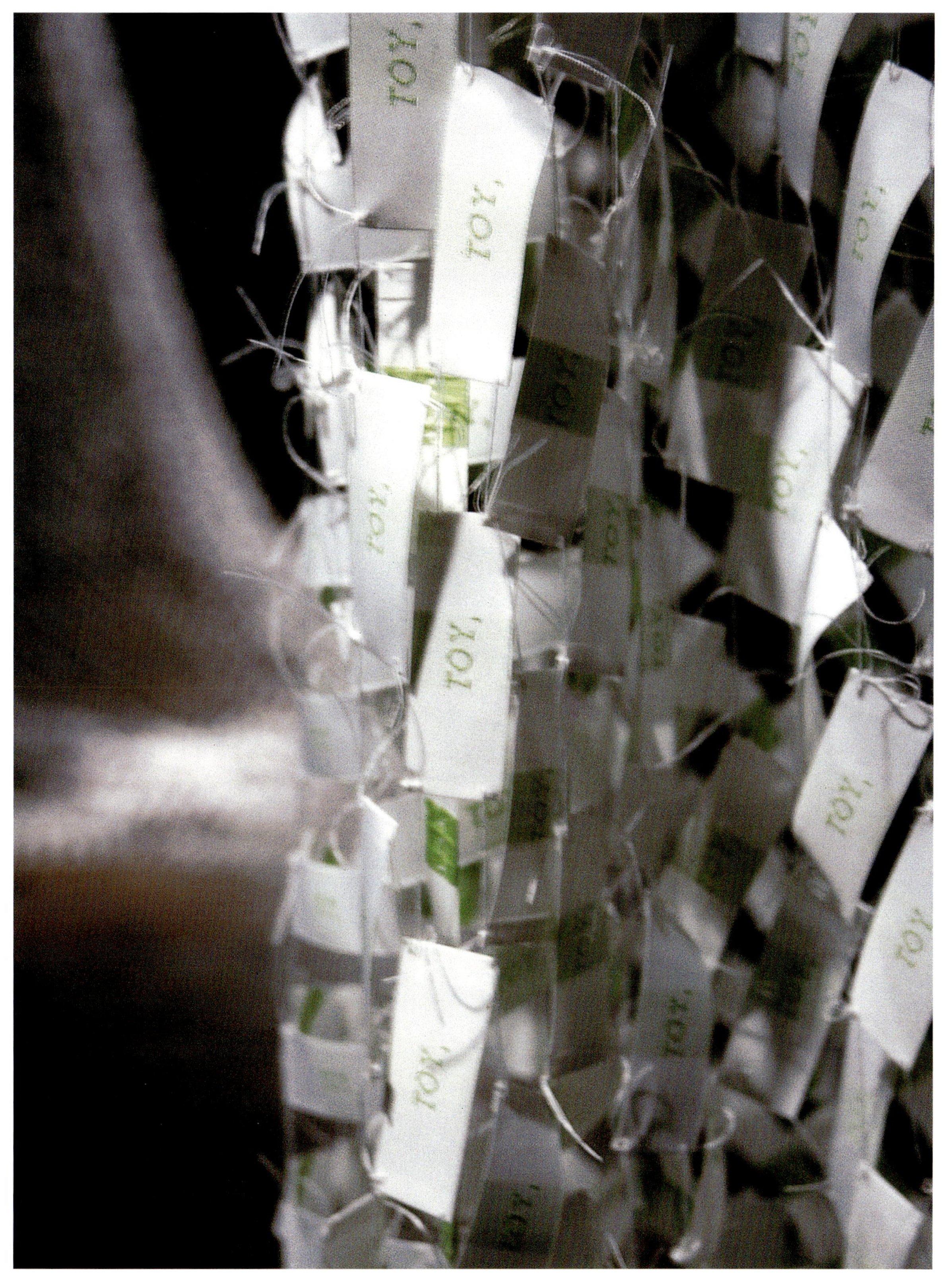

◂ PLATE 48 ***Toy, Dream, Rest**, 2003*

PLATE 49 ***Toy, Dream, Rest** (detail), 2003* ▸

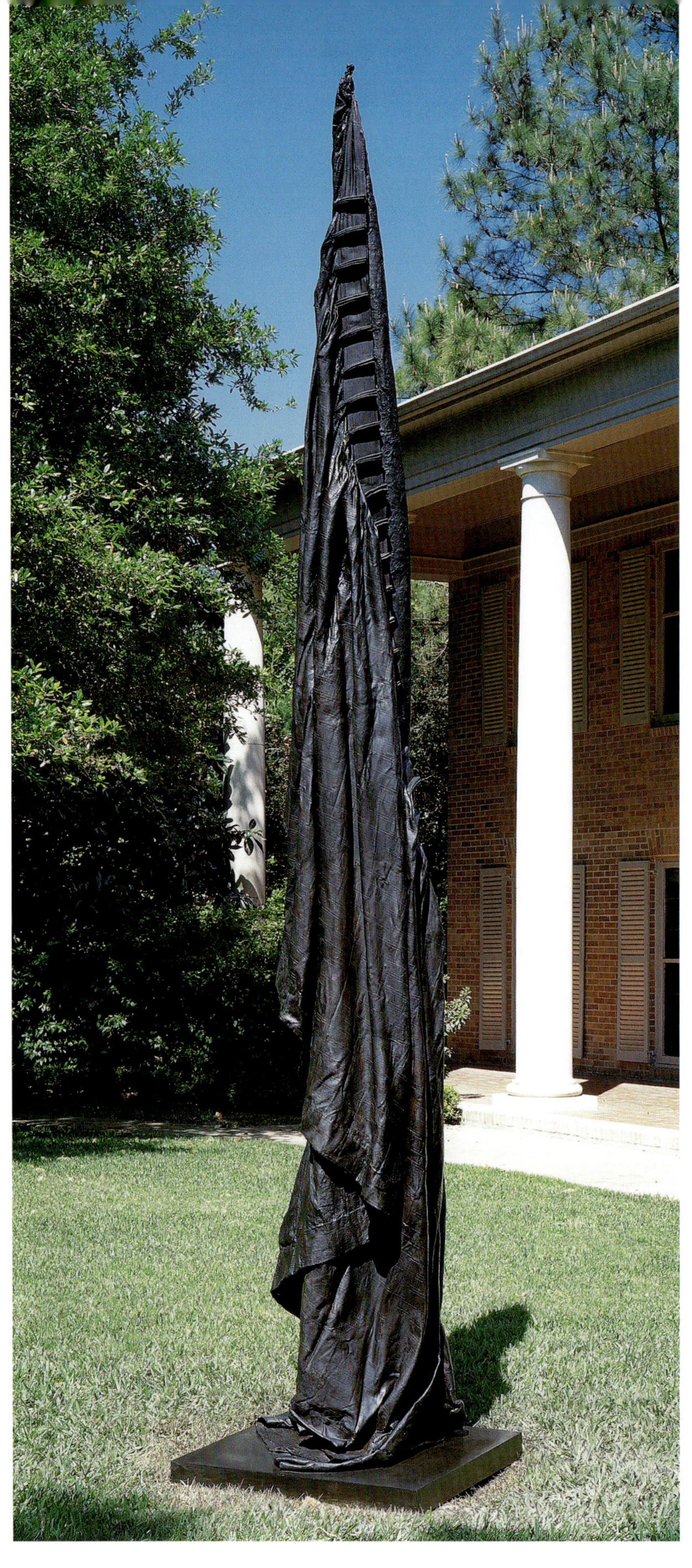

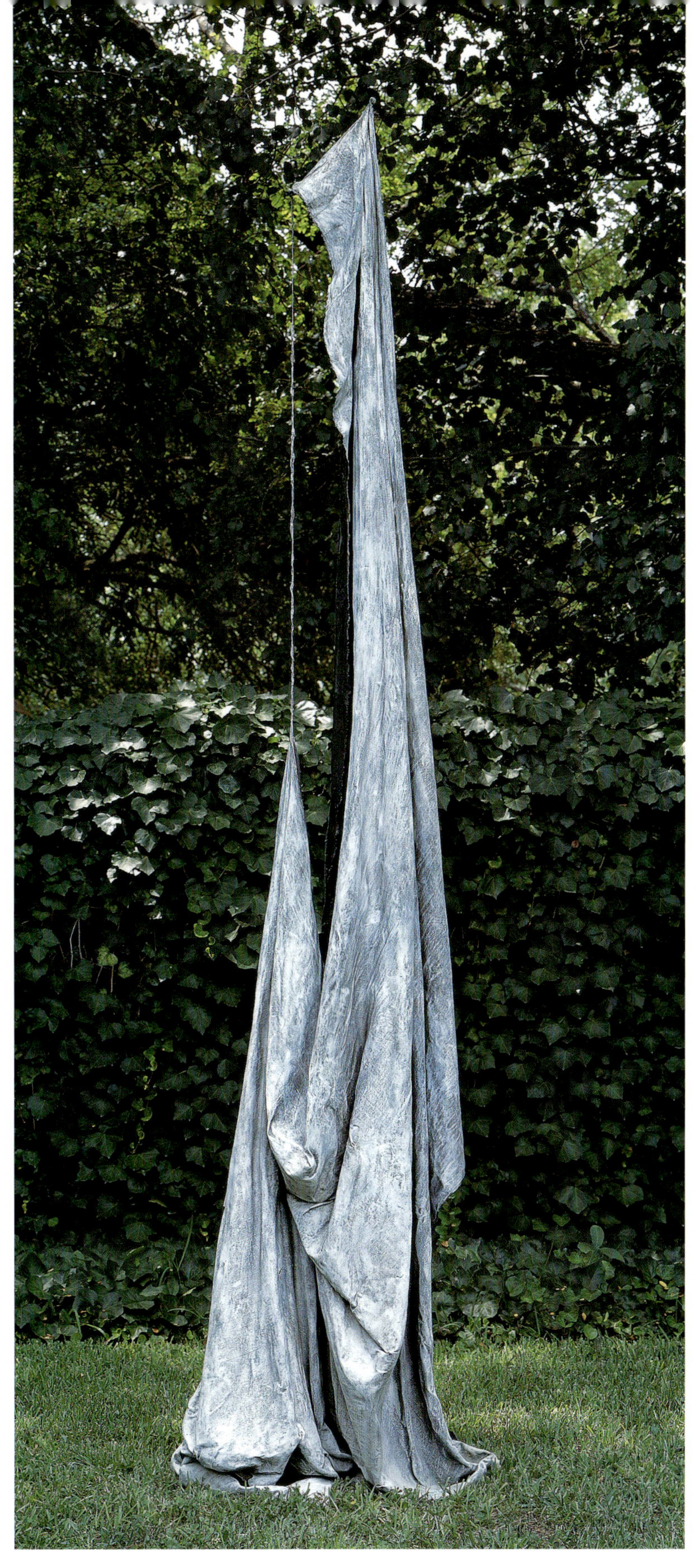

◂ PLATE 50 ***Black Drape***, *2002*

PLATE 51 ***Torn Flannel Duvet Cover,*** *2003* ▸

PLATE 52 ***Indian Fire***, *2003*

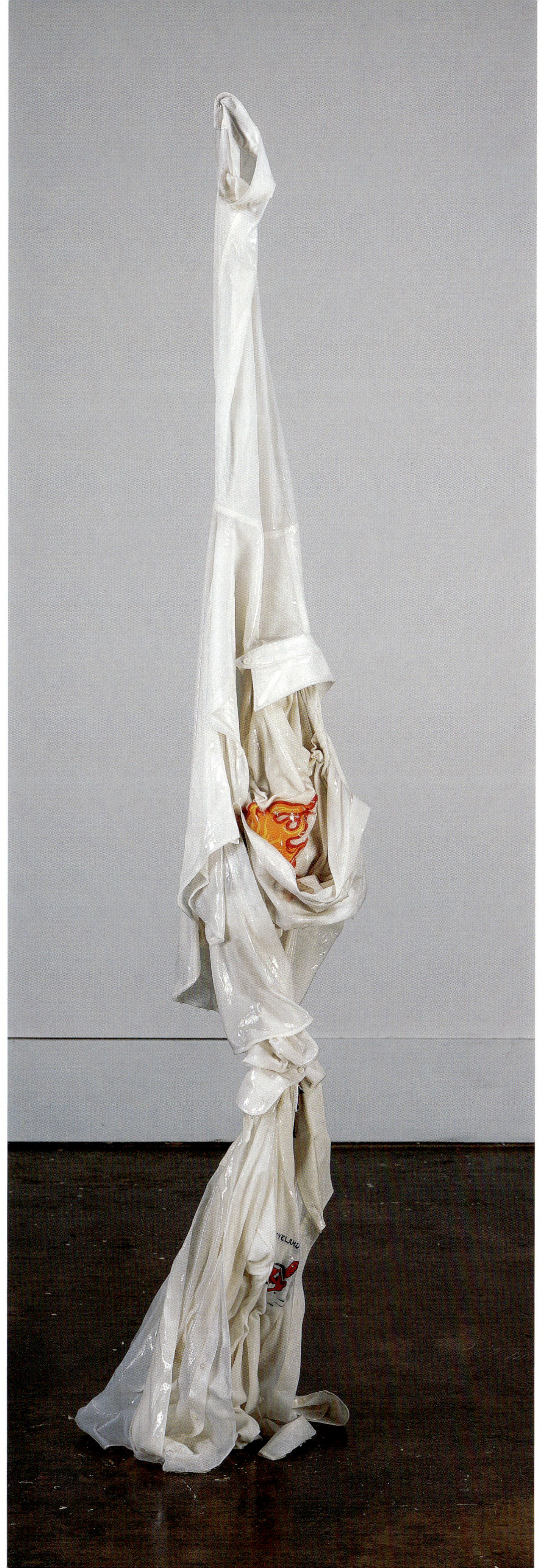

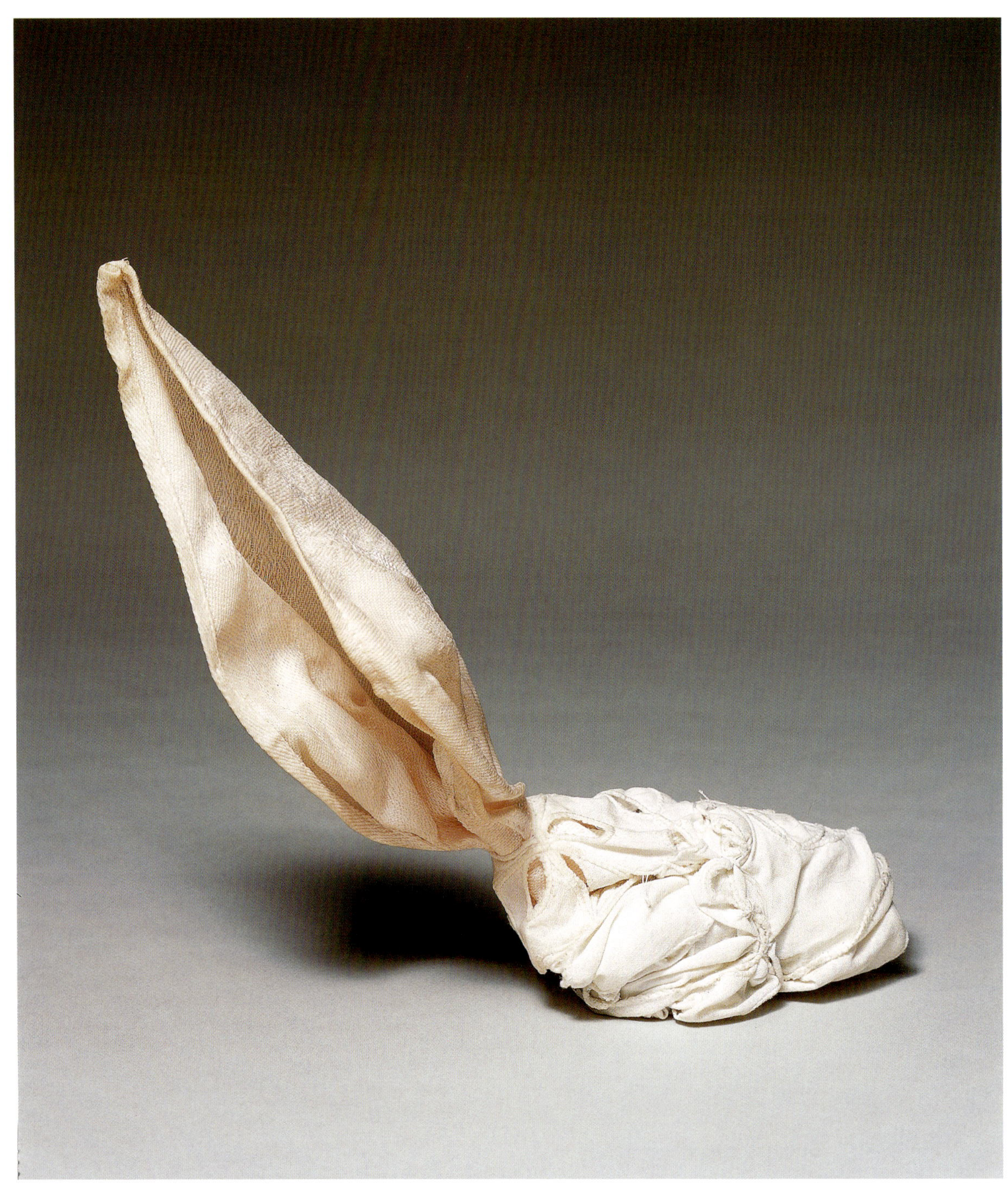

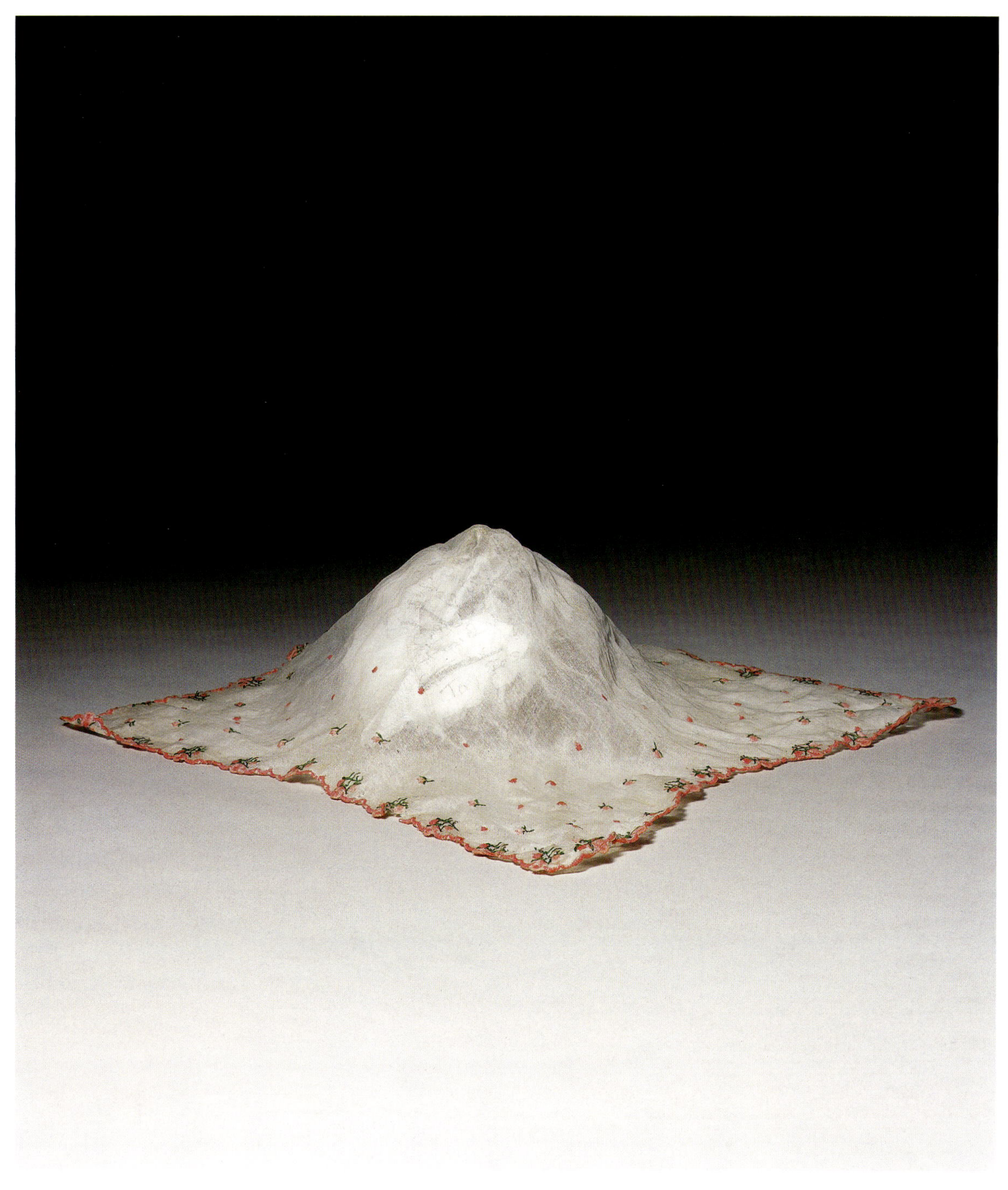

◂ PLATE 53 ***Kneel to Whisper in a Sow's Ear***, *2004*

PLATE 54 ***Meadow/Mountain/Idea***, *2004* ▸

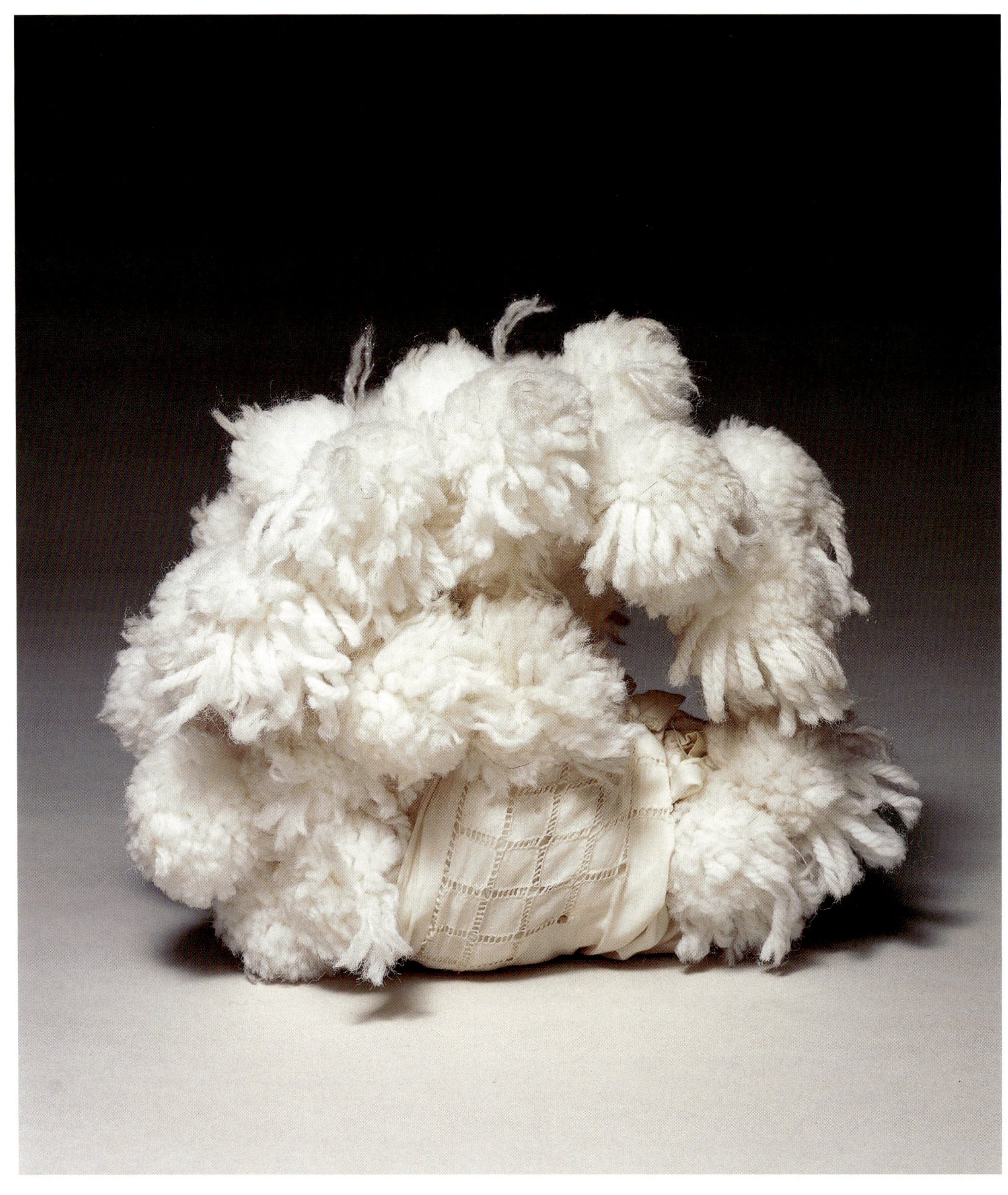

PLATE 55 ***Heart of Froth***, *2004*

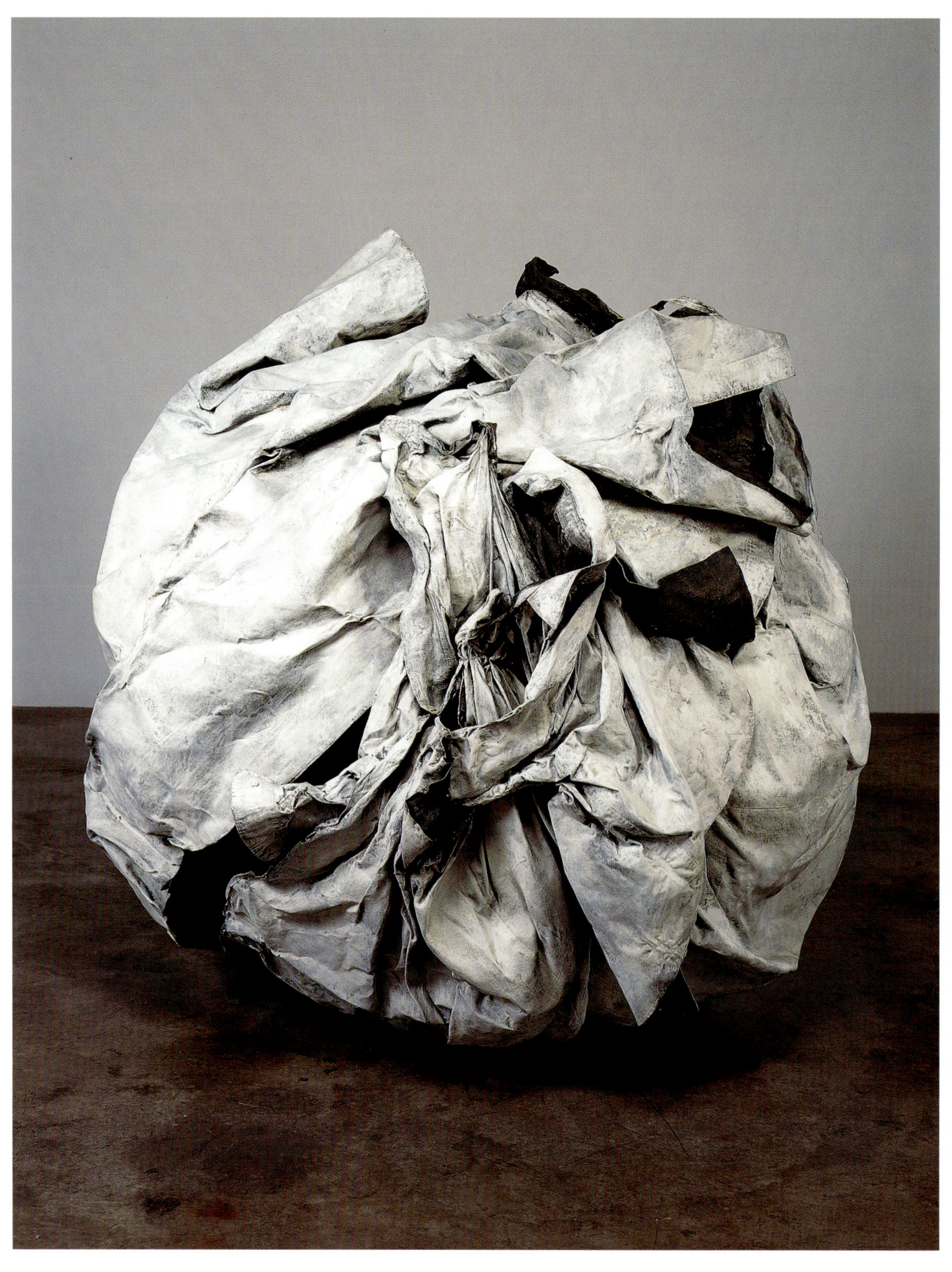

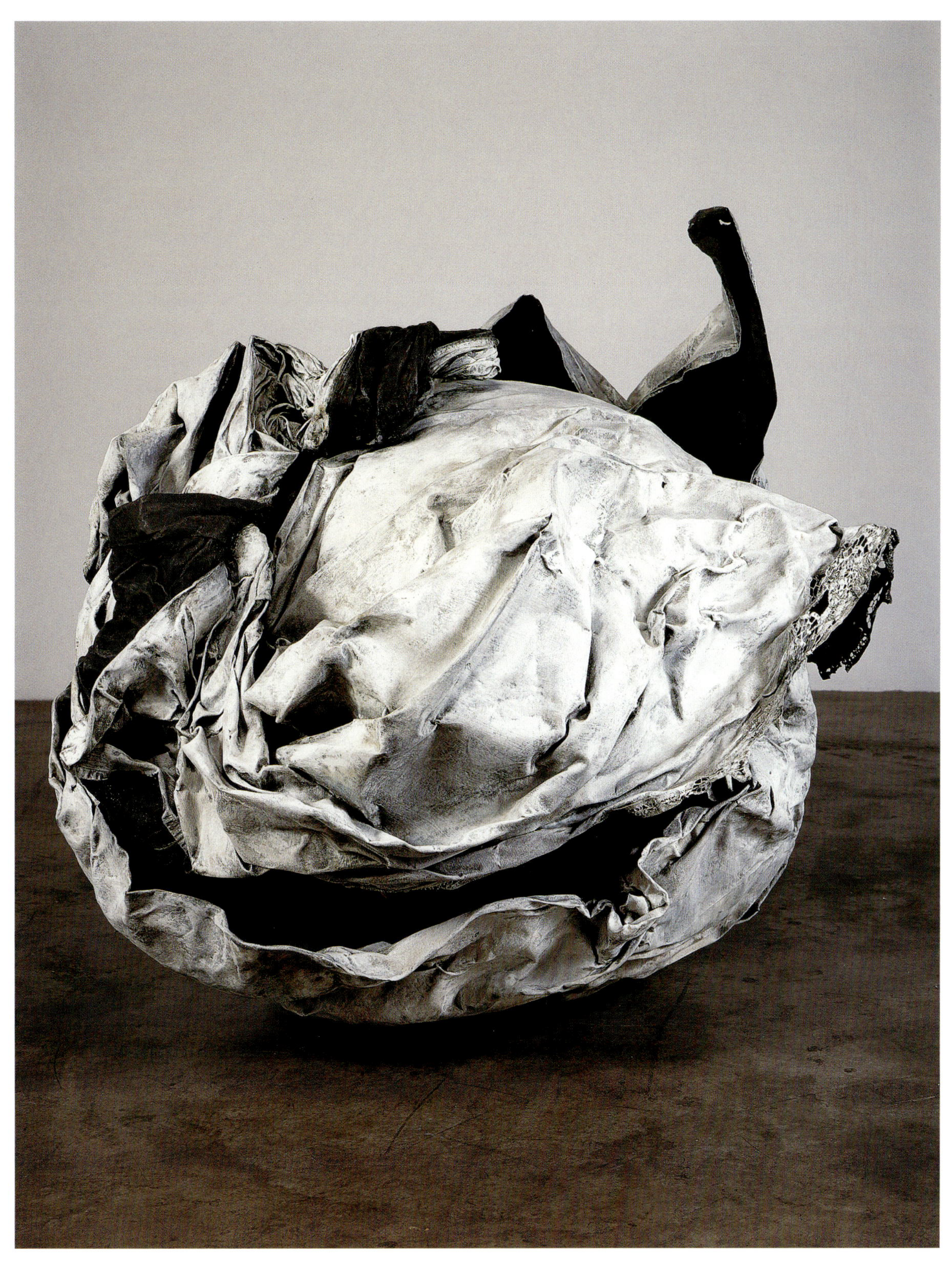

◄ PLATE 56 ***To Bring**, 2004*

PLATE 57 ***To Take**, 2004* ►

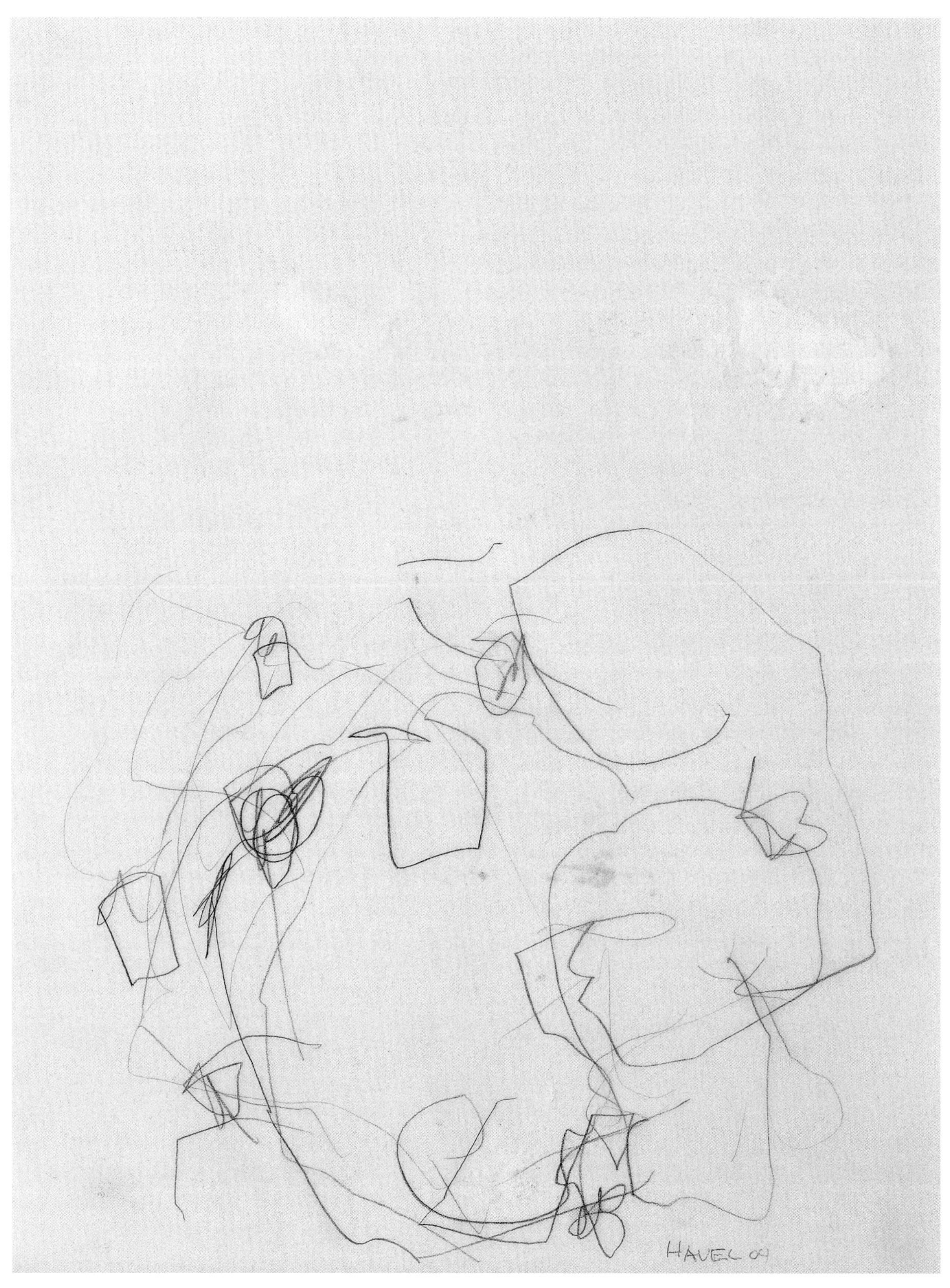
HAVEL 09

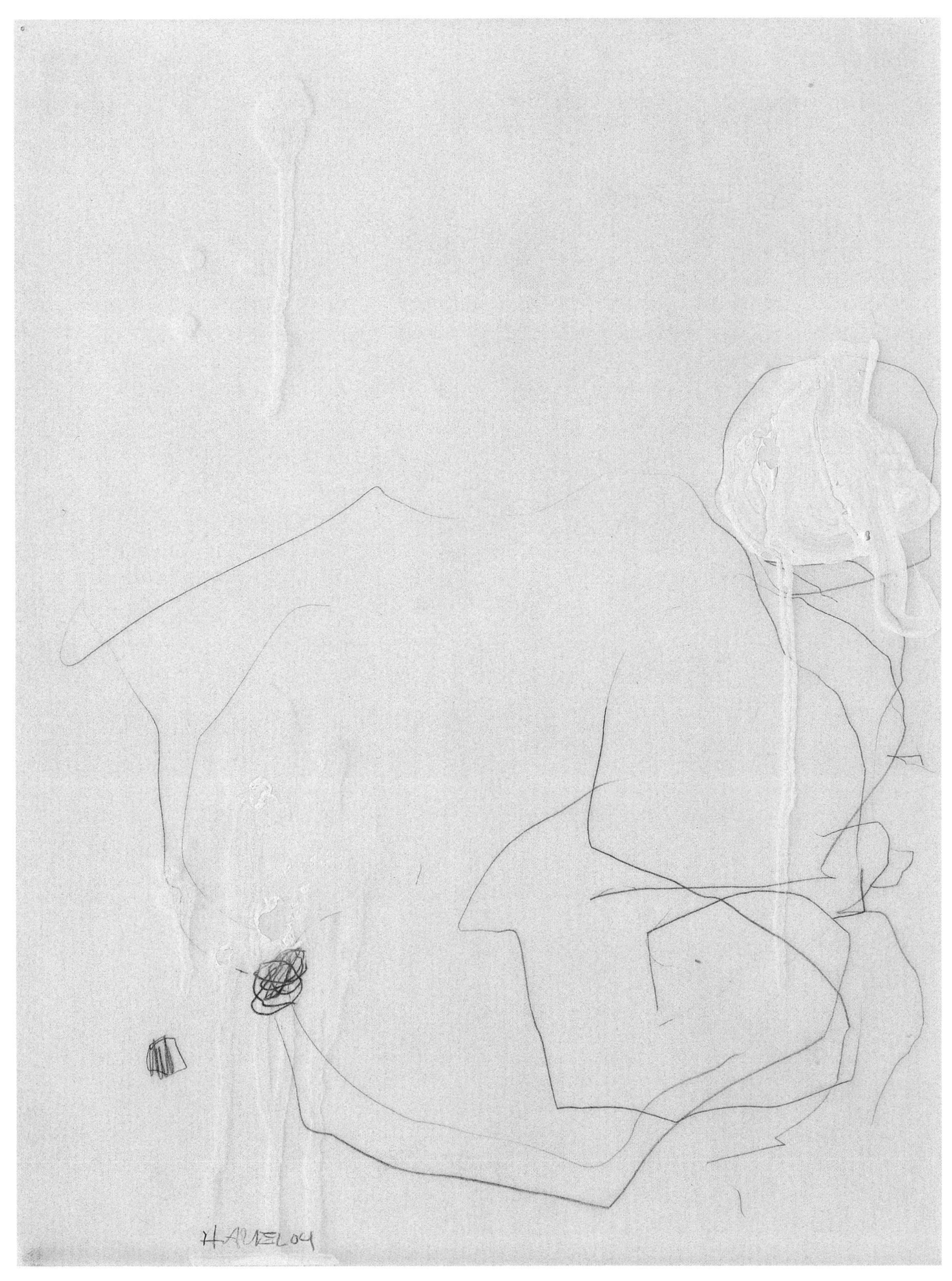

◀ PLATE 58 ***Bed Sheet Bundles**, 2004*

PLATE 59 ***Bed Sheet Bundles**, 2004* ▶

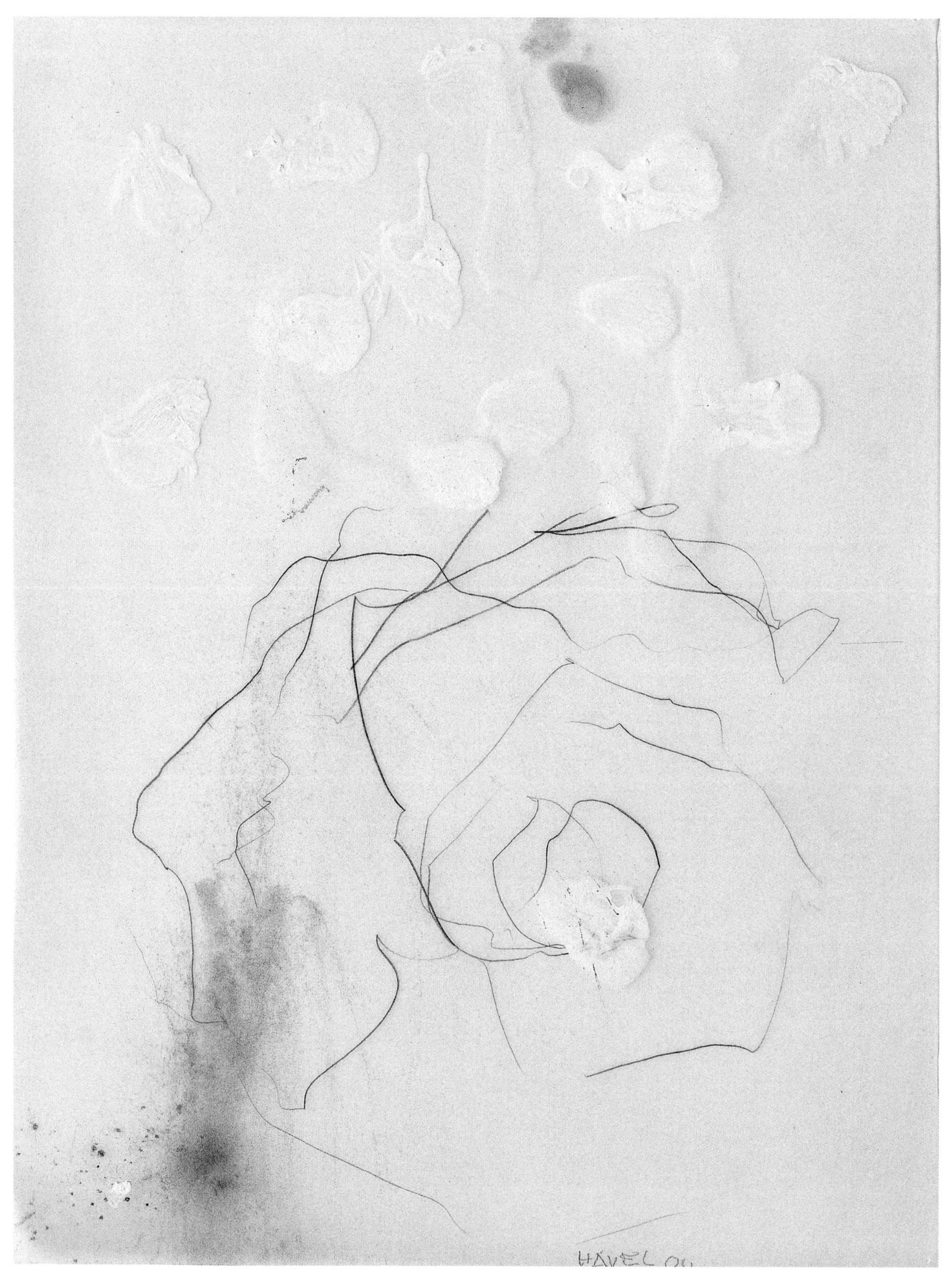
HAVEL 04

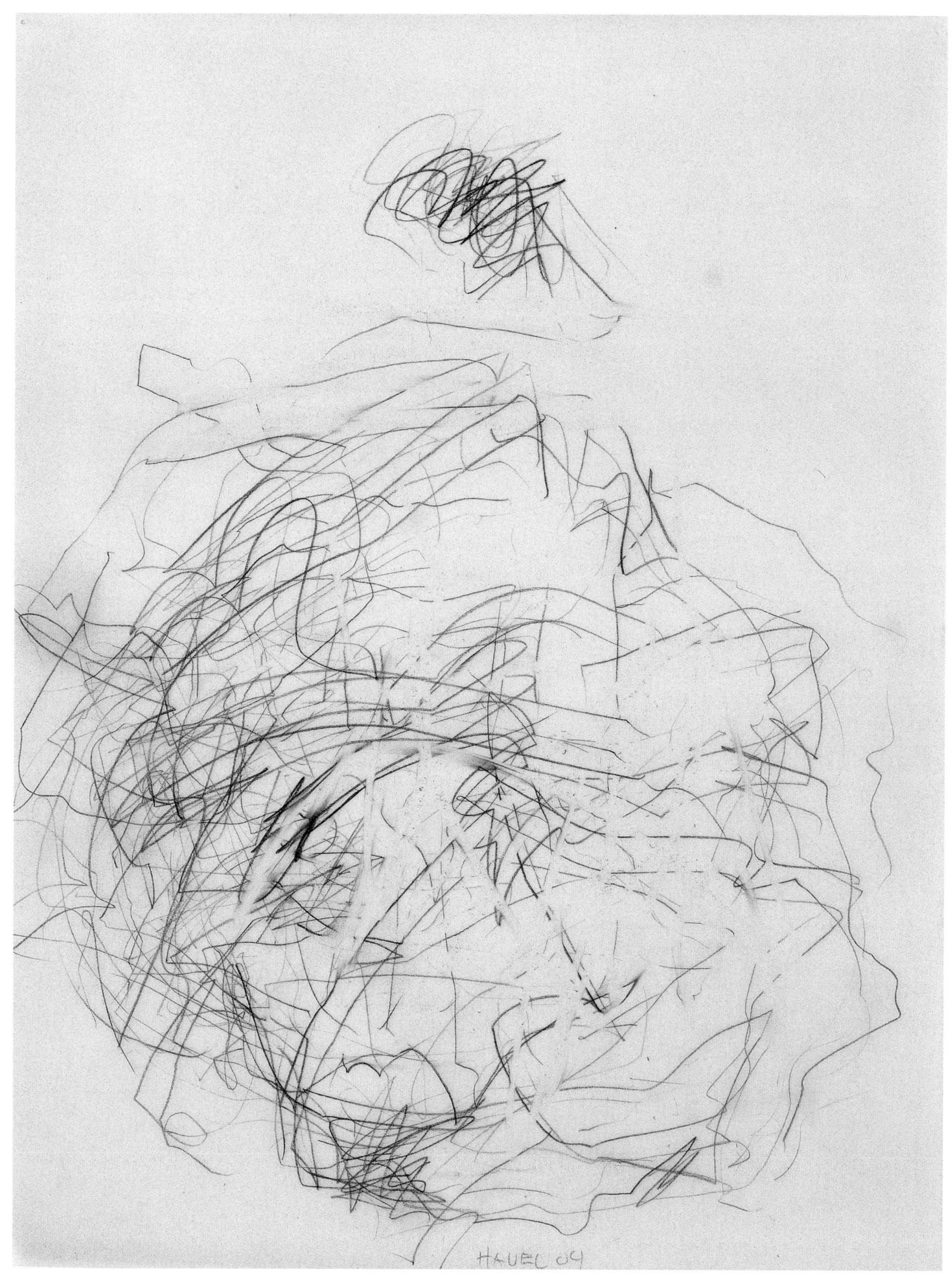

◀ PLATE 60 ***Bed Sheet Bundles**, 2004*

PLATE 61 ***Bed Sheet Bundles**, 2004* ▶

PLATE 62 *Exhibition*, ***To Bring/To Take***, *2003*

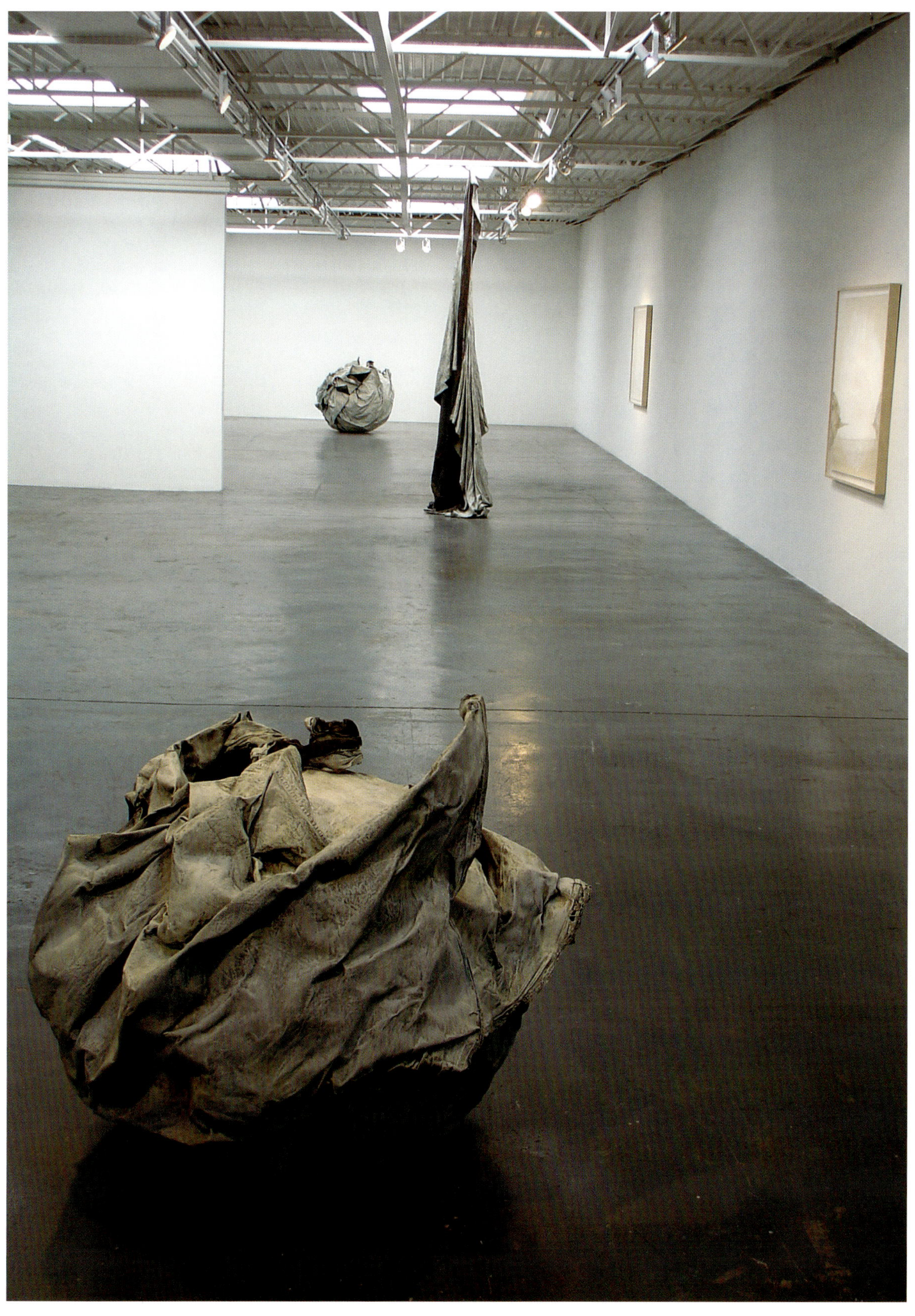

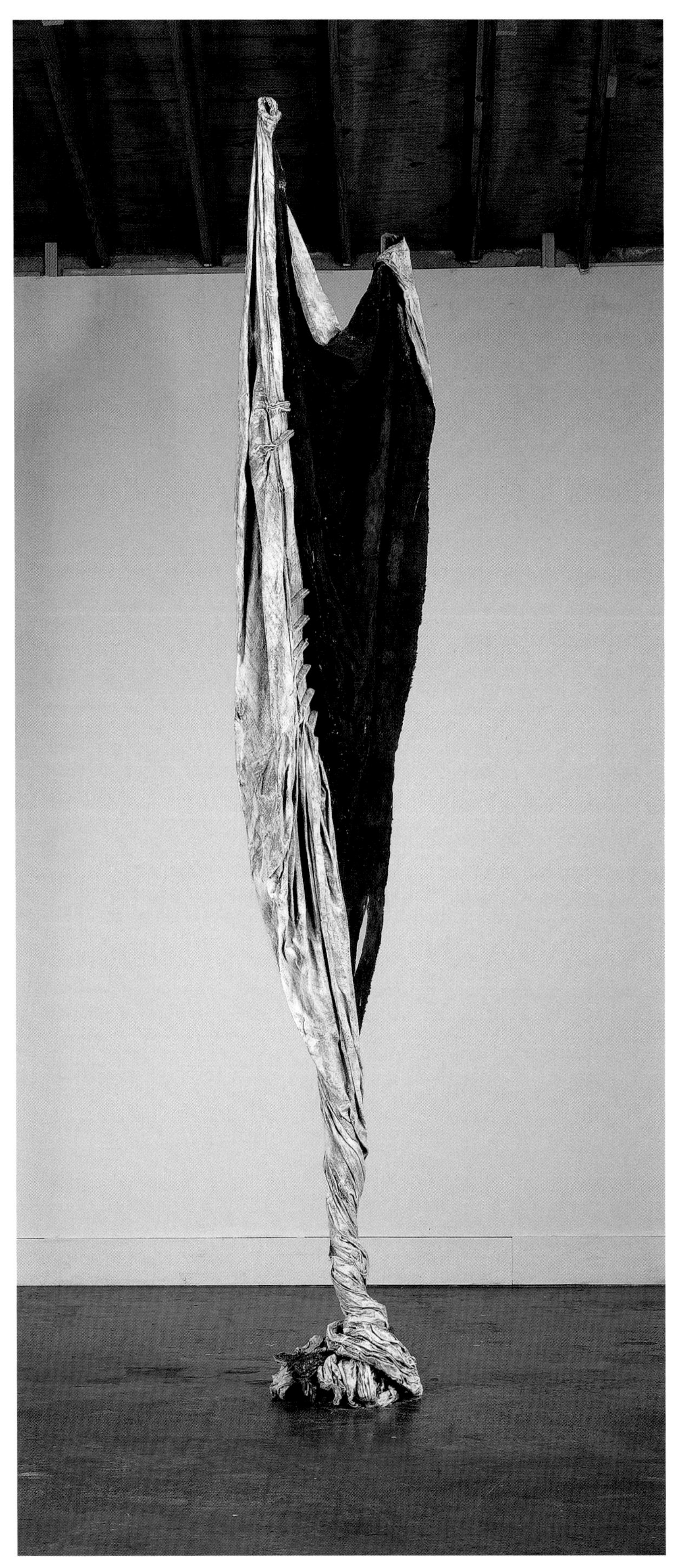

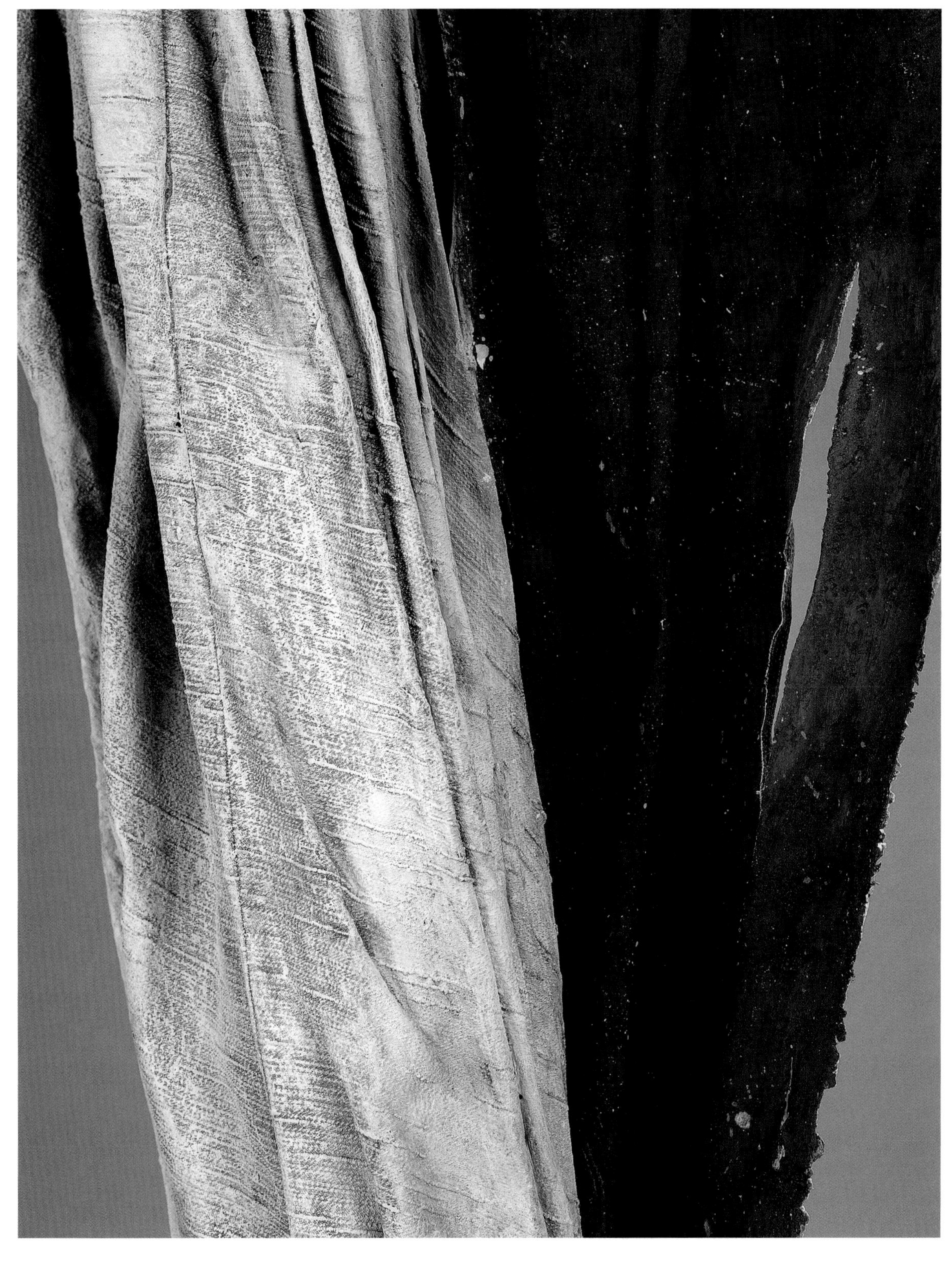

◀ PLATE 63 ***Torn and Twisted Curtain****, 2004–5*

PLATE 64 ***Torn and Twisted Curtain*** *(detail), 2004–5* ▶

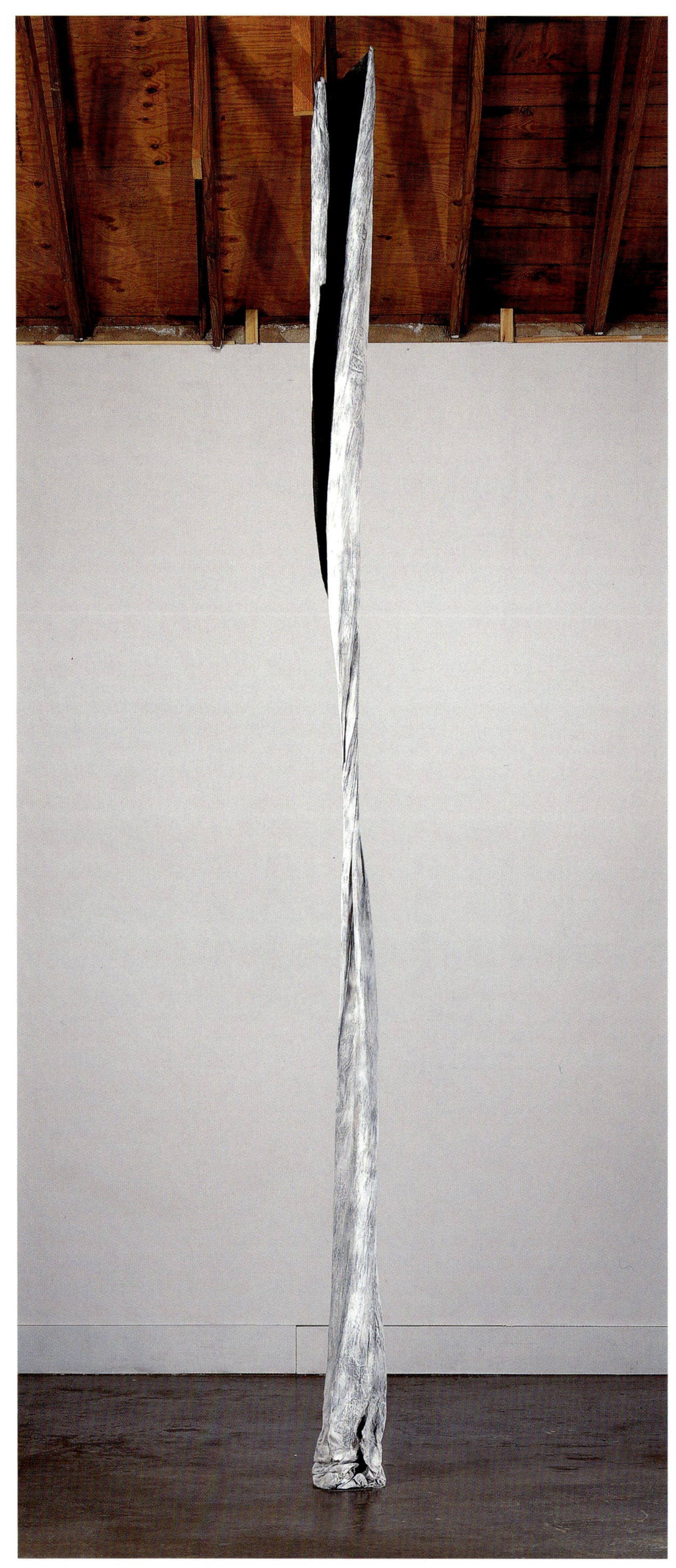

PLATE 65 ***Twisted Curtain****, 2004–5*

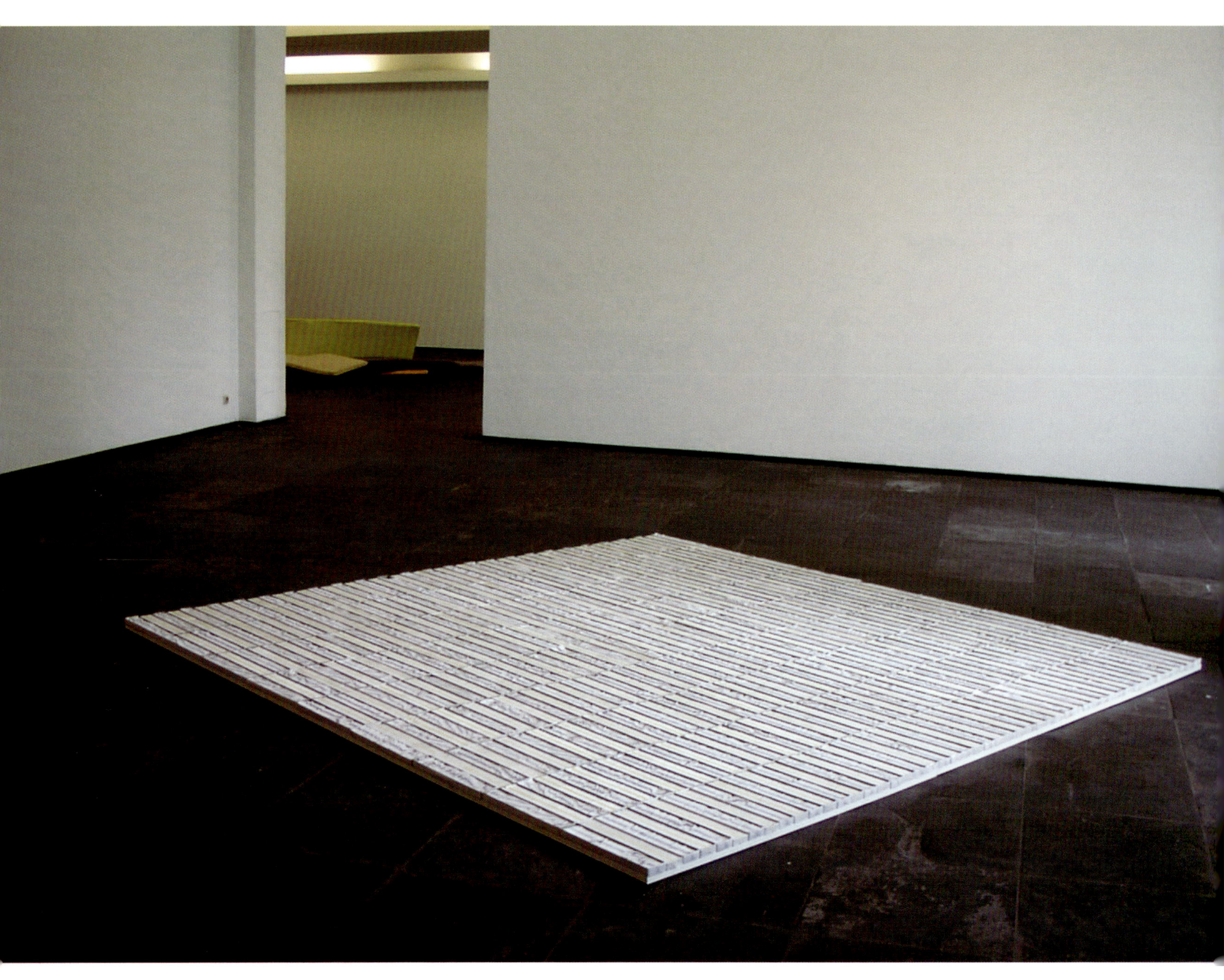

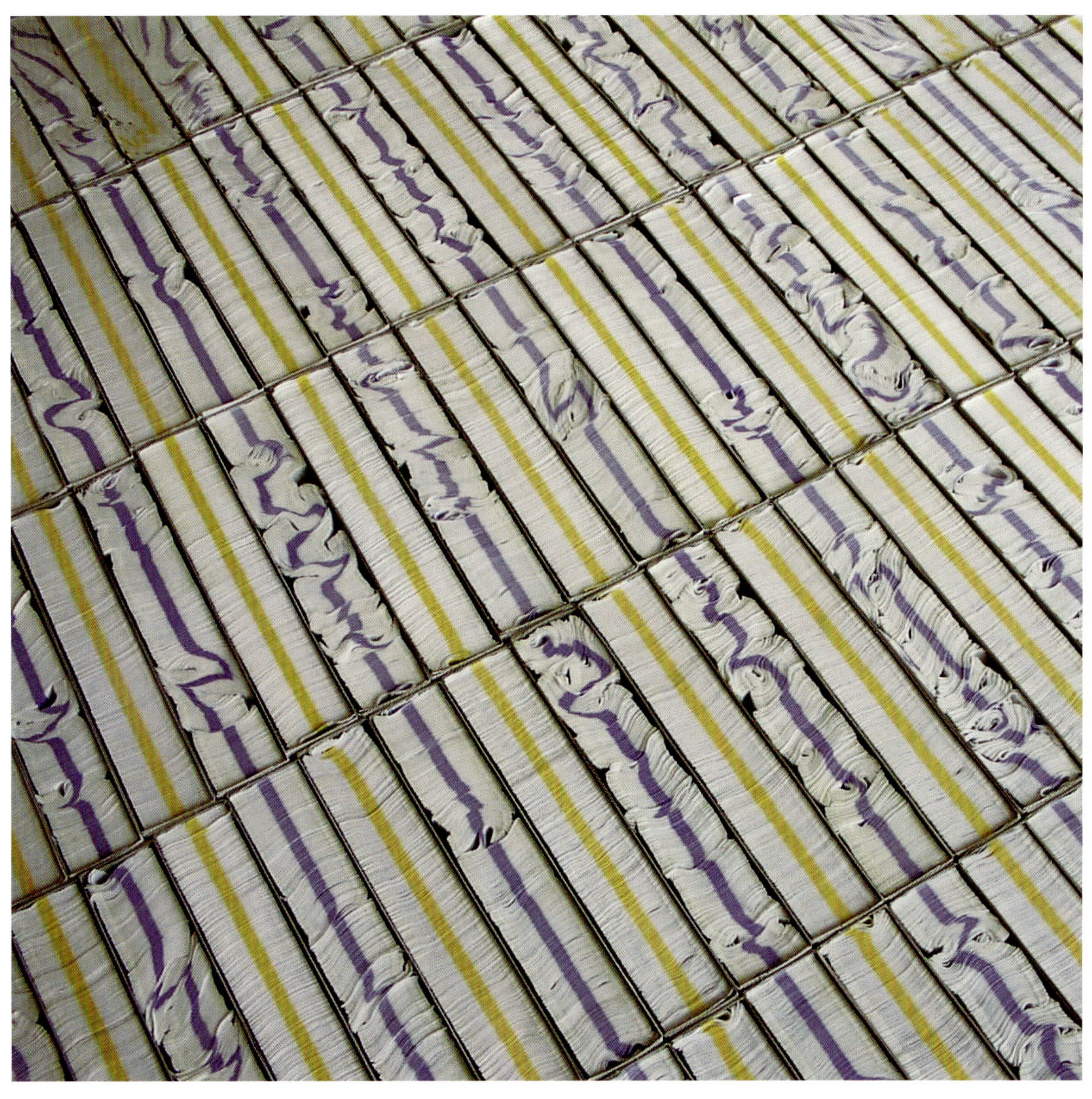

◂ PLATE 66 ***Lost and Lust***, *2004*

PLATE 67 ***Lost and Lust*** *(detail), 2004* ▸

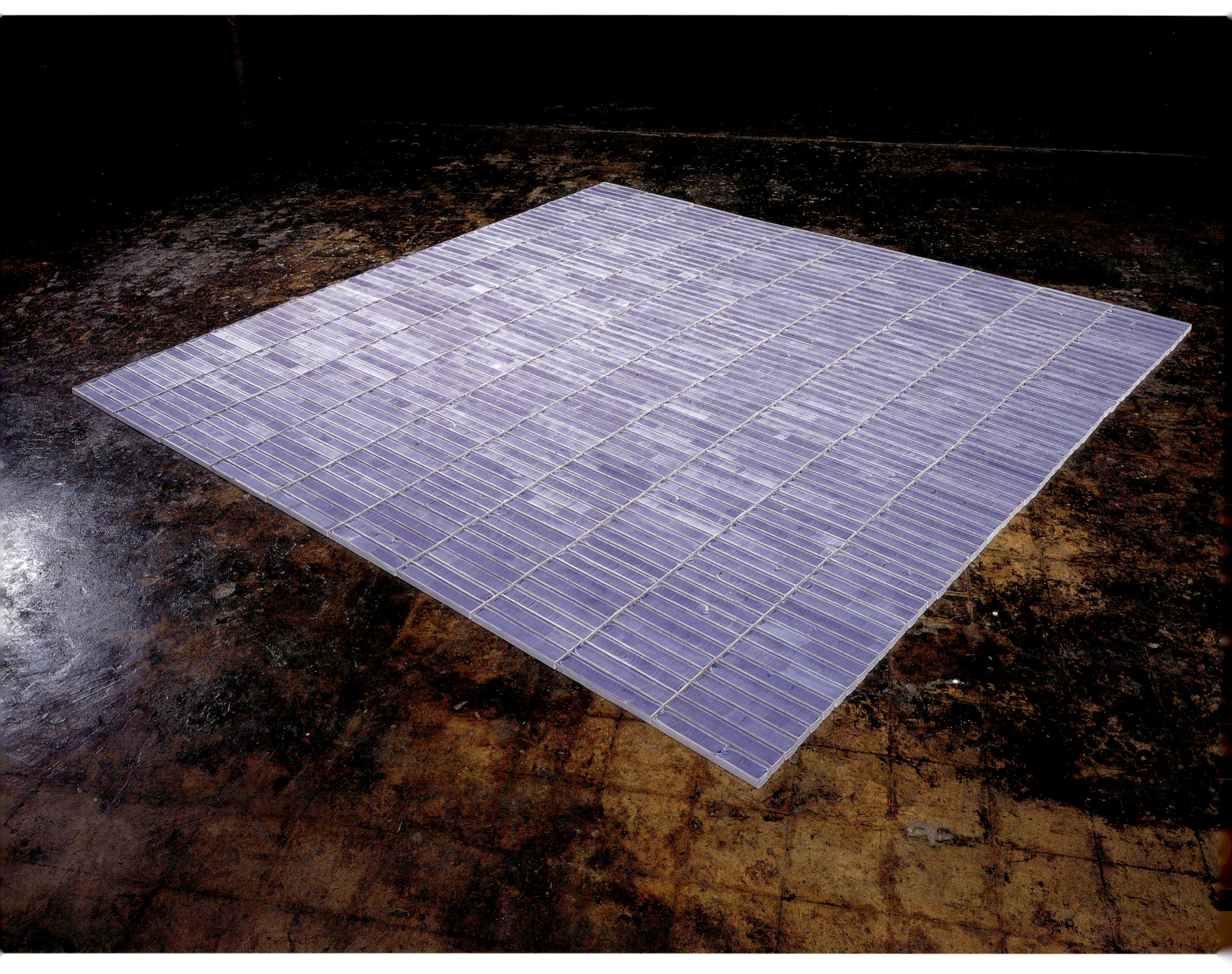

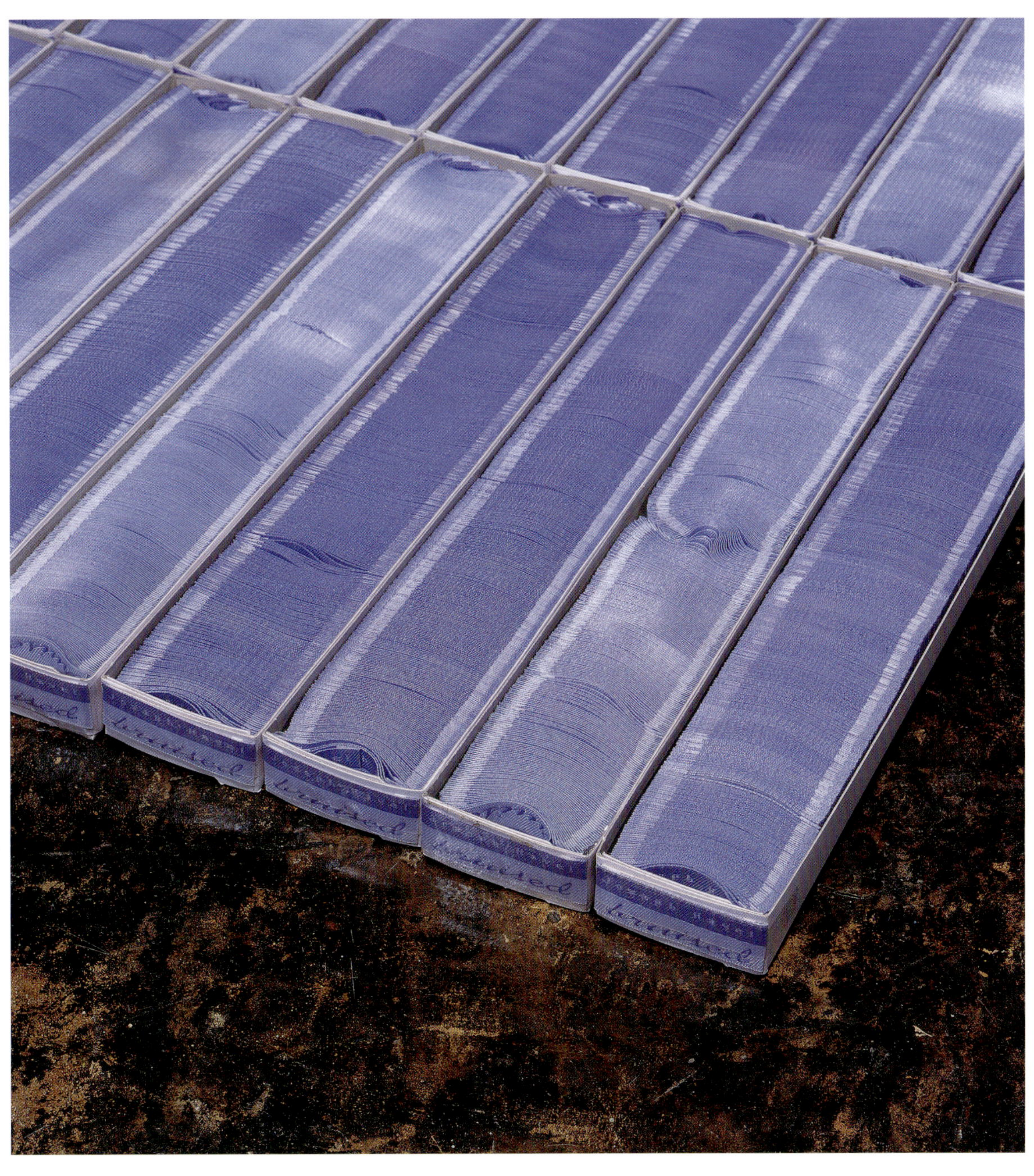

◄ PLATE 68 ***Bruised**, 2004*

PLATE 69 ***Bruised** (detail), 2004* ►

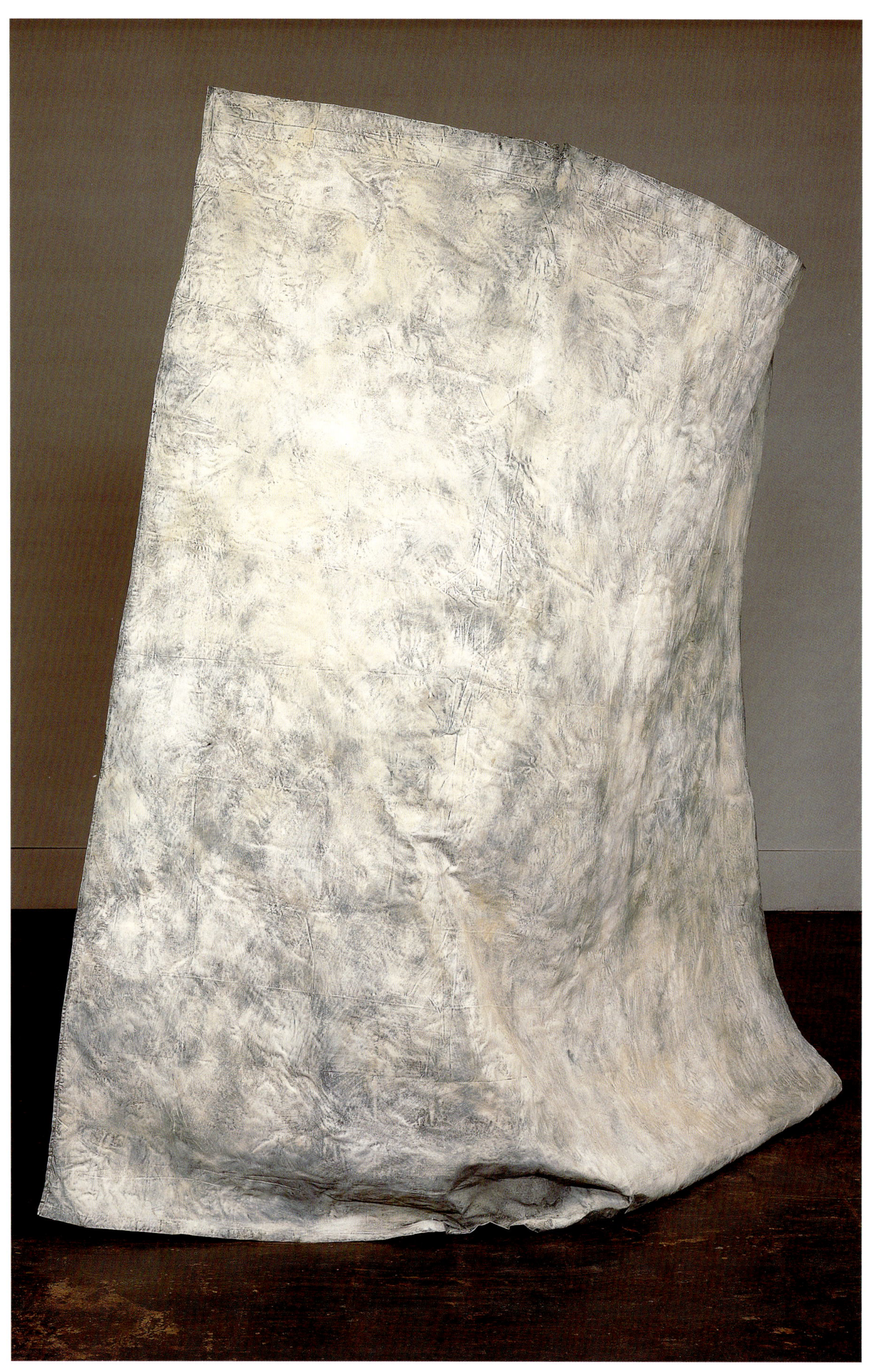

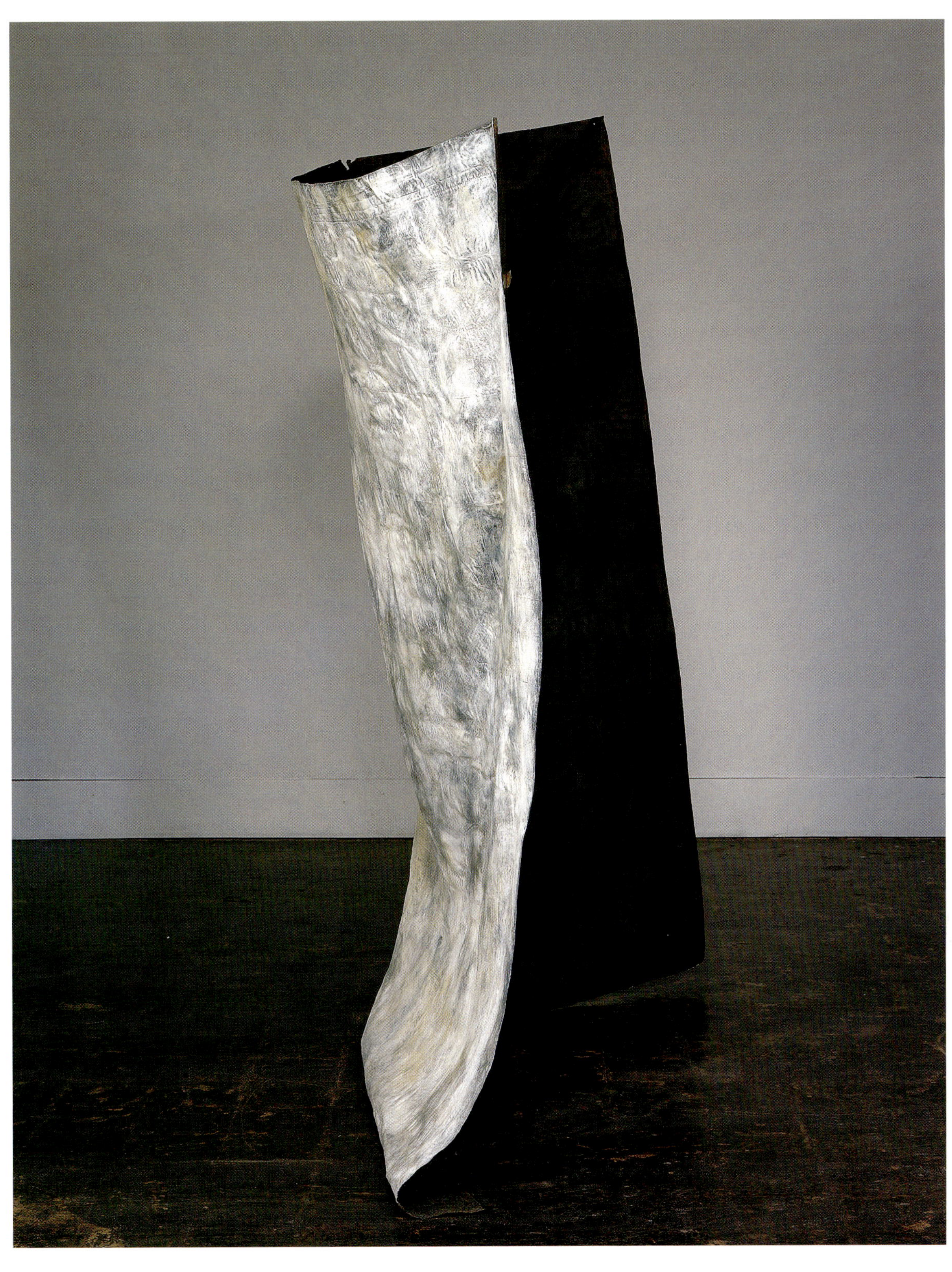

◀ PLATE 70 ***Wash***, *2004–5*

PLATE 71 ***Wash*** *(detail), 2004–5* ▶

◄ PLATE 72 ***Bed Sheet Drawing***, *2005*

PLATE 73 ***Bed Sheet Drawing***, *2005* ►

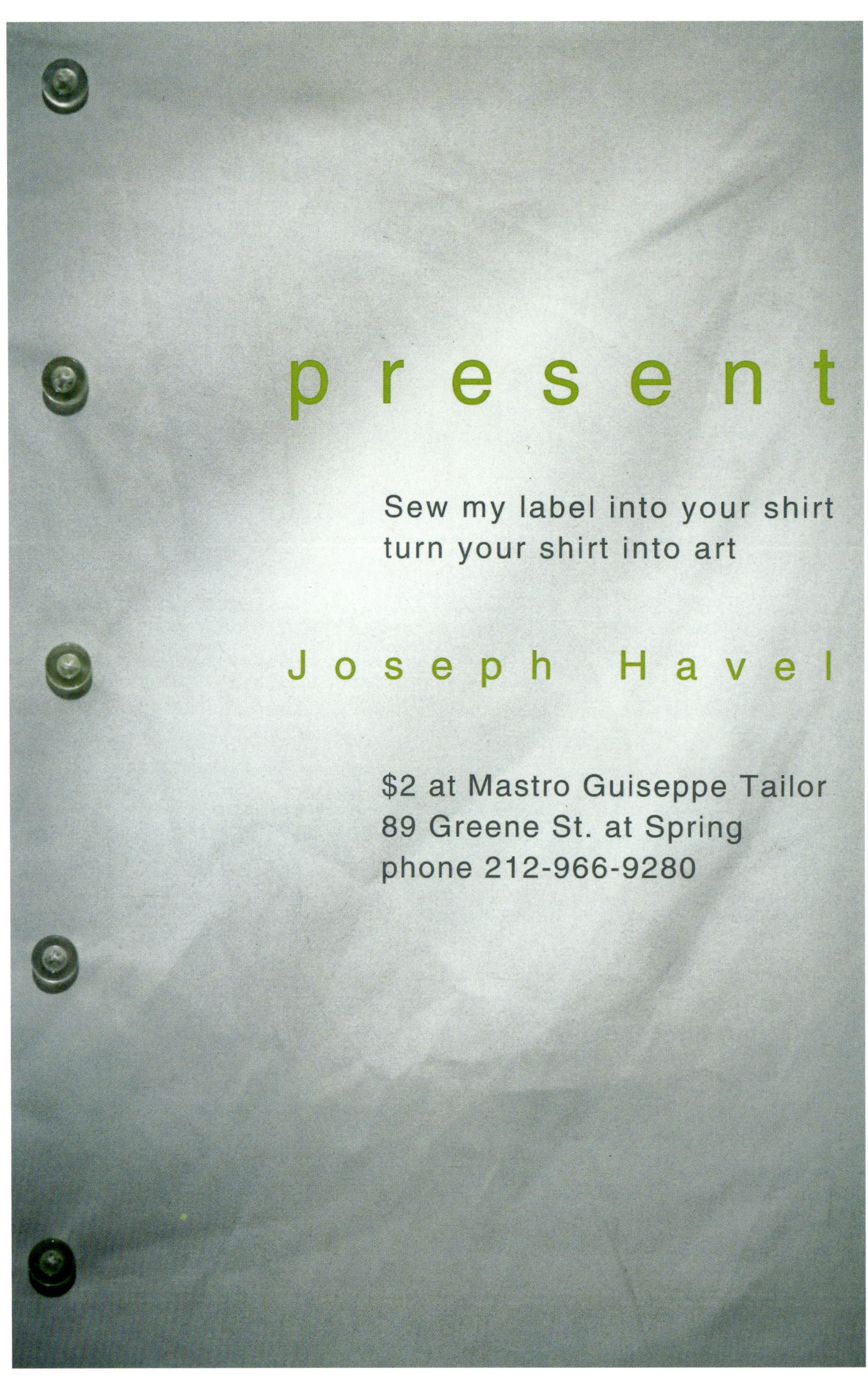
p r e s e n t
Sew my label into your shirt
turn your shirt into art
J o s e p h H a v e l
$2 at Mastro Guiseppe Tailor
89 Greene St. at Spring
phone 212-966-9280

PLATE 74

AN INTERVIEW WITH JOSEPH HAVEL

Peter Doroshenko
April 2005 | Houston, Texas

PETER DOROSHENKO:
Many of your current works have a rich lineage that can be traced to painting, drawing, and ceramics. What is the early history of these bonds that link your work to the history of art?

JOSEPH HAVEL:
When I entered undergraduate school at the University of Minnesota, I was interested in what I thought of as conceptual art but really was more like Fluxus. Early Claus Oldenburg happenings, and all of the props, drawings, and objects that remained as evidence after these performances, fascinated me. During my second year in school, I became obsessed with contemporary painting and drawing. At a certain period late in my undergraduate studies, one of my professors, Warren MacKenzie, got me interested in ceramics.

PD: Was there a sculpture class during that time period?

JH: I completed two sculpture classes; however, I found them very boring. At that time, sculpture was primarily focused on a strong man's aesthetic—welding and grinding metal or working with large stone blocks. Most of the art produced was secondary to the process.

PD: So you found a stronger connection to ceramics?

JH: Yes, I went to graduate school at Penn State for both ceramics and drawing. I made ceramic objects that became more sculptural over time. I liked the malleability of ceramics because it allowed me to create certain shapes and forms more closely associated with my painting and drawing.

PD: While you were taking ceramic courses, was your work always tied conceptually to painting and drawing?

JH: Yes. I never felt engaged with the history associated with ceramic sculpture during that formative time and because of that I felt free to consider larger questions about the nature of art.

PD: When did you decide to abandon ceramic sculpture completely?

JH: After graduate school, I moved to Sherman, Texas, to teach at Austin College. At first I continued to work with both ceramics and drawing. I found painting not as intimate or immediate as drawing, so I stopped working with that medium. Soon it became clear there was a limitation to the ideas I was able to explore in ceramics. I stopped making sculptures for about a year so I would have time to consider what any of the things I had been making had to do with my experience and identity. I continued to draw, went on sabbatical, and travelled for some time while examining issues and questions about other artists' work that had nothing to do with my practice—from the conceptual work of Bruce Nauman to the mannerist paintings of Bronzino. There were no great revelations during this time, but it did sway my drawing toward a narrative style. Basically I started drawing psychologically loaded still lives. These formed a mental bridge for me to rethink the object, the information that an object can carry, and how it mutates when presented as art.

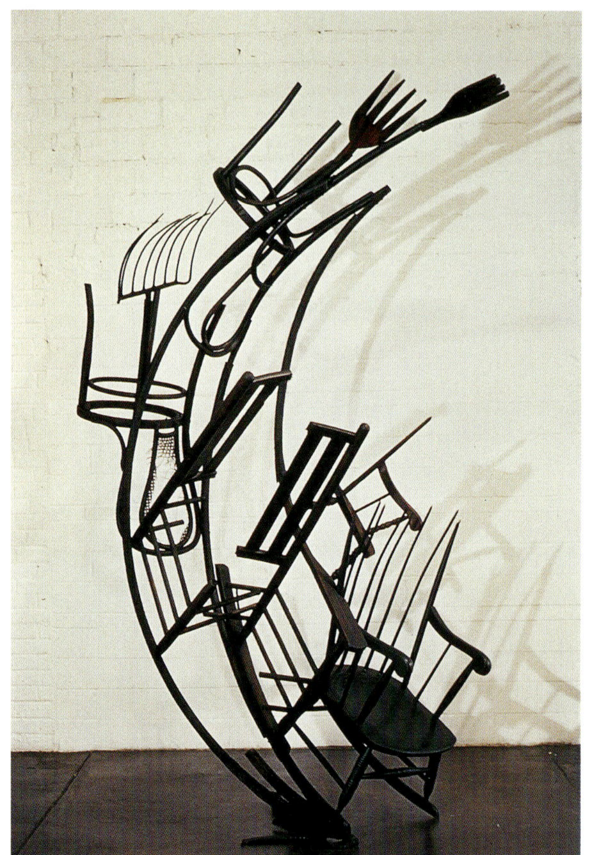

PD: Do you still have these drawings?

JH: No, these drawings were lost years ago. They were only important as a way to start to work three-dimensionally again. Through them I became interested in creating works that layered personal and historical information through visual poetry.

PLATE 75

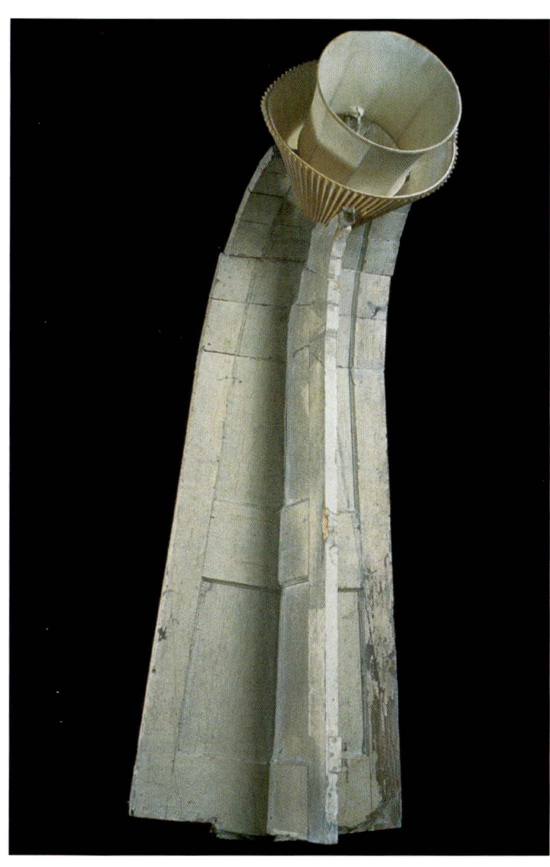

PLATE 76

PD: How did you start balancing these ideas and forms through assemblage?

JH: I started with objects that were readily available and that had associations suggesting relics or art-historical precedents. Objects such as trashed chairs formed an initial source for this visual poetry. After a period of time I tired of the sentimentality implied by the layering of history. It just seemed to take over the work and did not allow me to combine the references with the present. I was interested in surrealism, but I was not interested in creating such a direct parallel. I did not want to create insular artworks.

PD: Is that the moment you started working with lampshades?

JH: Yes, I began working with lampshades because I could find a better connection to the visual information I was interested in without making as predictable art references.

PD: Do you mean the information that is associated with the original use of the object?

JH: Yes. The aged wooden chairs had too much historically referential information, the lampshades seemed directly connected to their present use.

PD: As I think about those artworks, concepts of literature and music are incorporated. Is that the case?

JH: When I was in college, I came to the realistic decision that I was not good enough to be a professional musician after playing in various rock bands for many years. However, I remained interested in the way music could carry information that was immediately accessible. The same could be said for my interest in literature, especially poetry. I liked to

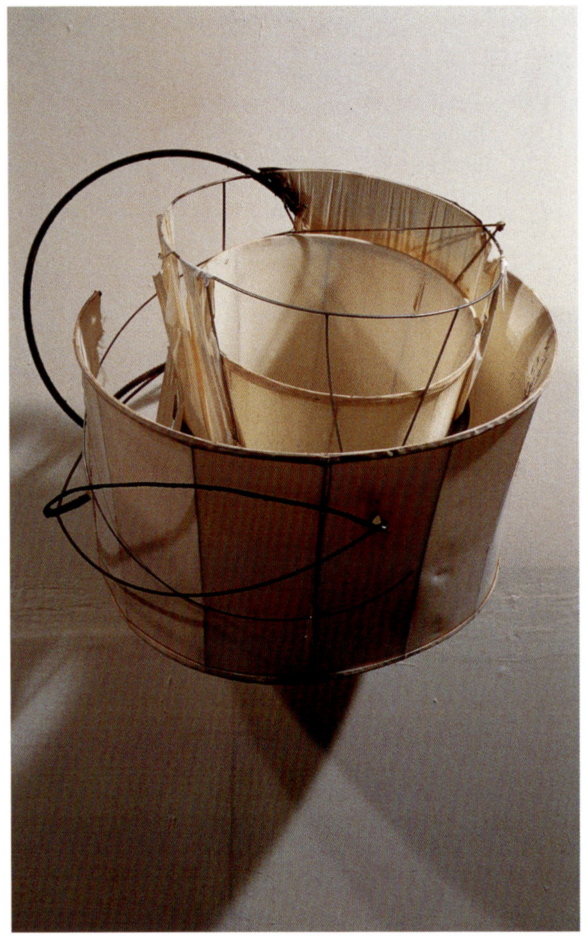

PLATE 77

read poetry and at times wrote some prose, but I knew early on that this augmented rather then replaced my art practice. I have incorporated aspects of both of these forms in my artworks.

PD: What poetry were you reading?

JH: I was reading confessional poets from the 1960s and 1970s, such as John Berryman, Robert Lowell, and Sylvia Plath. Their writing had a conversational voice, and they bent language in contemporary ways while remaining linked to the ambitions of grand literary achievement. So, when I was making many of my early drawings, I would use a poem as a source. Someone looking at the drawing would not necessarily know that, because I was not interested in illustrating a text, but it was a template of sorts.

PD: Was there ever a crossover to direct literary references?

JH: Occasionally a single poem, particularly from *The Dream Songs* by John Berryman, would be a direct source. I might even quote it or sample some element of the form or cadence. Later on in the label works I used direct photocopies from *The Dream Songs* to produce the brand names on the label.

PD: After your move to Houston in 1990, you continued working with lampshades as sculptural elements. Did the forms have anything to do with still-life paintings?

JH: Those works came from growing up as a white, suburban, middle-class youth in a family that moved from place to place accumulating things as we went along. I was also thinking about the seventeenth-century Dutch still lives painted for patrons who were part of a rising merchant class. I ironically referred to the lampshade sculptures as my Dutch flower paintings. The shapes of the flora and fruit in those paintings were a source but, more importantly, I was attracted to their sense of pending decay and

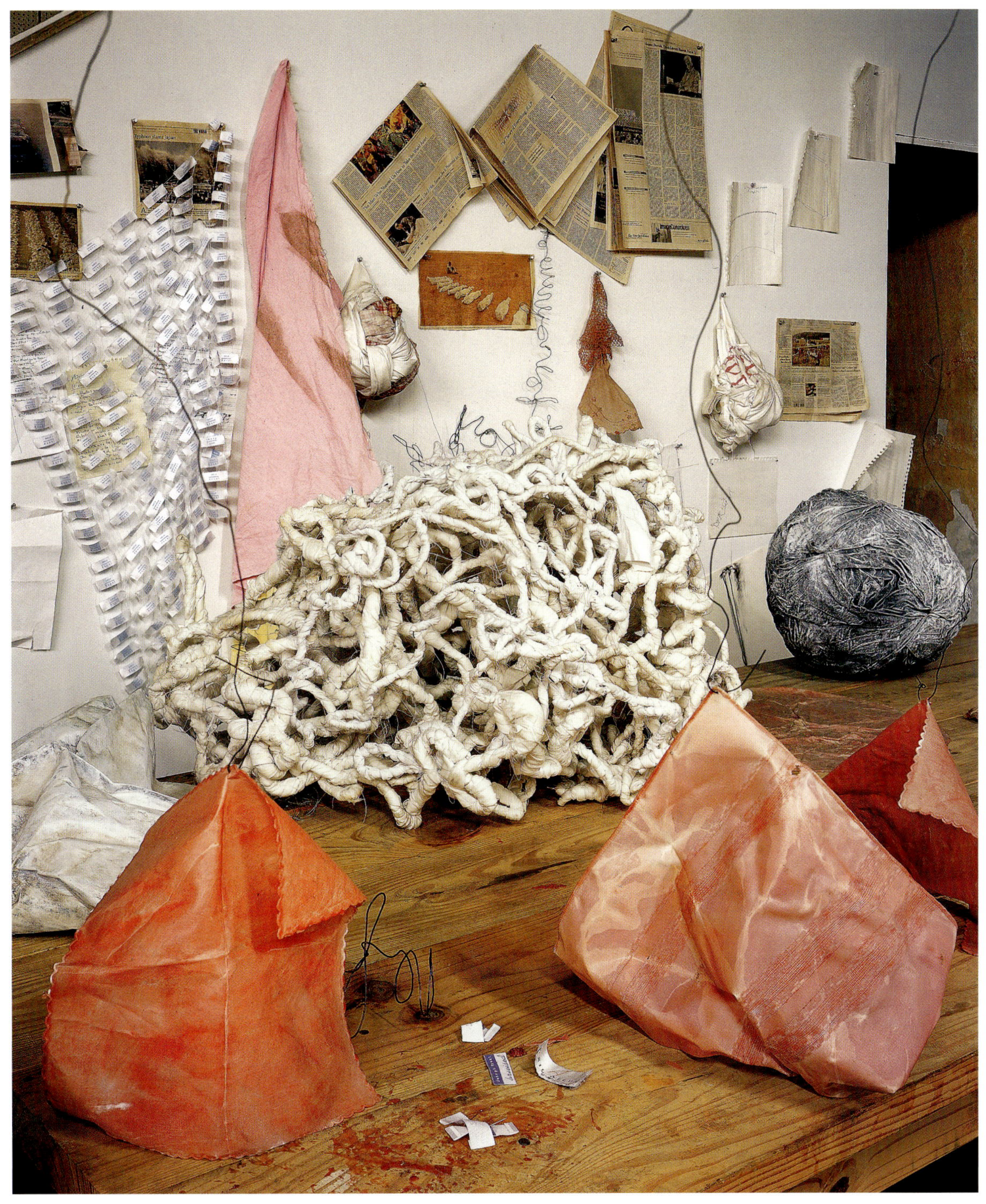

PLATE 78

mortality as it was presented in the everyday. I was trying to capture that in my objects. This expanded from flora to other biological sources, specifically viruses. The AIDS crisis was fully evident then, and I was thinking about errant biology and the way information spreads like an infection mutated as it travels. I made those works for about two years and then abruptly stopped making things for a few months.

PD: Maybe you had covered all the issues that were important at the time?

JH: After a while the works seemed a bit too spiritual, which was not my original intention.

PD: When did the use of white shirts become the focus of your work?

JH: On New Year's Day, 1993.

PD: That's very exact!

JH: On New Year's Eve I went to a resale shop and bought thirty used white shirts and the next day started to button them together. The precedent for this impulse came from when I was in high school. At that time I made a short, animated film about white shirts called *Sanforized*. The film, along with my drawings of white shirts, was connected to these happenings and performances I was thinking about. Only a couple of these happenings ever took place. I decided to revisit that small body of work from the early 1970s and expand on it with a more sophisticated vocabulary. I focused on the biological, economic, historical, and sociological issues surrounding the white shirt. I was also considering the dynamic between order and chaos, with the shirt being a fixed symbol in a shifting field. Finally, having grown up as a white, middle-class youth who had migrated to the suburbs in my formative years, I could anchor my intellectual considerations in personal experience.

PD: The color "white" has continued to be a dominant issue in your work. Did you do any initial research?

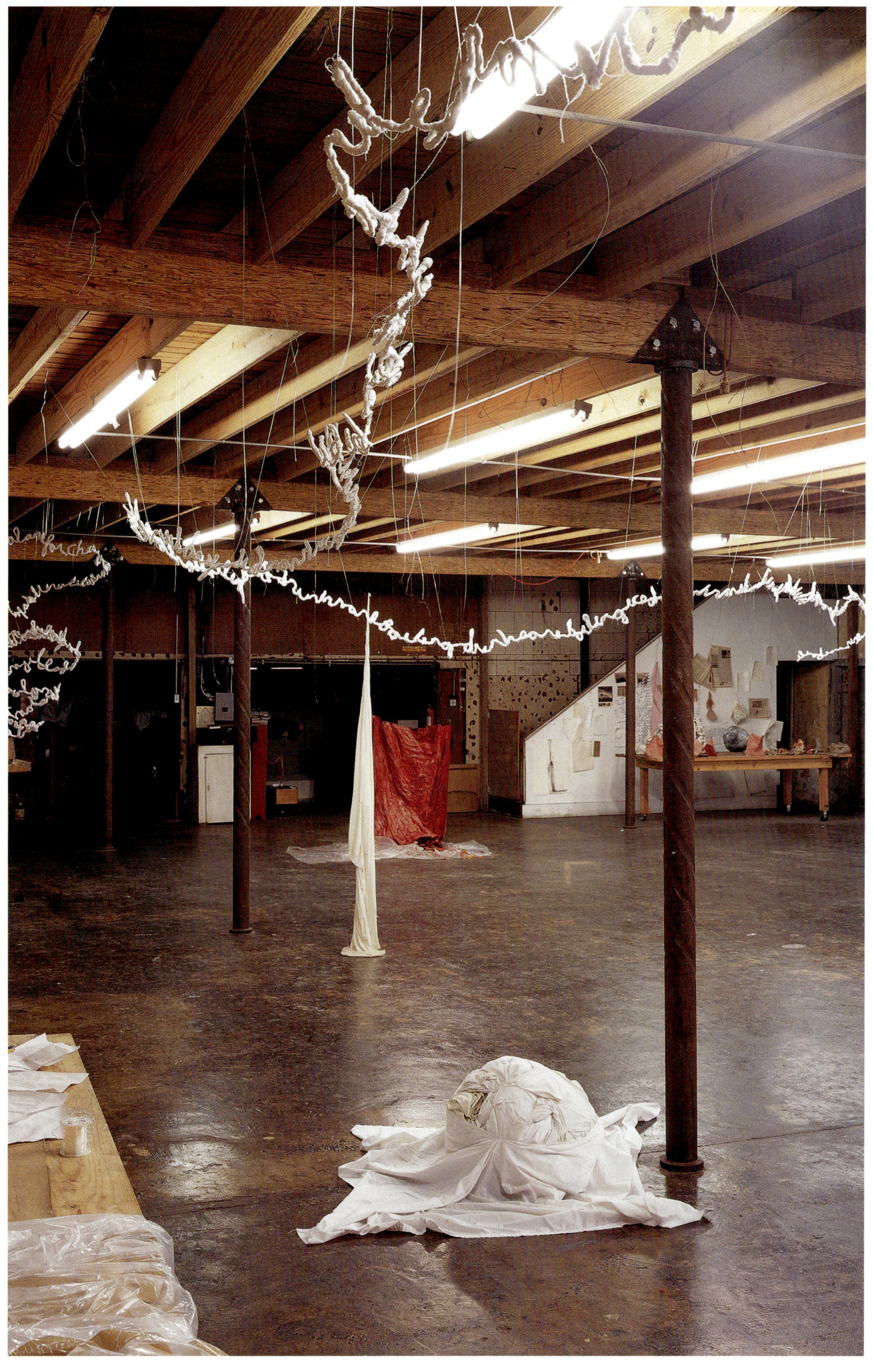

PLATE 79

JH: I studied the history of that color and its connection to the aristocracy, which favoured white clothing because of its association with cleanliness and because the labor class did not wear it. I also investigated the use of white in modernist architecture, particularly by Le Corbusier, who helped to establish white walls as a modernist standard. I was reading whatever contradicted the prevalent notion that white was neutral. Working as an administrator at an art school connected to one of the largest museums in the country personalized the social and political connections with white spaces and the authority of the white gallery.

PD: So, at that particular time, the lampshade virus works evolved into lampshades with white shirts sewn into them, and after a period of time only the shirts remained. With the use of white shirts, did the subject of the figure become important?

JH: In some ways the works were directly figurative because of the shirts, yet the final artworks were not of figures. The human form is implied by the clothing as well as by the verticality of the sculptures. I was most interested in reading through the figurative to the other information carried in the final work. Like poetry, a lot of information can be focused in a few lines and be carried almost subversively and certainly seductively by the rhythm, cadence, and overall form of each work.

PD: That points to a natural progression toward the use of the shirt labels.

JH: At first the labels were cut out of the shirts. Each label contained a lot of information that could reveal the year it was made, the design, the quality, and the class status of the garment. The label seemed to carry the genetic code of each shirt. When I pinned the labels on a wall, I was working visually—trying to make the best color field painting I could. I was trying to make a transcendent modernist grid, ignoring the data that was gathered, because it was going to be present no matter what I did.

PD: How did you decide to manufacture your own labels?

JH: I was in a group exhibition in New York called *Shopping*, and I had a tailor sew my own label design into other people's shirts. I wanted the work and the signature to be the same thing. I photocopied the word "present" as it appeared in Berryman's *Dream* Songs. The word had multiple pronunciations and numerous meanings, and all of them seemed to apply to an aspect of my work. I pinned a six-foot-square grid of the labels at Deitch Projects as a complement to the single labels available at the tailor's. The grid in the gallery was the same size as a standard Agnes Martin painting and functioned in a similar visual manner.

PD: Is that the exhibition in which you began using the labels to make large minimal wall paintings?

JH: Yes, the first "sculptures of paintings," as I called them, were large squares. Later some of them expanded to cover complete walls or were site specific. I think the largest one was *Lost* (plates 31 and 32). It measured 30 feet long, with more than 50,000 labels, and was exhibited in the 2001 Phoenix Museum Triennial. During the past nine years I have manufactured eleven labels based on words from Berryman poems or from Samuel Beckett short stories.

PD: There are also large floor sculptures made of labels. Are these related to minimalist sculptures?

JH: These works are *Bruised* (plates 68 and 69) and *Lost and Lust* (plates 66 and 67). They refer to Carl Andre's zinc plate floor pieces but are almost opposite in terms of their effect and associations. The labels are presented edge-up in the boxes they were shipped in and form a fragile field of rich color and unreadable words. I think they are a kind of failed minimalism.

PD: I see a formal correlation between the flat surfaces of the pinned label works and some of the bronzes, such as the MFAH commissioned work, *Curtain* (plates 28–30), or the recent bed sheet bronze, *Wash* (plates 70 and 71). How did the drapery pieces evolve in your practice?

JH: The draperies came out of the earlier shirt sculptures. At a certain time, I felt a little bit dead-ended in the political readings of the shirt works. I wanted to move away from specific political readings into less easily defined social and gender issues.

PD: A white drape doesn't carry the various sociopolitical codes that the shirts might?

JH: A white drape is a white drape. It's domestic, simple, and has a function. There is always an economic association with the kind of fabric the drape was made out of, but then that's it. From the beginning, the drape works created more opportunity for me to work abstractly. No matter in what form I would use the drape, it always took a neo-classical association and still it was just an ordinary object, a drape.

PD: Yet the final forms are not that easy of a read. Why is that?

JH: Viewers are given the chance to determine their own relationships to the associated classical values in a more ambiguous way. They have to decide something about themselves and their values rather than being told how they should feel.

PD: The figure may not always be the central image in your sculptures but even when invisible it still seems evident in the process. How conscious are you of leaving this trace of human activity?

JH: I think this is for the most part an extension of my interests and concerns and happens automatically. I am addressing the interface of my identity with social and cultural history, trying to ground it in intimate experience. This mirrors the way my art practice collapses into my private life. After all, the first bed sheet used for a sculpture was one I slept in and the first white shirt was one I wore.

PD: Formal art, poetry, science, social history, and economics tend to be the real foundation for all of your art production. This is very international in scope. Will the layering of different ideas and information continue to expand?

JH: I have always been interested in larger issues that can be given form and clarity through the discipline of art. Over the years I have been influenced by many other people, ideas, thoughts, and places in the world. The work will always continue to evolve as new information is brought into play.

PD: And yet, your work is very personal, very much about you.

JH: The best way to summarize the personal references is this: as if by wishing to make my works formally strong enough to be transcended, I become a virus in the works and my many interests make them coalesce into something else.

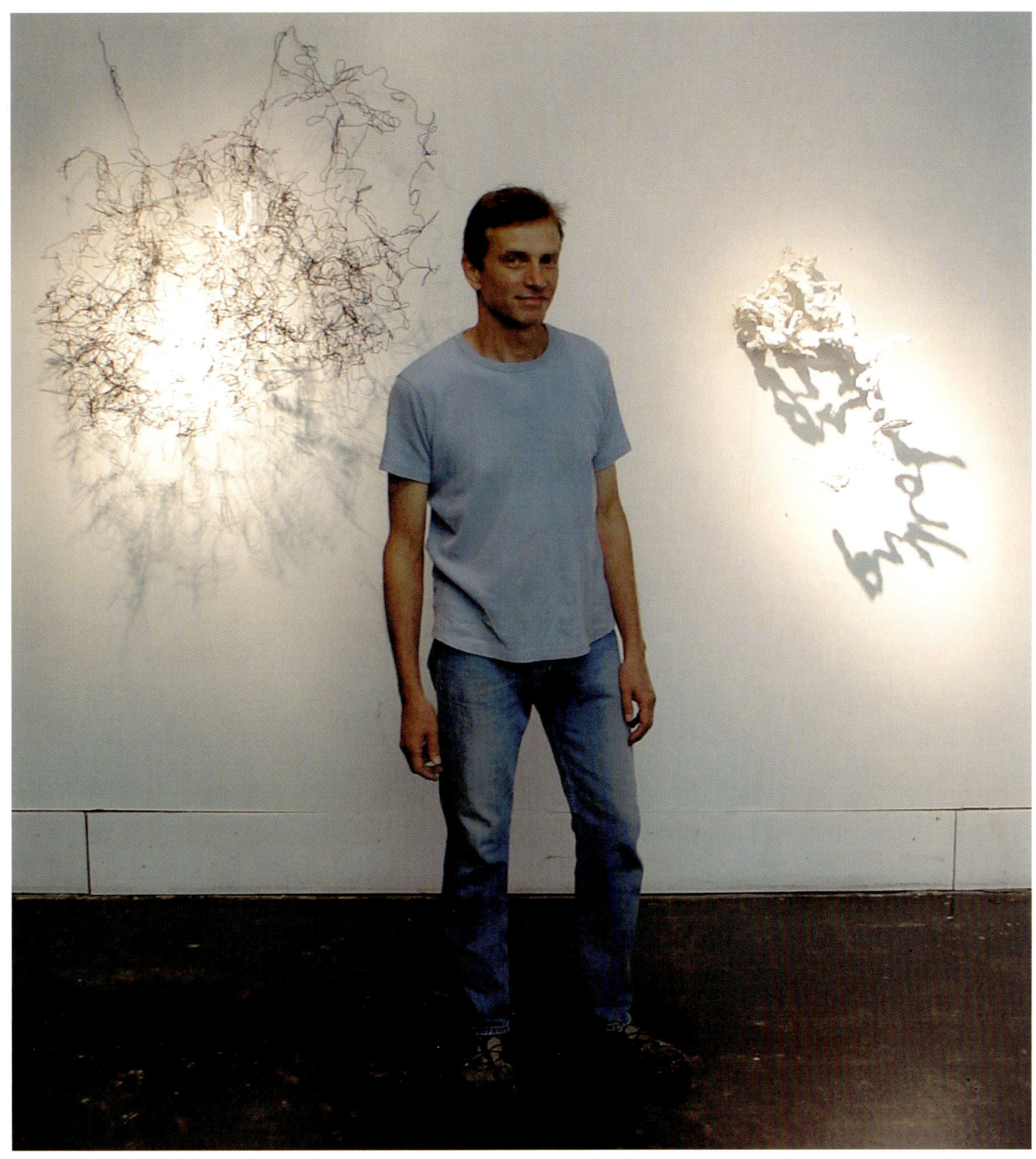

PLATE 80

Plate 74 ***Shopping Ad from Time Out magazine***
1993
Courtesy of the artist

Plate 75 ***Harvest***
1987
Wood chairs, steel and paint
96 x 66 x 44 inches
Collection of The Dallas Museum of Art

Plate 76 ***Narcissus***
1991
Wood doors, silk and cardboard lampshades, and paint
106 x 38 x 36
Collection of Michael Miller

Plate 77 ***Light Basket***
1991
Silk lampshades and paint
35 x 32 x 20 inches
Courtesy of the artist

Plate 78 ***View of Joseph Havel's studio***

Plate 79 ***View of Joseph Havel's studio with Drinks are Boiling, Iced Drinks are Boiling***
2005

Plate 80 ***Portrait of Joseph Havel in his studio***

1. ***Aura***
1995–96
Shirt collar, needle, thread, buttons
53 x 7 x 7 inches
Collection of Claire and Doug Ankenman

2. ***Three***
1996
Bronze with patina
114 x 19 1/4 x 14 inches
Collection of Beverly Kopp

3. ***Spine***
1996
Fabric shirt collars and monofilament
156 x 7 1/2 x 7 1/2 inches
Courtesy of Devin Borden Hiram Butler Gallery

4. ***Seam***
1995–96
Bronze
Dimensions variable
Courtesy of the artist

5. ***Laundered Pair***
1996
Bronze with patina
82 x 44 x 55 inches
Collection of Nancy M. O'Boyle

6. ***Un-Laundered Pair***
1996
Bronze with patina
86 x 45 x 45 inches
Collection of Jeanne and Michael Klein

7. ***February***
1996
Bronze with patina
94 x 10 x 10 inches
Collection of Dr. Carolyn Farb

8. ***Fleece***
1997
Shirt labels, thread, needles
29 x 21 inches
Collection of Dr. and Mrs. Bryan Perry, Dallas

9. ***Star***
1997–98
Bronze with patina
51 1/2 x 51 1/2 x 51 1/2 inches
Collection of Mr. and Mrs. Russell Hawkins

10. ***Moon***
1998
Fabric shirt collars and monofilament
21 x 21 x 21 inches
Collection of Suzanne M. Manns

11. ***New York Times, Financial, June 7, 1998***
1998
Bronze with patina
5 x 15 x 23 inches
Collection of Nina and Michael Zilkha

12. ***New York Times, Arts, June 7, 1998***
1998
Bronze with patina
5 x 15 x 23 inches
Collection of Frances and Peter C. Marzio

13. ***New York Times, Arts, May 31, 1998***
1998
Bronze with patina
5 x 15 x 23 inches
Courtesy of Dunn and Brown Contemporary

14. ***Drape***
1999
Bronze with patina
119 x 56 x 56 inches
Collection, Modern Art Museum of Fort Worth, Museum purchase, Sid W. Richardson Foundation Endowment Fund

15. ***Curtains***
1999
Bronze with patina
104 x 24 x 26 inches
Collection of Jeffrey and Toni Beauchamp

16. ***Table Cloth***
1999
Bronze with patina
77 1/2 x 11 x 12 inches
Collection of Blake Byrne, Los Angeles

17. ***Lost***
2000
Fabric shirt labels and steel pins
Dimensions variable
Courtesy of Devin Borden Hiram Butler Gallery

18. ***Bed Sheet***
2001
Fabric sheet and urethane resin
105 x 18 x 20 inches
Collection of Tim and Nancy Hanley

19. ***Black Drape***
2002
Bronze with patina
171 x 53 x 50 inches
Collection of Cornelia and Meredith Long

20. ***Fading Desire***
2002
Fabric shirt labels and steel pins
Two squares, each 144 x 144 x 2 inches
Courtesy of Galerie Gabrielle Maubrie

21. ***Torn Flannel Duvet Cover***
2003
Bronze with patina
126 x 48 x 33 inches
Collection of Mr. and Mrs. Robert H. Dedman, Jr.

22. ***Desire***
2003–4
Fabric shirt labels and thread
195 x 56 x 56 inches
Courtesy of Devin Borden Hiram Butler Gallery

23. ***Indian Fire***
2003
Fabric and urethane resin
92 x 38 x 34 inches
Courtesy of Galerie Gabrille Maubrie

24. ***Lost and Lust***
2004
Fabric shirt labels and cardboard
Collection of Stedelijk Museum voor Actuele Kunst (S.M.A.K.), Ghent, Belgium
1 x 120 x 120 inches

25. ***To Bring***
2004
Bronze with patina
53 x 57 x 55 inches
The Barrett Collection, Dallas, Texas

26. ***To Take***
2004
Bronze with patina
45 x 46 x 45 inches
Collection of Diane and Charles Cheatham

27. ***Bruised***
2004
Fabric shirt labels and cardboard
1 x 132 x 132 inches
Courtesy of Dunn and Brown Contemporary

28. ***Wash***
2004–5
Bronze with patina
105 x 103 x 23 inches
Courtesy of the artist

29. ***Twisted Curtain***
2004–5
Bronze with patina
198 x 25 x 18 inches
Courtesy of the artist

30. ***Torn and Twisted Curtain***
2004–5
Bronze with patina
192 x 53 x 22 inches
The Museum of Fine Arts, Houston, museum commission, gift of Nona and Richard Barrett, Nancy and Tim Hanley, Eliza Lovett Randall, Stanford and Joan Alexander Foundation, Claire and Doug Ankenman, Carol and Les Ballard, Toni and Jeff Beauchamp, Blake Byrne, Sara Dodd-Spickelmier and Keith Spickelmier, Kay and Al Ebert, Sam Gorman, Diana and Russell Hawkins, Janet and Paul Hobby, Karen and Eric Pulaski, Alice C. Simkins, Emily and Alton Steiner, Herbert C. Wells, Isabel B. and Wallace S. Wilson, Jill and Dunham Jewett, Karol Howard and George Morton, Jan Diesel, and Randee and Howard Berman, 2005.1051.

31. ***Fallen Reich***
2005–6
Fabric curtain and steel curtain rod
140 x 480 x 100 inches
Courtesy of the artist

EXHIBITION HISTORY AND SELECTED BIBLIOGRAPHY

Compiled by Michelle White

Joseph Havel

Born

Minneapolis, Minnesota, 1954

Education

M.F.A. Pennsylvania State University, University Park, 1979
B.F.A. University of Minnesota, Minneapolis, 1975

Awards and Grants

2004 Artadia Jury Award
1999 The Cultural Arts Council of Houston, Artist's Award
1998 American Institute of Architects, Houston, Artist of the Year
1995 The Louis Comfort Tiffany Foundation Award
1994 Cultural Arts Council of Houston, Artist's Award
1991 Dallas Museum of Art, Dozier Travel Grant
1987 National Endowment for the Arts, Artist's Fellowship

Selected Solo Exhibitions

2005 *Joseph Havel: The Arrival of the Bee Box.* Houston: Devin Borden Hiram Butler Gallery, 2–28 April

2004 *Joseph Havel: Lost/Lust.* Madrid: Project Rooms, ARCO, 12–15 February

To Bring/To Take: New Bronzes and Drawings. Dallas: Dunn and Brown Contemporary, 15 October–13 November

2003 *Joseph Havel: Desire with Lumps.* Houston: Devin Borden Hiram Butler Gallery, 22 March–6 May

Joseph Havel: Toy, Dream, Rest. Dallas: Dunn and Brown Contemporary, 16 May–14 June

Joseph Havel: Le Jeu du Travailleur. Paris: Galerie Gabrielle Maubrie, 22 November–10 January 2004

2002 *Joseph Havel: Desire.* Paris: Palais de Tokyo, 13 April–23 June

2001 *Joseph Havel: One Dozen Veils.* Dallas: Dunn and Brown Contemporary, 12 January–25 February

Joseph Havel: Lost. Houston: Devin Borden Hiram Butler Gallery, 1 March–28 April

Joseph Havel: Daydream Nation. Paris: Galerie Gabrielle Maubrie, 15 September– 30 November

2000 *Joseph Havel: New Sculpture.* Houston: Devin Borden Hiram Butler Gallery, 18 March–22 April

1999 *Joseph Havel, Lost: Shirt Labels, Nothing Photographs, Dream Drawings.* Galveston: Galveston Arts Center, 28 August–26 September

1998 *Joseph Havel: Woolen Lover.* Houston: Devin Borden Hiram Butler Gallery, 24 October–25 November

1997 *Joseph Havel.* Milwaukee: INOVA [Institute of Visual Arts], University of Wisconsin-Milwaukee Art Museum, 17 January–2 March

Joseph Havel. Annandale-on-Hudson, New York: The Center for Curatorial Studies Museum, Bard College, 15 June–24 August

Joseph Havel: New Drawings. Houston: Devin Borden Hiram Butler Gallery, 19 July–10 September

Joseph Havel: Weather. Dallas: Barry Whistler Gallery, 18 October–22 November (Brochure: Peter Doroshenko)

Joseph Havel: Commun. Paris: Galerie Gabrielle Maubrie, 8 November–20 December (Catalogue: Jérôme Sans)

1996 *Joseph Havel.* Huntington Beach, California: Huntington Beach Art Center, 13 April–16 June (Catalogue: Peter Doroshenko and David Pagel)

Joseph Havel. Kiev, Ukraine: Soros Center for Contemporary Art, October–December

1995 *Joseph Havel: Present*. Houston: Hiram Butler Gallery, 7 January–11 February

Corps Blanc: New Works by Joseph Havel. Dallas: Barry Whistler Gallery, 6 October–19 November

Joseph Havel. San Antonio: Blue Star Artspace, University of Texas, San Antonio Annex Satellite Space

1994 *Joseph Havel: Sculpture/New Bronzes.* Dallas: Barry Whistler Gallery, 4 March–16 April

1992 *Joseph Havel: New Bronze and Mixed Media Sculpture.* Seattle: Linda Farris Gallery, 6–30 August

Joseph Havel: Recent Sculpture. Houston: Davis/McClain Gallery, 18 January–22 February

1991 *Joseph Havel: Recent Sculpture.* Dallas: Barry Whistler Gallery, 14 September–19 October

1989 *Joseph Havel: Sculpture and Drawings.* Dallas: Barry Whistler Gallery, 28 October–25 November

Introductions 89. Houston: Davis/McClain Gallery, Summer

1988 *Joseph Havel: Sculpture.* Houston: Davis/McClain Gallery, 27 May–25 June

1987 *Joseph Havel: Sculpture.* Dallas: DW Gallery, January–5 February

Joseph Havel: Sculpture. San Marcos: Southwest Texas State University Gallery, 2–17 September

1984 *Joseph Havel.* Dallas: 500X Gallery

Selected Group Exhibitions

2004 *Borderlands: Images, Objects & Identity.* El Paso: El Paso Museum of Art, 25 January–18 April

Fight the Power. Paris: Galerie Gabrielle Maubrie, 24 January–6 March

5 *Years of S.M.A.K.* Ghent, Belgium: Stedelijk Museum voor Actuele Kunst, 1 February–18 April

Around the World in Forty Years: Selected Sculpture from Art in Embassies Program. Washington, D.C.: Department of State, 17 May–6 July

Objects of Our Desire: Sculpture from the Sheldon. Lincoln, Nebraska: Sheldon Memorial Art Gallery, University of Nebraska, 5 June–1 August

5th Anniversary Exhibition. Dallas: Dunn and Brown Contemporary, 10 September–9 October

Whiteness, A Wayward Construction. Charlottesville, Virginia: University of Virginia Museum of Art, 23 October–23 December; Laguna Beach, California: Laguna Museum, 23 March–6 July (Catalogue: Tyler Stallings, Ken Gonzales-Day, Amelia Jones, and David R. Roediger)

Patrons Choice: The Silver Anniversary of The Museum Collectors. Houston: The Museum of Fine Arts, Houston, 18 September–30 January 2005

Texas Vision: The Barrett Collection. Dallas: Meadows Museum of Fine Art, 21 November 2004–30 January, 2005

Joseph Havel/Richard Serra: Works on Paper. Houston: Devin Borden Hiram Butler Gallery, 20 November–20 December

2003 *Joining/Collage.* Houston: Devin Borden Hiram Butler Gallery, 12 July–10 September

White Hot. Houston: Devin Borden Hiram Butler Gallery, 9 August–10 September

Flip. Dallas: Dunn and Brown Contemporary, 5 September–4 October

25th Anniversary Show. Dallas: 500X Gallery, 6–28 September

Contemporary Texas Artists in France. Paris: Art in Embassies Program, U.S. Embassy, Residence Weber, January–December (Catalogue: Jeanne L. Phillips)

2002 *Labyrinths.* Houston: Devin Borden Hiram Butler Gallery, 12 January–27 February

Burning Desires: Acquisitions 1997–2001. El Paso: El Paso Museum of Art, 20 January–19 May (Brochure: Becky Duval Reese and William R. Thompson)

Escape from the Vault: The Contemporary Museum's Collection Breaks Out. Honolulu: The Contemporary Museum, 25 January–24 March

New Directions in Contemporary Art. Lincoln, Nebraska: Eisentrager-Howard Gallery, Department of Art and Art History, University of Nebraska-Lincoln, 13 May–5 July

Monochrome, Mostly. Arlington, Texas: Arlington Museum of Art, 30 August–28 September

Made in U.S.A. Houston: Devin Borden Hiram Butler Gallery, 8 June–8 August

Line. Houston: Devin Borden Hiram Butler Gallery, 10 August–12 September

Domestic: Artists Transforming the Everyday. Arlington, Texas: Arlington Museum of Art, 4 September–2 November

Systems Order Nature. Devin Borden Hiram Butler Gallery, 14 September–19 October

110 Years: The Permanent Collection at the Modern Museum of Fort Worth. Fort Worth: The Modern Art Museum of Fort Worth, December 2002–March 2003 (Catalogue: Michael Auping, Andrea Karnes, and Mark Thistlethwaite)

2001 *The Draftsman's Colors: Fourteen New Acquisitions from Johns to Chong.* New York: Whitney Museum of American Art, 3 March–8 July

Phoenix Triennial. Phoenix: Phoenix Art Museum, 28 July–23 September (Catalogue: Brandy Roberts and Beverly Adams)

Inside and Out: Contemporary Sculpture and Video Installation. Miami: Bass Museum of Art, 16 May–Ongoing

Black and White and a Little Bit of Color: Selections from The Contemporary Museum's Collection. Honolulu: The Contemporary Museum, 3 September–7 November

Space: Sculptor's Drawings, Drawings About Sculpture. Houston: The Museum of Fine Arts, Houston, 27 October–21 January 2002

2000 *Leandro Erlich, Terrell James, Joseph Havel and Dean Ruck: Four Artists from Houston,* Albany, Texas: The Old Jail Art Center, 22 January–15 April

V*ernon Fisher, Joseph Havel, Terrell James, Dean Ruck: Drawings.* Houston: Devin Borden Hiram Butler Gallery, 15 January–11 February

Showroom. Troy, New York: The Arts Center of the Capitol Region, 29 January–8 April (Catalogue: Ian Berry, curator)

Whitney Biennial of American Art. New York: Whitney Museum of American Art, 23 March–4 June (Catalogue: Maxwell L. Anderson, Michael G. Auping, Valerie Cassel, Hugh M. Davies, Jane Farver, Andrea Miller-Keller, and Lawrence R. Rinder)

Crossing State Lines: Texas Art from the Museum of Fine Arts, Houston. Houston: The Museum of Fine Arts, Houston, 23 September–18 March

Eight from Texas. New Orleans: Arthur Rogers Gallery, 7–28 October

1999 *Arbeiten auf Papier.* Karlsruhe, Germany: Galerie Rohloff, 15 January–12 Febuary

On the Ball: The Sphere in Contemporary Sculpture. Lincoln, Massachusetts: DeCordova Museum and Sculpture Park, 16 January–14 March

Texas Draws. Houston: Contemporary Arts Museum, 12 February–11 April (Catalogue: Lynn M. Herbert)

House of Sculpture. Fort Worth: Modern Museum of Art, 23 May–8 August; Museo de Arte Contemporaneo de Monterrey, Mexico (Brochure: Michael Auping)

Some Kind of Wonderful: Part I. Dallas: Barry Whistler Gallery, 5 June–3 July

Street Life. Houston: Project Row Houses, October 1999–March 2000

First Decade: Highlights from The Contemporary Museum's Collection. Honolulu: The Contemporary Museum, 6 November–3 January 2000

The XMAS Project. New York: Kent Gallery, 26 November–23 December

New Acquisitions. Dallas: Dallas Museum of Art

1998 *Interactions: Mark Gomes, Joseph Havel, Lisa Ludwig, Susan Schelle.* Reading, Pennsylvania: Freedman Gallery, Center for the Arts, Albright College, 26 March–28 April; Buenos Aires, Argentina: Centre Contemporaranea Borges (Catalogue: Christopher Youngs)

Visions. Dallas: Barry Whistler Gallery, 28 March–2 May

1997 *Works on Paper.* Dallas: Barry Whistler Gallery, 18 January–22 February

Serial Imagery. Dallas: Barry Whistler Gallery, 14 June–26 July

Landscape: The Pastoral to the Urban. Annandale-on-Hudson, New York: The Center for Curatorial Studies Museum, Bard College, 15 June–24 August

American Images: The SBC Collection of Twentieth-Century American Art. Houston: The Museum of Fine Arts, Houston, October–28 January 1998; Austin: The Austin Museum of Art, 14 Febuary–10 May 1998 (Catalogue: Betsy Fahlman, Walter Hopps, and Peter C. Marzio)

1996 *Three Visions.* Buenos Aires: El Centro Cultural Borges: June (Organized by Galveston Arts Center, Brochure: Clint Willour and Pampa Rissso-Patrón)

Shopping. New York: Deitch Projects, 5–21 September (Brochure: Jérôme Sans)

Shirts and Skins: Absence/Presence in Contemporary Art. Honolulu: Contemporary Art Museum, 4 December–2 February 1997

1995 *Das Pop.* Las Vegas: Donna Beam Gallery, The University of Nevada, 27 Febuary–21 March (Brochure: Dave Hickey)

Evocative Objects. Arlington, Texas: Arlington Museum of Art, 16 June–12 August

Gallery Artists Installation. Dallas: Barry Whistler Gallery, July–August

Joseph Havel and Lisa Ludwig: Material Differences. Galveston: Galveston Arts Center, 19 August–1 October

Joseph Havel/George Stoll/Meg Webster. Houston: Hiram Butler Gallery, 23 September–17 November

Twentieth-Century American Sculpture at the White House. Washington, D.C.: The First Lady's Garden, 28 September–15 March, 1996 (Brochure: Peter C. Marzio)

Genesis in Fire: Works from Green Mountain Foundry. Houston: The Glassell School of Art, The Museum of Fine Arts, Houston, 15 December–25 February 1996 (Brochure: Alison de Lima Greene)

1994 *Uncommon Objects.* Dallas: Barry Whistler Gallery, 17 June–30 July

Gallery Artists Installation. Dallas: Barry Whistler Gallery, August

Private Identity, Public Conscience: Contemporary Works from the Museum's Collection. Houston: The Museum of Fine Arts, Houston, 25 September–19 February 1995

Drawings. Dallas: Barry Whistler Gallery, 2 December–4 January, 1995

1993 *3-D Rupture: Dave Darraugh, Sharon Engelstein, Joseph Havel and Annette Lawrence.* Houston: Contemporary Arts Museum, 16 January–7 March (Catalogue: Peter Doroshenko and Lynn M. Herbert)

Summer Selections. Dallas: Barry Whistler Gallery, July–August

Sculptors & Paper. Hiram Butler Gallery, 7 August–11 September

Light. Dallas: Barry Whistler Gallery, 10 September–9 October

Virgil Grotfeldt/ Joseph Havel/ James Surls. Hiram Butler Gallery, 18 September– 22 December

Texas Contemporary: Acquisitions of the '90s. Houston: The Museum of Fine Arts, Houston, 19 September–21 November

Small Wonders. Dallas: Barry Whistler Gallery, 3 December–24 December

1992 *Urban/Suburban.* Arlington, Texas: The Arlington Museum of Art, 9 May–20 June

Thirty Prints. Dallas: Barry Whistler Gallery, 26 June–29 August

Out of Bounds: Contemporary Sculpture Takes Shape. Houston: The Museum of Fine Arts, Houston, 19 September–7 February 1993

Vernon Fisher/Joseph Havel/Douglas MacWithey. Dallas: Barry Whistler Gallery, 23 October–28 November

re: Creation, Re-Creation, Recreation: Art from Found Objects. Austin: Laguna Gloria Art Museum

1991 *An Anniversary Exhibition.* Dallas: Barry Whistler Gallery, 22 February–30 March

The State I'm In: Texas Art. Dallas: Dallas Museum of Art, 18 August–6 October

Ship Shapes: An Exhibition Celebrating the Texas Seaport Museum. Galveston: Galveston Arts Center, 30 November–5 January 1992 (Brochure: Clint Willour)

Material as Message. Houston: The Glassell School of Art, The Museum of Fine Arts, Houston, Winter (Brochure: Elizabeth Ward)

1990 *Ordinary as Extraordinary/Object as Subject.* Galveston: Galveston Arts Center, 1 September–14 October

Multiples. Houston: Davis/McClain Gallery, Winter

1989 *Another Reality.* Houston: Hooks-Epstein Gallery, 3 June–5 August; Little Rock: The Arkansas Arts Center, 17 August–1 October; San Antonio: Marion Koogler McNay Art Institute, 3 June–29 July 1990 (Catalogue: Surpik Angelini, Bert Long, and Thomas McEvilley)

A Century of Sculpture in Texas: 1889–1989. Austin: Archer M. Huntington Art Gallery, The University of Texas, 16 June–13 August; Amarillo: Amarillo Art Center, 2 September–22 October; San Angelo: San Angelo Museum of Fine Arts, 9 November–23 December; El Paso: El Paso Museum of Art, 13 January–31 March 1990 (Catalogue: Patricia D. Hendricks and Becky Duval Reese)

Works on Paper. Dallas: Barry Whistler Gallery, 15 July–9 September

The Artist's Eye. Houston: DiverseWorks, 10 November–30 December

Tracking Information: Drawings by Sculptors. Amarillo: Amarillo Arts Center, Fall

1988 *Joseph Havel Sculpture/Michael Miller Paintings.* Dallas: Barry Whistler Gallery, 27 May–25 June

X500X: A Tenth Anniversary Exhibition. Dallas: 500X Gallery, Winter

1987 *Found.* Houston: DiverseWorks, 30 May–11 July (Curator: Caroline Huber)

1986 *3 Sculptors—Francis Bagley, Linnea Glatt, Joseph Havel.* Sherman, Texas: Austin College

Art in the Metroplex. Fort Worth: Texas Christian University, September

1985 *Four Sculptors.* Texas City: College of the Mainland

1984 *Nine Sighted: Clay Sculpture in Texas.* Houston: Midtown Art Center, 17 November–22 December

1983 *Showdown: Perspectives on the Southwest.* New York: The Sculpture Center, 10 May–7 June (Organized by the Alternative Museum, New York, Catalogue: April Kingsley)

Houston Showdown. Houston: DiverseWorks, 4–30 November

1982 *Texas Sculptors Invitational.* Pensacola: Pensacola Community College

1979 *MFA Exhibition.* University Park: Pennsylvania State University Museum of Art

Selected Bibliography

2004 Hersant, Isabelle. "Joseph Havel: Habitus/corpus. Ou le Monde global habillé par l'esclave local." *Etc Montréal* 66 (June/July/August 2004): 76–79.

Sánchez, Marisa C. "Non-Places: An Interview with Joe Havel." *ARTL!ES* 44 (Fall 2004): 40–41.

Taylor, Stephanie. "Review: Borderlands: Images, Objects & Identity." *ARTL!ES* 42 (Spring 2004): 80.

2003 Haldane, David. "Exhibit Is Exercise in White Identity." *The Los Angeles Times*, 28 April 2003: B3.

Johnson, Patricia C. "Connecting Threads of Draped Bronze." *Houston Chronicle*, 2 August 2003: 1D+.

Myers, Holly. "White Noise, Where Race Meets the Sand: Laguna Beach." *LA Weekly* (25 April–1 May 2003).

Wolgamott, L. Kent. "Curtains!" *Lincoln Journal Star*, 13 April 2003: K6.

2001 Alexander, Paul. "Texas Lines 'em up." *Travel and Leisure* (February 2001).

Colpitt, Francis. "Report from Houston: Space City Takes Off." *Art in America* 88, no. 12 (October 2001): 128.

Daniel, Mike. "One Dozen Veils." *ARTL!ES* 30 (Spring 2001): 55.

French, Christopher. "Lost." *ARTL!ES* 30 (Spring 2001): 55.

_____. "Review." *ArtNews* (April 2001): 149.

Houston, Sam A. "The Man Behind the Curtain: Havel's Art Soars Above its Origins." *Houston Lifestyles and Homes* (June 2001), 55–57.

Nilsen, Richard. "Try, Try, Triennial Again." *The Arizona Republic*, 2 August 2001.

Sans, Jérôme, and Marc Sanchez. *Tokyobook* 2. Paris: Palais de Tokyo, 2001: 101.

Tyson, Janet. "Hot Spots, Texas." *Art Papers* 25, no. 4 (July/August 2001): 33, 34.

Vanesian, Kathleen. "Minimal Effort, Less Is Much More at the Phoenix Museum's Triennial." *Phoenix New Times*, 9–15 August 2001: 61.

2000 Coulter, Betsy. "Occasions to Live By: A Review of Project Row Houses, Round Eleven Street life." *Atopia* 0.66, 2000: 16–19.

Ennis, Michael. "Joseph Havel, Breaking the Mold." *Texas Monthly*, September 2000.

_____. "Northern Exposure." *Texas Monthly*, February 2000.

Finn, David. *20th-Century American Sculpture in the White House Garden.* New York: Harry N. Abrams, 2000.

Greene, Alison de Lima. *Texas: 150 Works from the Museum of Fine Arts, Houston.* New York: Harry N. Abrams, 2000.

Hoving, Thomas. "My Eye." *Art Net Magazine,* 7 April 2000: <http://www.artnet.com/magazine/features/hoving/hoving4-7-00.asp>.

Johnson, Patricia C. "They'll Take Manhattan." *Houston Chronicle*, 4 May 2000: D1+.

Kutner, Janet. "Work in Progress." *The Dallas Morning News*, 19 March 2000: 1C+.

Landay, Janet. *The Museum of Fine Art, Houston Visitor Guide.* Houston: The Museum of Fine Arts, Houston, 2000.

Lightman, Victoria. "Sculpture in Houston." *Sculpture Magazine* 19, no. 5 (June 2000): 26–31.

McCormick, Carlo. "Houston Journal." *Art Net Magazine*, 25 May 2000: <http://www.artnet.com/Magazine/reviews/mccormick/mccormick5-25-00.asp>.

Rush, Michael. "State of the arts." *Die Welt Online*, 16 May 2000: <http://www.welt.de/daten/2000/05/16/0516ad168200.htx>.

Schaernack, von Christiona. "Museums-Report Houston: Der Kunst-Clan von Texas." *Art Das Kunstmagazin* (March 2000): 38–50.

Schwartz, Therese. "Nirvana Takes a Holiday: The Whitney Biennial in 2000." *Arts4All Newsletter Online* 11, issue 12 (April 2000): <http://www.arts4all.com/newsletter/issue12/schwartz12.html>.

Shapiro, David. "Whitney 2000: Biennial Fever." *New York Arts Magazine Online*, 14 March 2000 <http://nyartsmagazine.com/41/Pages/18.html>.

Stoller, Ezra. *Whitney Museum of American Art.* New York: Princeton Architectural Press, 2000.

Tyson, Janet. "Remembering Green Mountain." *ARTL!ES* 26 (Spring 2000): 10–11.

1999 Johnson, Patricia C. "Millennial Biennial." *Houston Chronicle*, 9 December 1999: 1D+.

_____. "Streetlife, an international group of artists finds provocative ways to bring cultures together." *Houston Chronicle*, 24 October 1999: D8.

Kutner, Janet. "On Sculpture's Cutting Edge." *The Dallas Morning News*, 23 May 1999: 1C.

Tyson, Janet. "The 2000 Whitney Biennial: An Interview with Michael Auping." *ARTL!ES* 25 (Winter 1999–2000): 22-24.

_____. "House of Styles." *The Dallas Star-Telegram*, 23 May 1999: D1+.

_____. "House of Sculpture." *ARTL!ES* 23 (Summer 1999): 48.

Vogel, Carol. "Surprises in Whitney's Biennial Selections." *The New York Times*, 8 December 1999: B1+.

1998 Sans, Jérôme. "Review: Joseph Havel." *Art Press* 231 (January 1998): viii.

1997 Akhtar, Suzanne. "'Weather' Takes the Workday World by Storm." *San Antonio Star-Telegram*, 2 November 1997: H8.

Aukeman, Anastasia. "Shopping." [Deitch Projects, New York] *Art News* 96 (January 1997): 116, 118.

Daniel, Mike. "Clothes Encounters." *The Dallas Morning News*, 17 October 1997.

Kutner, Janet. "Joseph Havel at Barry Whistler." *The Dallas Morning News*, 25 October, 1997: 12 C.

Lightman, Victoria. "Joseph Havel" *Sculpture* 16, no. 7 (September 1997): 80–82.

Norklun, Kathi. "Landscape: The Pastoral to the Urban." *Woodstock Times*, 7 August 1997: 10.

Raynor, Vivien. "Landscapes That Celebrate Their Makers." *The New York Times*, 10 August 1997.

Smith, Roberta. "Hudson Valley Conversation." *The New York Times*, 18 July 1997.

1996 Belenky, Oleksandr. "Don't Disregard Your Old Shirts!" *Day* [Kyiv, Ukraine], 2 February 1997.

Curtis, Cathy. "Vision, Reach and Grasp." *The Los Angeles Times*, 24 December 1996: F1+.

_____. "History and Colors, Collars." *The Los Angeles Times*, 23 April 1996.

Goldman, Robert. "Artist's Diary." *Art Net Magazine*, 24 August 1996: <http://www.artnet.com/magazine/features/goldman/goldman9-24-96.asp>.

Morse, Marcia. "Shell Game." *Honolulu Weekly*, 18–24 December 1996.

Rose, Joan. "'Shirts and Skins' flawed, but well worth seeing." *The Honolulu Advertiser*, 15 December 1996: F8.

Sans, Jérôme. "Shopping" (catalogue). *Time Out* [New York], 4–11 September 1996.

Shaw, Edward. "Innocents Abroad: U.S. Artists in Buenos Aires." *Buenos Aires Herald*, 16 July 1996.

Vanderknyff, Rick. "The Starch of Triumph." *The Los Angeles Times* (O.C. Edition) 17 April 1996: F1+.

Wilson, Wade. "Artistic Migration." *Where* [Dallas], July 1996.

1995 Davenport, Bill. "White on White." *Public News*, 18 October 1995.

Doroshenko, Peter. "Joseph Havel in Conversation with Peter Doroshenko." *ARTL!ES* 7 (June/July 1995): 26–29.

Johnson, Patricia C. "Havel's shirts collar sense of fresh air." *Houston Chronicle*, 12 January 1995: 1C+.

_____. "Espousing 'Material Differences.'" *Houston Chronicle*, 20 August 1995: D8+.

Tyson, Janet. "A Stitch in Time." *Fort Worth Star-Telegram*, 5 July 1995.

1994 Kutner, Janet. "Turning images into ideas: artists find messages in the commonplace." *The Dallas Morning News*, 10 March 1994: C1.

1993 Alspaugh, Leann Davis. "Contemporary Arts Museum 3-D Rupture Exhibition." *Museum and Arts* (January 1993): 18–21.

1992 Chadwick, Susan. "Sculptors show their mettle." *The Houston Post*, 6 February 1992: F1+.

Johnson, Patricia C. "Fine Craftsmen Turn to Bronze." *Houston Chronicle*, 26 January 1992.

_____. "A 'Rupture' with Tradition." *Houston Chronicle*, 16 January 1992.

Kutner, Janet. "Ironies in the Fire." *The Dallas Morning News*, 10 November 1992: C1+.

McBride, Elizabeth. *Artspace* 16, no. 3 (May/June 1992).

1991 Chadwick, Susan. "Dallas Museum gives three Houston artists cash awards." *The Houston Post*, 3 June 1991.

_____. "Materials are Art's Message at Glassell." *The Houston Post*, 25 January 1991.

Ennis, Michael. "Buried Treasures." *Texas Monthly*, October 1991.

Johnson, Patricia C. "Exhibit Offers Collage of Emotions." *Houston Chronicle*, 7 February 1991.

Kutner, Janet. "Visual Relief." *The Dallas Morning News*, 22 September 1991.

Mitchell, Charles Dee. "Bluebonnets and All." *The Dallas Observer*, 19 August 1991.

Tyson, Janet. "Deep in the Art of Texas." *Fort Worth Star-Telegram*, 21 September 1991.

1990 Davidow, Joan. "Joseph Havel: Balancing Act." *Detour Magazine*, March 1990.

Jarmusch, Ann. "Critic's Choice." *The Dallas Times Herald*, 6 July 1990.

Johnson, Patricia C. "Blue Venus and Moon Delight Eye." *The Houston Post*, 13 January 1990.

_____. "Humble Objects Make Powerful Sculptures." *Houston Chronicle*, 13 January 1990.

Kutner, Janet. "A Cut Above." *The Dallas Morning News*, 20 June 1990.

_____. "State of the Art: DMA's Texas exhibit covers a lot of territory, but omissions are many." *The Dallas Morning News*, 1 December 1990.

_____. "Bountiful New Harvest for the DMA." *The Dallas Morning News*, 1 December 1990.

McBride, Elizabeth. "Multiples." *Art News* 89, no. 5 (May 1990): 224.

Tyson, Janet. "Wood in All Its Forms." *Fort Worth Star-Telegram*, 24 June 1990.

1989 Bacigalupi, Don. "Houston Letter." *Contemporanea* (December 1989): 31.

Chadwick, Susan. "Sculpting with Poetic License." *The Houston Post*, 21 July 1989: D1+.

Johnson, Patricia C. "Introductions Gains Strengths." *Houston Chronicle*, 13 July 1989: D1.

_____. "In Reality It's Just Too Much." *Houston Chronicle*, 14 June 1989.

1988 Roberts, Tre. "Review, Joseph Havel: Sculpture." *Art Papers* (September/October 1988): 64–65.

Mitchell, Charles Dee. "Joseph Havel at Barry Whistler." *Art Space* 53 (September 1988).

1987 Kutner, Janet. "New Directions for Two Local Artists." *The Dallas Morning News*, 31 January 1987.

Johnson, Patricia C. "Found Objects: Junk or Junque?" *Houston Chronicle*, 28 June 1987: I5.

PUBLIC COLLECTIONS

Artpace, San Antonio
The Jack S. Blanton Museum of Art, The University of Texas at Austin
The Contemporary Museum, Honolulu
The Dallas Museum of Art
El Paso Museum of Art
The Federal Reserve Bank, Dallas
Ministry of Culture, France
The Modern Art Museum of Fort Worth
Musée d'art et d'industrie, Roubaix, France
The Museum of Fine Arts, Houston
Sheldon Memorial Art Gallery, University of Nebraska, Lincoln
Stedelijk Museum voor Actuele Kunst (S.M.A.K.), Ghent, Belgium
The South Texas Institute for the Arts, Corpus Christi
Whitney Museum of American Art, New York

INDEX

Note: The titles of artworks are in *italics.* Titles of works not by Havel are followed by the artist's name in brackets, e.g., *Bed* (Rauschenberg). For works other than sculpture the medium is also shown in brackets, e.g., Berryman, John, *The Dream Songs* (poems).

Page numbers in italics are for illustrations, e.g., *Bed Sheet* 13, *76*, 96-7

COPYRIGHT AND REPRODUCTION CREDITS

FIGURES

Figure 1
© Lynda Benglis/Licensed by VAGA, New York, NY

Figure 2
Scala/ Art Resource, NY

Figure 3
Alinari/ Art Resource, NY

Figure 4
© Robert Rauschenberg/ Licensed by VAGA, New York, NY

Figure 5
© CNAC/MNAM/Dist. Réunion des Musées Nationaux/ Art Resource, NY; photo by Jacques Faujour; © 2005 Artists Rights Society (ARS), New York/ ADAGP, Paris

Figure 6
© Courtesy of the artist and CRG Gallery, New York; photo by Lynn Rosenthal

Figures 7, 8, 12, 13, 15
Thomas R. DuBrock

Figure 10
© 2005 Joel Shapiro/Artists Rights Society (ARS), New York

Figure 11
© Réunion des Musées Nationaux/Art Resource, NY; photo by Gérard Blot/C. Jean

Figure 14
Digital image © The Museum of Modern Art/Licensed by SCALA/Art Resource, NY; © 2005 Artists Rights Society (ARS), New York/VG Bild-Kunst, Bonn

Figure 16
© Courtesy of the Artist and Roberts and Tilton, Los Angeles

Figure 17
© Courtesy of the Artist

Figure 18
© The Estate of Eva Hesse. Hauser & Wirth Zürich London

Figure 19
© Carl Andre/Licensed by VAGA, New York, NY; photo by Phillip Scholz Ritterman

PLATES

Plates 5, 6, 7, 11, 18, 19, 20, 43, 44, 49, 62, 65, 75, 76, 77, 78, 79
Joseph Havel

Plates 24, 34, 35, 36, 37, 38, 39
Steve Denny

Plates 25, 26, 31, 32, 48 (and cover/jacket detail)
Fraser Stables

Plate 27
Jerry L. Thompson, courtesy Whitney Museum of American Art, New York

Plates 40, 41, 42
Marc Domage/Tutti

Plates 58–61, 72–73
Thomas R. DuBrock

Plates 66, 67
Peter Doroshenko

Plate 74
Joseph Havel and Charles Wiess

Plate 80
Ken King

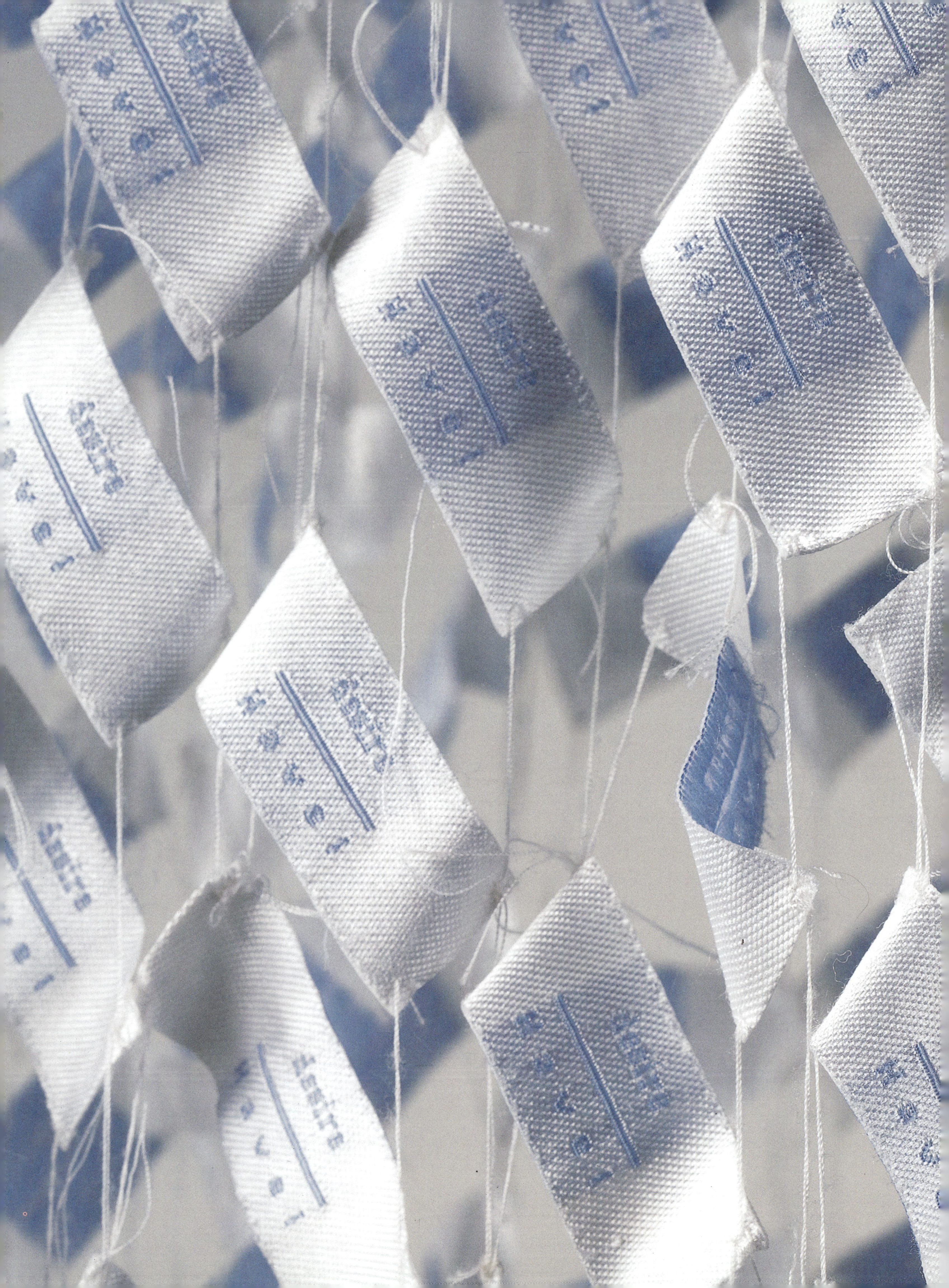